REBELS, MERCENARIES, and DIVIDENDS

The Katanga Story

REBELS, MERCENARIES, and DIVIDENDS

The
Katanga
Story

by SMITH HEMPSTONE

FREDERICK A. PRAEGER
Publisher • New York

BOOKS THAT MATTER

Published in the United States of America in 1962
by Frederick A. Praeger, Inc., Publisher
64 University Place, New York 3, N.Y.

© Smith Hempstone 1962

Library of Congress Catalog Card Number: 62-15792

Printed in the United States of America

CONTENTS

MAPS

FOR MY PARENTS

REBELS, MERCENARIES, and DIVIDENDS

The Katanga Story

Then I heard the boom of the blood-lust song
And a thigh-bone beating on a tin-pan gong.

—Vachel Lindsay, *The Congo*

INTRODUCTION

THE KATANGA story is not a pleasant one to tell. It is a tale of savagery, deceit, false morality, power politics, smugness, and plain incompetence. The U.S. is deeply involved in this story and not, to my mind, creditably involved. The position of the Kennedy Administration is that the U.S. completely supports the United Nations in the Congo and Katanga. That, however, cannot be a substitute for a just and effective American policy. World peace has been threatened by the Katangan problem and probably will be for some time. The foundations of the United Nations have been shaken by it, and a wedge has been driven between the NATO powers. Consequently, Katanga deserves our attention.

This is not intended as an apologia for President Moise Tshombe or his regime. I am probably more aware of the weaknesses of the man and his government than many of those who criticize him most vociferously. Although I have some friends among them, I am not particularly fond of the Belgians as a group, either at home or in Africa. Collectively, I far prefer—among others—Spaniards, Sudanese, Somalis, and Austrians. Nor is the *Union Miniere du Haut-Katanga*, the mining complex which dominates Katanga's economic life, a particular friend of mine. Although its representatives invariably have been kind to me, they have, on occasions, demonstrated all the arrogance and evasive-

3

ness frequently characteristic of corporations enjoying a monopolistic situation.

I first came to Katanga four years ago, after spending a month in a grass-roofed hut on the Kasai-Katanga border, shaking off a particularly persistent case of dysentery. Since then, I have been to Katanga more times than I can remember, including three visits during the past year. I was witness to both the September and the December fighting in my capacity as African correspondent of the *Chicago Daily News*. I know Tshombe personally. My life has been threatened by his gendarmes. I have few illusions about him or about Katanga. Yet I also know his good qualities, his intelligence, bravery, and racial tolerance. I know that his government, with all its faults, has the one essential characteristic of any administration and one too seldom encountered in Africa: the capacity to govern. I remember Katanga as it was in happier days, with mines working, shops open, children in school, churches full. I remember it as the U.N. and the U.S. made it in December, with mortar shells falling in the parks where people used to walk, machine guns stuttering in the deserted, smoke-filled streets. If you listened hard then, you could hear a thigh-bone beating on that tin-pan gong.

It is a commentary on America today that I should feel compelled to say that I do not belong to the American Committee for Aid to Katanga Freedom Fighters, am not a member of the John Birch Society, am not in the pay of the Katangan Government or *Union Miniere*, and really could not care less about the fluoridation of water. I am a registered Republican, although I did not vote Republican in the 1960 Presidential election. I do believe that the United Nations has a role to play in the world today—I had the privilege of fighting in a just war under its banner in Korea —and I believe the U.S. should remain in the international organization. I do not believe, however, that the U.N. is, or should be, regarded as a sacred cow endowed—through the laying on of political hands—with a supranational in-fallibility. When it becomes sacrilege to criticize the U.N. (or the U.S. Government, for that matter), the organiza-tion has lost its usefulness. The U.N. is not, to my mind, automatically a power for good in the world. It was cre-ated primarily to provide the machinery for the peaceful solution of international problems. If it is to be used for the adjudication of domestic disputes by majority verdict, only international anarchy can result. The U.N. has an immense capacity for good or evil, depending entirely on how it is used. If it is to be used to implement or condone aggression, as it has been in Katanga and in Goa, then it is a power for evil. It cannot, of course, act more morally or more effectively than the nations which constitute it. When the U.N. abandons the rule of law and permits the unbri-dled pursuit of national passions, no matter how popular these passions may be, it becomes worthless as an instrument for world peace. The U.S., in this regard, bears a heavy responsibility, both because of its membership in the Se-curity Council and its heavy financial support.

I state all this only because spokesmen of the present Administration have found it convenient to tar with the brush of neo-fascism all those who find the position of the U.N. and the U.S. in Katanga to be morally and practicably indefensible. Some Administration spokesmen apparently find dissent intolerable. I would have thought that we, as Americans, would have had quite enough of that sort of thing with Senator McCarthy. You do not have to be a white supremacist or to favor the impeachment of the Chief Justice of the U.S. Supreme Court, to have a feeling of re-vulsion and sadness about what the U.N. and the U.S. have done and are doing in Katanga. One serves neither one's country nor the U.N. by saying they are right when they are wrong.

Not since the Spanish Civil War have men of so many Western nations come from the corners of the earth to fight each other and die in a remote and alien land. Seldom, since the Iberian blood-bath has the essential nature of the struggle been so little understood by so many. This book is an attempt to place Katanga in perspective, to show what it is and why it was inevitable that it should become the ideological and physical battleground it is today. To my knowledge, no book of this nature has yet been published in English. Consequently, I have had to rely largely on my own experiences in Katanga, United Nations proceedings, documents provided by *Union Miniere*, Katangan Government statements, private sources, and press reports. Insofar as background information on pre-independence days, the records of the Belgian Government have been helpful.

No doubt, as time passes, others who participated on one side or the other in the Katangan adventure will write books which will help to fill in the gaps. The consequences of this battle for Central Africa are fraught with such dangers that it is to the advantage of all free men that the whole truth should be known.

S. H.

April 19, 1962
Karen, Kenya
East Africa

I

M'SIRI'S GHOST

"I will feed fat the ancient grudge I bear him.
He hates our sacred nation; and he rails,
Even there where merchants most do congregate."
— WILLIAM SHAKESPEARE,
The Merchant of Venice

EVEN IN the days long ago, when the rest of the Congo was covered by a vast inland sea, men lived in the broken hills of Katanga, on the shores of that great water. It is the only part of the Congo where scientists have found a continuous record of human habitation stretching from the pebble culture of the Early Lower Paleolithic Period through the hand-axe cultures of the Lower Paleolithic, the polished stone culture of the Neolithic, and the ancient Bantu civilizations of the Lualaba River Valley.

Sometime toward the end of the first millennium, the Bantu peoples, from whom the people not only of modern Katanga but of most of the Congo are descended, moved into the Congo from the northeast, probably from the Nile Valley. No one knows the reason for this great folk movement, but it is probably that the Bantu moved south under pressure from the Nilotic and Hamitic peoples.

The Bantu advance should not be thought of in terms of an army marching toward a definite objective. The movement was in the form of waves, which rolled across Ka-

7

tanga, ebbing and flowing like the tide, from at least the tenth century on. The principal folk migrations had ended by the fourteenth century but considerable movement was still taking place when white men reached Katanga 400 years later. One group would move into an area, destroy or absorb the local inhabitants, build villages, and plant crops. Such a group might remain for generations in one locality before moving on again. Meanwhile, other groups would have surged past and around it, leap-frogging it, pushing on ahead in the never-ending search for new lands.

Although Katanga lay in the direct path of these Bantu invasions, which reached South Africa's Great Fish River before clashing with the northward-trekking Afrikaners in the nineteenth century, the geographical features of Central Africa diverted and impeded the Bantu tide. One arm of the invasion blunted itself, broke up, and dissolved in the great rain forests of the Congo. The other, blocked to the west by the water barrier of Lakes Tanganyika, Mweru and Bangweulu, swept south through the Rhodesias toward the Zambezi and Limpopo River valleys. Katanga was too high, cold, and dry to suit the Bantu, its soil too poor. Consequently, although those Bantu to the west of the string of lakes which dot the Great Rift Valley undoubtedly used Katanga as a corridor to the south, relatively few settled there permanently. Those who did stay easily conquered the original Stone Age inhabitants, who may have been pygmies. The Bantu knew how to work metal and to make weapons from it, and this gave them a technological advantage in war almost comparable to that exercised today by the nuclear powers over those nations limited to conventional armaments.

So the Bantu came to Katanga, settled there, moved on, were replaced by others until gradually, sometime in the second millennium a more or less resident group took root. There followed the organization and consolidation of political power: Kingdoms took shape, dynasties were created, spheres of influence gradually formed, and tribal rivalries arose.

The great rivals for power in medieval Katanga, as they are today, were the Baluba and Lunda tribes. The first great Bantu kingdom created was the Baluba empire, founded sometime in the fifteenth century by Kongolo Mukulu, a rather disagreeable despot who was beheaded by his own subjects after he threatened to kill his eldest son, of whom he was jealous. At its apogee, the Baluba empire, which lasted for 200 years, was larger than Belgium, Holland, and Luxembourg combined. It stretched from the present site of Albertville on Lake Tanganyika to the Bushmaie River within the borders of modern Kasai and south to about the 10th degree of latitude. This is still the Baluba heartland but geography has played an unfunny joke on the tribe: Instead of being the nucleus of a strong state, the Balubas today find themselves a hated minority trisected among northern Katanga, southern Kasai, and southern Kivu.

Although the Baluba empire lasted in a truncated form until the last years of the nineteenth century, when intrigues against the Belgians resulted in its dissolution, the Balubas ceased to be the dominant force in Katanga in the sixteenth century with the rise of the Lunda empire.

The Lundas, under their great chief Mwata Yamo, ruled over a kingdom even larger than that of Kongolo Mukulu. Mwata Yamo's domain extended from Angola in the west, included much of Kasai, the southern half of Balubaland, and arched south through Katanga and present-day Northern Rhodesia. The Lunda empire at its peak was considerably larger than Portugal. Like their archenemies the Balubas, the Lundas' success was based primarily on their military skill and their talent for political organization.

The Lunda empire began to disintegrate at the end of the seventeenth century as Katanga found itself gripped in the twin pincers of the slave trade, which by then had become a huge international business (the *coup de grâce* was ad-

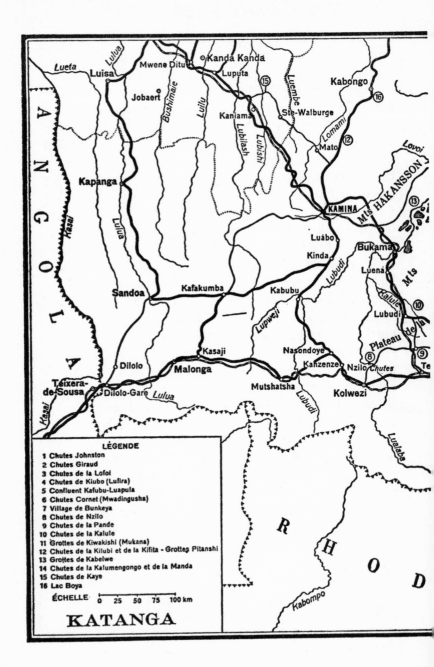

LÉGENDE

1 Chutes Johnston
2 Chutes Giraud
3 Chutes de la Lofoi
4 Chutes de Kiubo (Lufira)
5 Confluent Kafubu-Luapula
6 Chutes Cornet (Mwadingusha)
7 Village de Bunkeya
8 Chutes de Nzilo
9 Chutes de la Pande
10 Chutes de la Kalule
11 Grottes de Kiwakishi (Mukana)
12 Chutes de la Kilubi et de la Kifita - Grottes Pitanshi
13 Grottes de Kabelwe
14 Chutes de la Kalumengongo et de la Manda
15 Chutes de Kaye
16 Lac Boya

ÉCHELLE

0   25   50   75   100 km

KATANGA

ministered by the Chokwe tribe, formerly allied with the Lunda; the rebellion of this tribe of hunters and warriors in 1887 resulted in the eclipse of the Lundas for seventy-five years). Slaves had first been taken only from the more populous areas, such as the banks of the Congo. But as the supply dwindled and local inhabitants grew more wary, it became necessary to launch expeditions into the remote parts of the interior in search of "black ivory." From Portuguese Angola in the west came expeditions led by *pombieros,* half-caste traders in the service of the Portuguese. From Zanzibar in the east came Arab slavers who crossed Lake Tanganyika and pressed into northern Katanga in their search for African women for the harems of Muscat and Oman. Both the Portuguese and the Arab slavers, of course, had firearms, and no Bantu kingdom could stand up against them. In the first half of the nineteenth century, it is estimated that 7.5 million Congolese slaves (150,000 per year) —many of them from Katanga—were shipped to the New World from West African ports. The Arab trade to the east was far less than this, but certainly at least a number equal to that actually shipped must have died in attacks on native villages or in the long march to the coast.

About the middle of the nineteenth century, at the height of the chaos into which the slave trade had plunged Katanga, a third tribal force, which exists to this day, projected itself into the midst of the Baluba-Lunda rivalry. This was the Bayeke tribe. According to Bayeke storytellers, the tribe originated in Unyamwezi (central Tanganyika). Following a wounded elephant, a party of Bayeke hunters trekked into what today is Katanga. There they saw some copper ingots, which they purchased and took back with them to their chief, whose name was Kalassa. Kalassa, who recognized the value of the ingots, trekked into this new country and made friends with its ruler, Chief Katanga, after whom Tshombe's nation is named. Kalassa made many trips between his own country and that of Chief Katanga. So that the knowledge of the source of the copper ingots would not be lost, he took with him on these later trips his son, Ngelengwa, also known as Mushidi, Msidi, Mchire or M'Siri. It is by the last of these versions of his name that Kalassa's son is best known. M'Siri, whom Kalassa had decided to leave in the new country to supervise his trading operations, was given land for himself and his bodyguard by Chief Katanga. Later, two of M'Siri's brothers joined him at his settlement, which was called Lutipula. M'Siri was brave and successful in battle against his enemies and those of Chief Katanga, and Katanga finally gave him his favorite daughter in marriage. M'Siri repaid the old chief's kindness by poisoning him and defeating Katanga's son in battle. He kept on good relations with the Lunda but attacked and defeated the Baluba Chief Cazembe, who lived north of the Luapula, thus securing his right flank. By diplomacy, he gained the adherence of many tribes. Others he smashed, building on the bedrock of his courage and daring a warrior empire larger than Czechoslovakia. M'Siri's writ ran from the Luvua River in the north to the Congo-Zambezi watershed in the south, from Lake Mweru and the Luapula River in the east to the Lualaba River in the west. One day, a defeated chief warned M'Siri that the whites would come "to eat his gold." But for the moment, Katanga belonged to M'Siri.

M'Siri was not content to be just a military figure. He gained a monopoly on the traffic in slaves, ivory, copper, salt, and iron. These he traded for arms and ammunition, which enabled him to defeat still more tribes and thus to acquire more slaves to trade for additional armaments. M'Siri traded with the coastal Arabs of East Africa, with Rhodesian, Tanganyikan, Ugandan, and Angolan tribes, and with the Portuguese. His capital, Bunkeya, the palisades of which were topped with the skulls of his enemies, became the greatest trading mart in Central Africa. At the height of M'Siri's power, Bunkeya had a population of 20,000. The Bayeke chief, who kept a harem of 600 wives (including the Portuguese half-caste Maria da Fonseca), could field an army of 10,000 warriors, 3,000 of them armed with rifles. M'Siri's desire for wives had political as well as sexual and social implications: Like any medieval European monarch, he secured his position by marriage with the wives and sisters of his barons and of chiefs defeated by him in battle. He even sent an emissary to the Portuguese governor of Angola in Luanda, demanding one of his daughters in marriage, a request that was refused.

This, then, was the state of affairs in Katanga when two rival European powers began to take an interest in its colonization: This vast country of open savannahs and broken hills, twice the size of West Germany but only lightly populated (seven people to the square mile today), was harried from east and west by slavers; the great rival empires of the Balubas and the Lundas had collapsed; M'Siri, the Bayeke chief from Tanganyika, his courage turned to sadism in his old age, represented the one focal point of authority. It was with him that the European powers would have to deal.

In 1876, King Leopold II (1835–1909), Belgium's vigorous, ambitious, money-loving monarch, summoned representatives from Europe and America to Brussels to launch the International African Association. The catalyst for this meeting had been Henry Morton Stanley's epochal travels through the Congo two years earlier. The ostensible purposes of the Association were humanitarian, scientific, and commercial. It adopted its own flag (a gold star on a blue field) and sent Stanley to the Congo to make treaties with the chiefs and to undertake the building of a railway into the interior.

Britain, Portugal, France, and Germany were all interested in the sovereignty of the Congo. Rather than see one of their rivals already holding territories in Africa grab the Congo, all four agreed that the so-called Congo Free State should become Leopold's personal property. The Congo did not become a Belgian colony. Instead, Leopold II became king of Belgium and of the Congo, an important distinction. The Congo did not become a Belgian colony until 1908, when Leopold transferred his rights to the state. This decision, confirmed at the Berlin Conference of 1885, had been anticipated—perhaps made inevitable—three years earlier by the U.S. recognition of the "sovereignty" of the International African Association. The U.S. was the first nation to recognize the Association's flag, preceding even Belgium by a year. Thus it can be seen that American intervention in Congolese affairs is nothing new.

But there were men and interests who were displeased by the decision to hand the Congo to Leopold II, and were not prepared to accept it. One of these was Cecil Rhodes (1853–1902), the great British empirebuilder. Rhodes' great ambition (aside from procuring the return of the United States to the British empire) was to create a north-south British-African axis stretching from Egypt to the Cape of Good Hope, through which a railway was to be built.

To achieve this end, he had to secure Bechuanaland on the northern flank of the Transvaal Republic, keep the Afrikaners out of the Rhodesias, break the Portuguese claim to a corridor linking their possessions in Angola and Mozambique, seize Katanga, and checkmate the Germans in Tanganyika. Katanga offered an additional prize in that it had been known for nearly two centuries that the region contained copper.

Rhodes was able to talk Britain into proclaiming a protectorate over Bechuanaland in 1885. In exchange for a free hand in Swaziland, he induced the Afrikaners to drop their claims north of the Limpopo. His own men moved into what is today the Rhodesias in 1890, thus preventing the forging of a link between Angola and Mozambique. Rhodes was to lose Tanganyika to Germany but to win the right of transit across the Central African lakes to British Uganda. There remained only the question of Katanga.

The Berlin Conference had given Leopold the Congo basin as his private preserve. But no one had bothered to delimit the Free State's boundaries. Under the principle established at Berlin, the acid test was to be "effective occupation." This meant getting to M'Siri first and getting his "X" as signature on a treaty. It meant establishing border posts and military camps.

European explorers had wandered on the fringes of Katanga for decades. The Portuguese explorer de Lacerda had seen Lake Mweru by 1798 (and had died on its shores). Another Portuguese, Joaquim Rodriquez Graca, explored the Lunda empire, Upper Kasai, and the Upper Lulua River between 1843 and 1845. The great Scottish missionary David Livingstone wandered around Lakes Mweru and Bangweulu and explored the Upper Luapula River in 1867 and 1868. Five years later, the little-known British explorer Verney Cameron made the first crossing of Africa from east to west, spending three years on his journey from Zanzibar to Angola, during which he passed through the middle of Katanga, discovered the course of the Lukuga River, and reached the Lualaba at Nyangwe, the great Arab slaving headquarters. When Stanley started his history-making trip down the Congo in 1874, he launched his boats at Kasongo, a few miles north of what is today the Katanga border. Six years later, two German explorers, Pogge and Wissmann, penetrated northwestern Katanga in the vicinity of the Upper Kasai and Lomami rivers. Two of their countrymen, Reichard and Bohm, reached M'Siri's capital at Bunkeya in 1884. In the same year, the Portuguese explorers Capello and Ivens walked through southern Katanga on their way from Angola to Mozambique.

As the last decade of the nineteenth century approached, many explorers of many nationalities knew something about Katanga. Some had passed through the heart of the country; but none had signed treaties with the chiefs, no posts had been established. Since 1798, when a Portuguese governor of Rios de Sena, a district of Mozambique, wrote that a Goan trader had visited Chief Cazembe near Lake Mweru—a man who "owns copper and gold mines and is at war with a chief whose land produces brass"—it had been known that there was copper in Katanga. The natives forged small crosses of copper which they used for currency (three of these appear on Katanga's flag). But no one was aware of the wealth of the country, although Leopold seems to have had more than an inkling of it.

The problem, from Leopold's point of view, was to find the money to finance Belgian expeditions to annex Katanga. As has been mentioned, the Congo Free State was his personal real estate and did not belong to Belgium. Consequently, it was up to him personally to finance the exploration and development of the Congo, not to the Belgian Government. As it happened, things were not going well for Leopold financially in the Congo: The railway into the interior was proving far more expensive than had been anticipated, the Congolese rubber quotas were not being met, his forces were involved in expensive campaigns against the Arab slavers in the east. In short, Leopold just did not have enough ready cash to finance the acquisition of Katanga. Nor could he afford to wait: In 1890, two of Rhodes' agents, Alfred Sharpe and Joseph Thomson, reached M'Siri's capital at Bunkeya, Thomson coming from the south and Sharpe swinging around the northern edge of Lake Mweru and approaching from the northeast. Both had sought treaties with M'Siri that would annex Katanga to Northern Rhodesia. Both had failed. Sharpe had entered Bunkeya dressed in shabby clothes and accompanied by an unimpressive escort, so M'Siri assumed that the Englishman was lying when he described the power and majesty of Britain and the advantages to be had by accepting its protection. But Leopold realized that Sharpe might not be so unlucky the next time.

The Belgian King huddled with the directors of the *Societé Generale de Belgique*, Belgium's largest business concern. The financiers agreed to the formation of a corporation called the *Compagnie du Congo pour le Commerce et l'Industrie* (CCCI), which was to assist Leopold in the development not only of Katanga but of the whole Congo. It soon became obvious, however, that Katanga posed certain problems that set it apart from the rest of the Congo. Consequently, CCCI spawned another corporate child, the *Compagnie du Katanga*. To this organization, as to the other great chartered companies of the past, was delegated a part of the monarch's sovereignty. Its directors agreed to annex and develop in Leopold's name as much of Katanga as the company could lay its hands on. In return, in a 99-year agreement signed in 1891, Leopold granted the *Compagnie du Katanga* concession rights over one-third of the territory it was able to annex. Thus, out of the pressures of power politics and the inadequacies of a monarch's purse was born the partnership between high finance and government that exists in Katanga to this day.

The *Compagnie du Katanga* performed its end of the bargain with dispatch and efficiency. Between 1891 and 1893, four separate Belgian expeditions fanned out through Katanga. Although there were individual failures, the total effect was to make Katanga Belgian rather than British.

The first expedition, under Paul Le Marinel, made straight for Bunkeya in an attempt to bring M'Siri to heel before he could change his mind and accept British protection. The M'Siri of Le Marinel's day had grown old, senile, and sadistic. The command of his armies and the government of his country he now left to his sons and lieutenants, while he indulged in orgies of cruelty within his palace of mud and thatch. Women were thrown into pits full of starving dogs for M'Siri's pleasure. Men were buried up to their necks and left to die. The hearts were cut from M'Siri's living wives and given the Chief to suck, after which he spewed the blood in the faces of his favorites as a mark of honor and affection. One Belgian who reached Bunkeya described M'Siri's antics this way:

"Human hearts, still beating, were thrown into mugs of *pombe* (native beer), which were then enjoyed by the entire court. Men were tied to trees, and when they groaned in hunger, were given their own ears, nose, and arms to eat, and perished after devouring themselves."

Terror ruled in Bunkeya, and the situation outside M'Siri's capital was not much better. There was famine in the land, and the vassal tribes were restive. One of these, the Basangas, infuriated at the news that the daughter of their chief had been killed by M'Siri during one of his orgies, rebelled, killed all the Bayekes within their territory, and marched on Bunkeya, which they partially destroyed by fire. M'Siri was saved only by the last-minute arrival of his largest army, which had been locked in combat with the hated Balubas.

M'Siri was not in any mood for discussions with Le Marinel—an agent of the Congo Free State, not of the Belgian financiers. Le Marinel, who had arrived at M'Siri's capital on April 18, 1891, spent six exasperating weeks in Bunkeya (during which M'Siri destroyed most of the Belgian expedition's ammunition by setting its depot afire) before M'Siri even deigned to see him. When he did, the old Bayeke Chief rejected out of hand Le Marinel's offer of Belgian protection and ordered him to leave the country. Being short of ammunition, Le Marinel had no choice but to march away.

At the time, a British missionary named Daniel Crawford was living in Bunkeya. With him Sharpe had left M'Siri's unsigned treaty of British protection on the understanding that Crawford would do what he could to get the Bayeke Chief to sign, and, at the same time, would forestall any Belgian attempt to annex Katanga. It is not known how much Crawford influenced M'Siri to reject Le Marinel's overtures but he is supposed to have played a key role.

A few months after Le Marinel's departure, a second Belgian expedition under Alexandre Delcommune descended the Lomami River to Five Degrees South Latitude, marched east to the Lualaba (the principal tributary of the Congo), followed it into Katanga, crossed the rugged Hakansson Mountains, and worked its way up the Lufira Valley to Bunkeya, arriving there on October 6, 1891. Delcommune, an agent of CCCI, had no better luck than Le Marinel: M'Siri turned him down and ordered him to leave the country. But although Delcommune withdrew from Bunkeya, he did not leave Katanga. Instead, he marched east toward Lake Mweru, explored it, and continued north to Lake Tanganyika, turning west at the present site of Albertville, from which he followed the Lukuga Valley back to the Upper Congo River (there called the Lualaba).

Delcommune's failure to leave Katanga immediately so enraged M'Siri that, under Crawford's urgings, he decided to accept British protection. Crawford immediately dispatched a letter to Sharpe, Rhodes' representative, telling him of M'Siri's change of heart and advising him to come immediately to Bunkeya to claim Katanga for Great Britain.

Unknown to M'Siri, Crawford, or the runner carrying Crawford's letter, yet a third Belgian expedition, this one under the auspices of the newly-formed *Compagnie du Katanga*, was at that very moment approaching Bunkeya. This expedition was led by William Stairs, a Nova Scotian who had served with Stanley. Stairs' party intercepted the messenger bearing Crawford's letter to Sharpe. These men were playing for big stakes, and Stairs had no compunctions about reading the letter. He realized immediately that the game was up: M'Siri would either refuse to see him or would delay him until a British expedition arrived to annex Katanga. Stairs, although a British subject, was loyal to his employers: He made a forced march to Bunkeya, reaching M'Siri's capital on December 14, 1891. Stairs confronted M'Siri and made him the usual presents but demanded that the old Chief abdicate. M'Siri, in a rage, withdrew to a village an hour's march from Bunkeya. The following day, Stairs sent Captain Bodson, his Belgian assistant, after M'Siri, with instructions to bring him back to Bunkeya. M'Siri apparently threatened Bodson, who drew his revolver and shot down the old Bayeke Chief. Bodson, in turn, was slain by Masuka, one of M'Siri's sons. Bunkeya, however, remained calm, and Stairs was able to negotiate with M'Siri's eldest son and successor, Mukanda, who accepted the flag of the Congo Free State as the price of being allowed to rule the Bayeke.

At this point, the fourth, and perhaps the most important Belgian expedition (also under the auspices of the *Compagnie du Katanga*) was nearing Bunkeya, which it reached on January 30, 1892, five weeks after M'Siri's death. This expedition was led by Lucien Bia, assisted by Emile Franqui (after whom Port Franqui on the Kasai River is named), and Jules Cornet, a young geologist. At this point, Stairs, weak from starvation and wracked with fever, left Bunkeya for Africa's East Coast with the survivors of his expedition. He reached Chinde, in Mozambique at the mouth of the Zambezi, where he died while waiting for a ship. Stairs' name is forgotten now. The Belgian Government does not even list his name among those of the sixty-six explorers who opened up the Congo. Le Marinel, Delcommune, Bia, Franqui (who later became managing director of *Union Miniere*), and Cornet all have towns, dams, or other public works named after them in Katanga; Stairs has none. Yet without this obscure Nova Scotian, Katanga today might be a part of British Northern Rhodesia. The course of history was altered when Stairs intercepted and read Crawford's letter. Men are dying in Katanga today because of that footnote to history, although few of them would recognize Stairs' name.

While Stairs lay dying on the shores of Mozambique, Bia completed the Nova Scotian's work of exploration and treaty-making before dying himself of starvation and disease. With M'Siri out of the way and his warriors exhausted by famine, the last obstacles to Leopold's dream were removed; Katanga became a part of the Congo Free State. Cornet (1865–1929), meanwhile, was taking extensive geological soundings. The extent of Katanga's mineral wealth, until then only guessed at, overwhelmed him. He kept his findings a close secret until he was able to report to Leopold. The Belgian King was so amazed at the stories the young geologist told him that he ordered Cornet's findings kept a state secret until 1894, when Belgium and Britain finally delimited the boundary between Katanga and Northern Rhodesia. It was as well that Cornet and Leopold kept their silence: The border comes within a few hundred yards of the richest of all Katanga's mines, the Prince Leopold mine at Kipushi.

To develop and exploit Katanga, the *Compagnie du Katanga* and the Congo Free State vested their rights to the territory in the *Comité Special du Katanga* (CSK), with the objective of capitalizing them and sharing the profits. Anxious to keep on the good side of the British financiers, CSK granted prospecting rights to Tanganyika Concessions Ltd., a company created by Rhodes. This partnership with the British led to the formation of the much-maligned (and little understood) *Union Miniere du Haut-Katanga*, which handles the actual exploitation of Katanga's mineral wealth.

This is not the place to discuss the role of *Union Miniere* in the development of Katanga. What is sufficient for the moment is to understand the historic role which the *Societé Generale*, CCCI, *Compagnie du Katanga*, CSK, and *Union*

Miniere (all nearly—but not quite—the same) have played in Katanga; this may help us to understand why *Union Miniere* does—and, of necessity, must—assume responsibilities beyond those of a normal commercial company.

Remember that *Union Miniere* and its corporate ancestors have not just done business in Katanga; they have created Katanga. From that fateful day when Bodson shot M'Siri, *Union Miniere* has not only been involved in Katangan politics, *Union Miniere*, in a very real sense, *is* Katanga. It cannot help it. It is a destiny it cannot escape. Its dams, its highways, its mines, its treatment plants all recall the names of the men who made Katanga what it is today. Many of those working for the company now in Elisabethville, Kolwezi, and Jadotville are sons and grandsons of the men who opened up Katanga. They can no more sit by and allow Katanga to collapse than a Cabot, a Lodge, or a Kennedy can disavow a responsibility toward Massachusetts. If there is blame to be apportioned, surely it can only concern the manner in which such a responsibility is carried out, not the acceptance of the responsibility.

If we can appreciate that the men and the companies who discovered Katanga, annexed it, mined its riches, built its cities, dams, highways and schools, and left their bones in its arid soil enjoy a special responsibility in Katanga, then we have come a long way toward understanding what is happening in Katanga today.

As *Union Miniere*'s actions today are only an extension of its former role, the anatomy of African politics in Katanga can be read in the country's past. The fundamental rivalries today are exactly what they were in the sixteenth century: a struggle for power between the Lunda tribe—represented by Moise Tshombe (who is a member of the Lunda royal house and the son-in-law of the Lunda paramount chief)—and the Balubas—represented by Jason Sendwe, who has ties to the royal family of the Balubas. The third angle in the triangle is Tshombe's tough Minister of the Interior and viceroy, Godefroid Munongo. Munongo comes naturally by his toughness, his antipathy for Balubas, and his talent for governing: He is old M'Siri's grandson. When Munongo speaks, his voice is that of the warlike Bayeke tribe, a few of whose old men can still remember M'Siri, under whom the tribe had wealth and power.

Lunda, Baluba, Bayeke. These have been the roots of power and the sources of conflict in Katanga for five hundred years. Arresting or killing Tshombe and Munongo cannot alter this power structure one iota. The Balubas may rule in the north but they will never control the south. Sendwe is no alternative to Tshombe. Were Tshombe and Munongo to disappear, the Lunda and Bayeke royal families would simply throw up other men whom the tribes would follow. For historic reasons, the Bayeke and the Lunda have usually found themselves in alliance. For one thing, both of these tribes are Swahili-speaking while the Baluba speak Tshiluba, which, with Swahili, accounts for two of the Congo's four *lingua francas* that enable the country's 200 tribes to communicate with one another (the other *lingua francas* are Lingala and Kikongo). To be lasting, then, any Katanga settlement must have the support of the Balubas, Lundas, Bayekes, and of *Union Miniere*. Despite protestations to the contrary, U.N. (and U.S.) policy has had the result—if not the intention—of weakening these last three legs of power while supporting the first. This is why it can never succeed.

Insofar as Katanga's relations with the rest of the Congo are concerned, a host of factors—ethnic, linguistic, geographic, economic, and political—have conspired to create a feeling of separateness in Katanga. With the exception of the Balubas, who also live in Kasai and Kivu provinces, the ethnic ties of the Katangan tribes are with the south, not the north. The vigorous Lunda tribe, for example, is neatly bisected by the Katanga–Northern Rhodesia border, and Tshombe's father-in-law, the Lunda paramount chief, has tribesmen in Northern Rhodesia. This is also true of Katanga's white population: Only about 60 per cent of Katanga's whites are Belgians, the rest being Britons, Americans, Rhodesians, and Italians, with close ties to the whites across the border in Northern Rhodesia. Swahili, a language little spoken elsewhere in the Congo, is the *lingua franca* of Katanga.

One has only to study maps to understand Katanga's separateness from the rest of the Congo. First of all, one must appreciate the vast distances and areas in which we are dealing. It is farther from Leopoldville to Elisabethville than it is from Paris to Prague. If superimposed on a map of Europe, the Congo would blanket most of the NATO powers. Katanga itself is twice the size of West Germany. But it is not only a matter of distances. Katanga is a different type of land from the rest of the Congo, and the man is a fool who does not know that the nature of a land influences the character of its people. Most of the Congo is flat forest country, hot and humid. Katanga is high, cool (the average temperature in Elisabethville is 68° F.), arid savannah. The navigable reaches of the Congo River system, the arteries that tie together the remainder of the country, grasp at Katanga like a gnarled hand. But they do not reach it: Katanga's natural lines of communication lie to the south and west.

The economic development of Katanga, which we shall explore at greater length later, has been entirely different from the rest of the Congo. Because of its vast mineral wealth, Katanga has been the scene of heavy foreign investments in the form of mines, metallurgical plants, secondary industry, communications, and ancillary social services. This is fortunate because, in agricultural terms, Katanga is the poorest of the six Congolese provinces. The result in human terms is that Katanga has a considerable white population (35,000, or 29 per cent of the Congo's whites before the general exodus in 1960; the percentage must be twice that high now), a large and relatively advanced African wage-earning class, and a considerable population of "foreign" (non-Katangan) Africans, attracted by the economic and social opportunities available there. Although Katanga's whites could hardly be described as raving liberals, they have over the years established a tradition of toleration, mutual respect, and easy race relations with the Africans. It is worth noting that in 1958, a year-and-a-half *before* independence, Elisabethville was the only one of the Congo's seven cities to have an African majority on its city council. This tradition of racial cooperation, which exists nowhere else in the Congo, has also contributed to the Katangan feeling of separateness.

In political terms, this historical feeling of exclusiveness has been expressed, first, by Katanga's whites, and later by its Africans, in the demand for greater autonomy. Granted that to a considerable degree this has been, and is, based on a perhaps understandable reluctance on the part of the Katangans to share their mineral wealth with the rest of the Congo. But this has been only a part of the story. All the other factors mentioned have contributed to the Katangan feeling that they are—and ought to be—separate from the Congo.

To imply—as United Nations and State Department spokesmen have done—that Tshombe is the father of Katangan secession and that the whole movement would collapse without *Union Miniere*'s support indicates that these gentlemen are either lamentably uninformed about Katanga, or that they choose to ignore the facts of history for political purposes. The roots of Katangan separatism run deep. Tshombe and pro-Tshombe *Union Miniere* officials are only the logical and visible flowers produced by the shrub. M'Siri's ghost dances in Katanga tonight.

And now on to present-day Katanga.

II

MODERN KATANGA

"Stormy, husky, brawling,
City of the Big Shoulders."

—CARL SANDBURG,
Chicago

To travel by car from Kasai into Katanga is to pass from one world into another. My wife and I had been in the central Congo for many weeks, gripped in the green, depressing hands of the rain forest, relieved only by an occasional sandy savannah. At last, south of Luluabourg, as you near the Katangan border, you shrug off the forest. The transition is so quick that it is almost imperceptible. You drive through the forest, come upon a clearing larger than any you have seen before—then a belt of open country studded with grotesque ant hills and broken by patches of woods—and then the forest is gone almost before you realize it. It is replaced by mile on mile of monotonous scrub bush, neither honest trees nor open grassland but thick, level-topped expanses of gnarled bushes with only a little grass growing beneath them.

You rattle across the Lubilash River, which (like all of Katanga's rivers except the Lukuga) flows from south to north, and soon you are in Kaniama, one of Katanga's twenty-four departments and part of Grands Lacs Province. It was here that Tshombe's gendarmerie threw back the

Congolese National Army when it attempted to invade Katanga in November, 1961. Kaniama itself is a desolate, hot little village (altitude 2,821 feet) boasting three small hotels with a total of fourteen rooms, fundamentally a railroad town, the northernmost Katangan stop on the route of the *Compagnie des Chemins de Fer du Bas-Congo au Katanga* (BCK). BCK, which employs 16,000 workers, and its companion companies, the *Compagnie des Chemins de Fer Katanga–Dilolo–Leopoldville* (KDL) and the *Chemin de Fer Katanga* (CFK), are corporate children of the *Societé Generale de Belgique*. Among them, they have 1,500 miles of standard-gauge (3'6") track (more than half of the Congo's total or 4 per cent of all of Africa's). They carry 60 per cent of the Congo's freight tonnage, about 5 million tons per year. Much of the BCK-KDL net is electrified.

The *Comité Special du Katanga* used to run an agricultural school here that taught tobacco farming to young Belgian colonials, enticed to Katanga by COBELKAT (*Societé de Colonisation Belge au Katanga*), the Belgian colonization society. The center has long since closed, and the district is in a state of anarchy. It will probably remain in this condition for some time to come. Kaniama marks the border between the lands of those ancient enemies, the Lundas and the Balubas. These are the marches of the Lunda heartland and they stretch west from the Lubilash into Angola and south almost to the Rhodesian border, the homeland of the Lundas' other ancient enemies, the Chokwe.

To the south of Kaniama, along a slowly climbing road now no longer sandy but of red laterite sprinkled with mounds of elephant droppings each the size of a birthday cake, lies Kamina, yet another department of Grands Lacs, the capital of which (also called Kamina) lies fifteen miles from the former Belgian military base, now held by the United Nations. Kamina is a dreary but important railway center from which a line branches off to the east, eventually reaching Albertville on Lake Tanganyika. In the old days, Kamina had a population of 2,400 whites and 27,000 Africans; most of the whites and some of the Africans have now left. Kamina—like Kaniama—is primarily a railroad town (it has its *Hotel de la Gare*, a forlorn place, in addition to two other hostelries, the *Aviateurs* and the *Welcome*). A good deal of cotton is grown in the surrounding countryside (although it is 800 feet higher than Kaniama), and there is an ugly little industrial center, its grubbiness somewhat relieved by the yellow-blooming cassias that line its streets. Kamina—like Kaniama—is a tribal-border area. To the west are the Lunda, to the south, in the Lubudi River Valley, are the Bene Mitumba and Munongo's Bayeke, and, separated from the last two tribes by the ragged, scrubby flanks of the Hakansson Mountains, the Balubas. But these Balubas, it should be noted, are allied to Tshombe. They helped themselves to a good many rifles and machine guns when the Belgians left the Kamina military base and under their Chief, Kasongo Nyembo, have proved a thorn in the side of the United Nations garrison ever since. The basis of the alliance between Tshombe and Kasongo Nyembo is simple: Tshombe sees to it that Kasongo Nyembo gets a bit of ammunition, keeps his gendarmerie off, and gives the Baluba Chief the right to take what he can by force of arms from the United Nations. In short, Kasongo Nyembo is a sort of robber-baron of the M'Siri stamp, who owes only nominal allegiance to Tshombe. The arrangement suits both men.

Southeast of Kamina, you cross many small streams and drop through the Hakansson Mountains (3,608 feet) in a series of hairpin turns into the southernmost extremity of the Lualaba River Valley. The Lualaba, which becomes the Congo when it enters Kivu Province (hereafter, I shall refer to the Lualaba as the Upper Congo), is the historic invasion route toward Upper Katanga, which was probably used by the Bantu. It is the route down which the Congolese National Army, supported by the United Nations, has made a few tentative jabs.

The Upper Congo rises near Musofi in the hills on the Rhodesian border west of Elisabethville at an altitude of about 4,700 feet. It chatters through the hills, tumbling down one cataract after another, until, north of Kolwezi, it reaches the N'Zilo Gorge, where it is harnessed by the great Delcommune Dam that provides power for *Union Miniere's* mines. At some spots the gorge is only 90 feet wide but it cuts 1,300 feet into the earth. The Delcommune, which has created a lake that stretches 65 miles upstream, and its companion, the Le Marinel Dam on the Seke, a tributary of the Upper Congo, are only two of four dams which ultimately will put the river's strength to work. And it is a great strength: After it enters the N'Zilo Gorge, the Upper Congo plunges 1,550 feet in 43 miles. At the end of the gorge, the river emerges onto the plain, where it is joined by the Lubudi River, and flows sedately to the north. At Bukama, 414 miles from its source, the Upper Congo, there about a hundred yards wide, is crossed by a steel bridge that carries the BCK railway north to Kamina. At Bukama, situated on the river's right (east) bank, you are at one of the lowest points in Katanga: The altitude is only 1,886 feet and the weather is usually hot and muggy. But directly to the south the Manika Plateau, the homeland of the Balembwe and the Basanga tribes, rises to more than 5,000 feet. Bukama is the capital of the department of the same name and it, too, is part of Grands Lacs Province. The lakes from which the province takes its name stretch north along the course of the Upper Congo, mostly just to the east of it, like a string of muddy pearls. There are more than thirty of them, the largest being Lake Upemba, which covers 93 square miles. South of Lake Upemba and to the east of the river is the Upemba National Park, nearly three million acres of what used to be completely unspoiled nature reserves, into which no human visitors were allowed.

In recent months, however, there has been some skirmishing between rival tribes and no one really knows what the situation is now. Bukama, which has a landing strip, a radio-telegraph station, a few shops and two hotels (the *de la Marine*, which boasts cold running water, and the *Bukama*, which is bone-dry), is an important strategic center presently held by the Katangan forces. Not only do the railroads and roads from Kamina and Elisabethville meet here to be funnelled across the Upper Congo on Bukama's steel bridge (the only bridge across the river for hundreds of miles) but the town is also the highest navigable point on the river. When it can be done—the level is often too low during the dry season that lasts from April to November—it takes four days to make the 398-mile run downstream to Kongolo, where rapids again block the river. North of Bukama, the Upper Congo enters the Kamolondo depression, which is 155 miles long and about 30 miles wide. Here it breaks up into a number of channels that thread their ways to the bird-thronged lakes that dot the countryside. Lake Kisale—covered with water lilies—is perhaps the best known of these, if only because it is the one through which the Upper Congo flows from one end to the other. At Lake Kisale the Upper Congo is joined by its first important eastern tributary, the Lufira, which also rises near Musofi. Like the Upper Congo, the Lufira is harnessed by the Cornet and Bia dams, which provide power for the Jadotville area.

After Lake Kisale, the Upper Congo meanders through flats choked with papyrus and head-high elephant grass. Crocodiles doze on the mudbanks and buffalo can be seen resting among occasional clumps of trees. About 300 miles north of Bukama, at Ankoro, the capital of Luvua Province, which sits on the left bank, the Upper Congo is joined on the right by the Luvua River, navigable 100 miles upstream as far as Kiambi. The Luvua drains Lake Mweru, which in turn draws water from Lake Bangweulu by means of the Luapula River.

At Kabalo, the river steamers connect with the railway from Albertville. Beyond Kabalo, and twenty-four miles south of the town of Kongolo, the Upper Congo is joined by the Lukuga River, which drains Lake Tanganyika. Lake Tanganyika, in turn, is fed by the Ruzizi River from Lake Kivu. Just north of Kongolo, Katanga's northernmost town, navigation is blocked by a series of five stretches of rapids, collectively and somewhat extravagantly named *Portes d'Enfer*, which squeeze the river to a width of 100 yards. Kabalo, in the Kongolo Department of Luvua Province, is important primarily as a communications center. As has been noted, the railway from Albertville to Kamina passes through it. From Kabalo, the railway continues north through Kongolo on its route to Port Franqui. Kongolo, situated on the left bank of the Upper Congo, never had a population of more than 300 whites. But it was an important center with a military base, airfield, hospital, and radio-telegraph center. It is Bahemba, Basonge, and Baluba country, and the tribesmen grow coffee, bananas, rice, and cotton on the fertile plains on both sides of the river. Kongolo was evacuated by the Katangan gendarmes in November of 1961, Congolese army units moved in, and the Balubas pretty much ran amok in the town until the United Nations forces restored at least a semblance of order.

Two-hundred-and-fifty miles to the east of the river is Lake Tanganyika. Living in the hills which skirt the lake (in north to south order) are the Bakalanga, Batumbwe, Batabwa, and Bashila tribes. The two lakeside Katangan towns are Albertville and Baudouinville. The former is the more important; the latter, backed up against the Marungu Mountains, which reach an altitude of 6,500 feet, is the more scenic. Albertville, perched on the hills overlooking Lake Tanganyika, is the oldest Belgian city in Katanga. It was founded in 1891 by Captain (later Baron) Jacques de Dixmude as a jumping off place for the Belgian Anti-Slavery Society's crusade (called by Cardinal Lavigerie) against the Arab slavers on Lake Tanganyika. The town began as a small fort five miles south of the Lukuga River, a sluggish reed-choked stream that drains Lake Tanganyika into the Upper Congo. The war against the Arabs, who had their headquarters at M'Toa, just north of the Lukuga, lasted three years before the slavers were finally expelled. Before the arrival of the Belgians, M'Toa had been quite a town. From 1860 until 1894, it was the largest Arab port on the western side of Lake Tanganyika, the world's second deepest (after Baikal) lake and the turntable for the Arabs' slave and ivory caravans passing to and from Zanzibar and the Congo. It was also the point where European explorers bound for the Congo from Africa's East Coast assembled their caravans. As early as 1882, nine years before M'Siri's death, M'Toa had an English Protestant mission called "Plymouth Rock," which later moved to Kawala Island opposite the town. It was not, in fact, until 1915, when the railway from Albertville to Kabalo was completed, that Albertville passed M'Toa in importance.

Today, Albertville, at an altitude of 2,575 feet, is the capital of the Katangan province of Tanganyika, which is composed of the departments of Albertville, Baudouinville, Nyunzu, and Moliro. Before the 1960 troubles, Albertville had a population of 1,400 whites and 25,000 Katangans. But many of the whites have since fled across the lake to Kigoma in the face of the advancing United Nations and Congolese National Army troops. Albertville has a cement factory, the Greinerville coal mine, large railway repair shops, pleasant homes built into the hillside, and a drydock larger than a football field and big enough to handle any ship on the lake. The drydock used to be a popular place to swim until they drained it one day and found two large and rather belligerent crocodiles thrashing around on the bottom.

On the Luvua plains, between Lake Tanganyika and the Upper Congo, lies the important (2.5 per cent of the world's production) tin-mining town of Manono. Manono, which before the troubles had a population of 650 whites and 30,000 Africans, was literally built from scratch. There was nothing there before the *Compagnie Geologique et Miniere des Ingenieurs et Industriels Belges* (GEOMINES) began to exploit the tin just before World War I. The mine is an open-pit affair and is heavily mechanized. The ore is refined and exported as ingots which are more than 99 per cent pure. Aside from the tin works, perhaps the most striking thing about Manono is its fruit trees. The entire town is studded with mangos (more than 50,000 at last count), orange, lemon, guava, and papaya trees that perfume the air, afford shade, and provide food for the population. Manono is Bakunda country, a tribe allied to the Balubas. The Katangan Government was forced out of the town in 1960 and terrible atrocities were perpetrated by the tribesmen. Later, Katanga's White Legion recaptured the town. Recently, it was evacuated again by the gendarmerie.

South of the Luvua Valley, between the Upemba Park and Lake Mweru, you climb again onto that series of high plateaus, separated by the valleys of the Luapula, Kafuba, Lufira, Dikiluwe, Lualaba, and Musonoi rivers, that is Upper Katanga, undulating savannah and bush country occasionally studded with mountains and splotched by marshy clearings called *dembos*. The scenery is less monotonous and the air is fresher. Here, east of the 5,577-foot high Kundelungu Mountains, lives another section of the Bayekes, the Batembos, the Bashilas, and the Baushi. Beyond them and into the Congo pedicle (the strip of land which juts into Rhodesia like an accusing finger), is the land of the Babemba, the eastern Lundas, the Balambas, and the Balalas. All of these tribes have kinsmen living across the border in Rhodesia and they are solidly pro-

Tshombe. West of the Lufira River Valley, which nearly
bisects Upper Katanga, live the Bakaondes, Luenas, Minun-
gus, and the western Bayekes. Again, Tshombe enjoys the
support of the majority of these tribesmen. Always remem-
bering that local quarrels and rivalries often make for ex-
ceptions, it is fair to say that Tshombe is strong south of
the 9th Parallel, weak in the forests north of it. It is this
southern heartland of eroded streams, deep valleys, cool
plateaus, and tumbling rivers that produces most of Katanga's wealth. Its three principal cities are Kolwezi, Jadotville, and Elisabethville, the capital.

Of these three towns, Kolwezi is the least known to the
foreigner and the most attractive. Had the colonial period
lasted another decade, it might well have become the most
important. At an altitude of 4,733 feet, Kolwezi has about
the best climate of any town of the Congo: The mornings
are brisk, the air sparkles, and an open fire feels good at
night. The town (with a population of 4,100 whites and
70,000 Africans) was not built until 1938 when the western
copperfields began to be exploited. Kolwezi—the capital
of Lualaba Province—straddles the railway that leads from
Elisabethville through Angola to Lobito. It boasts a copper
concentrator, a metallurgical plant, and, near it, the mammoth Delcommune and Le Marinel hydroelectric schemes.

With 5,000 whites, Jadotville before independence had
the third largest concentration of Europeans in the Congo.
Only Leopoldville and Elisabethville were ahead of it. Thus,
Jadotville was one of three Congolese cities with the official rank of a municipality. The city, 87 miles northwest
of Elisabethville, has been little damaged by the fighting
in Katanga (just as Kolwezi has not been badly damaged)
and most of its whites are still there. Jadotville, which has
an African population of 75,000, lacks Elisabethville's quiet
charm but it partially compensates for this in its more
picturesque setting amid rugged, eucalyptus-clad hills (its
altitude is 4,166 feet). The Franqui and Bia dams are near

Jadotville, and the town's industrial complex, which includes an ore concentrator, a metallurgical plant, a cement
factory, and extensive workshops, is the largest in Katanga.
For generations, natives had smelted the copper found near
Jadotville. The town was founded in 1927 and called
Likasi (its native name) until 1931, when it was renamed
after Jean Jadot, *Union Miniere*'s first chairman. The town
is the capital of the province of the same name.

Which brings us to Elisabethville, the capital of Katanga,
named after King Albert I's queen. It was founded in 1910
by General Emile Wangermee, Katanga's first governor.
When I came there four years ago, I had expected to find
a Big-Shouldered city like Sandburg's Chicago, a rough,
brawling town reminiscent of the American West of the
post-Civil War period. There is just a touch of this atmosphere in the Rhodesian mining towns like Chingola,
Kitwe, and Ndola across the border, but nothing could be
further from the truth about Elisabethville. Although the
city creates the impression of being not quite finished, of
coming half-baked from the oven, the overriding atmosphere is one of primness, of order, of pleasant, prosperous
but dull suburban living. The Times Square of Elisabethville is the intersection of the *Avenues de l'Etoile* and
Royale. On one side is the much fought-over pie-shaped
post office. Bookshops, the *Au Royal* sidewalk cafe, and
the monument to the dead of the two World Wars fill the
other corners. The feeling that Elisabethville (the native
name for the city is Lubumbashi) is half-finished, comes
from the curious juxtaposition of shops: You buy a Dior
gown in a smart shop; its neighbor is an automobile repair
works.

A block away from the post office, at the intersection of
the *Avenue de l'Etoile* and the *Avenue Fulbert Youlou*
(named after Tshombe's good friend, the President of the
ex-French Congo) is the Grand Hotel Leopold II. Behind

the *Leo Deux* is the railway station, and, stretching away to the east, the industrial area.

Driving west on the *Avenue de l'Etoile*, one comes to a symbolic intersection. To one side is the headquarters of the *Union Miniere du Haut-Katanga*. To the other is Tshombe's palace, the political nervecenter of the country. Without the support of the other, neither would be possible.

The *Union Miniere* compound, dominated by the 492-foot chimney of the smelter (the highest in Africa and third-tallest in the world) and the huge slag heap, stretches away to the southwest. On the north flank of the compound is the mining company's Lubumbashi native housing sector; to the south are the municipal native residential quarters of Katuba, Kenya, and Albert. These are pleasantly wooded townships with their own stores, churches, and social centers. Despite the Belgian boast that racialism has no part in their philosophy, it is worth noting that "persons of color" were required by law to live in areas set apart for them. This means either in company quarters or in a *cité indigène* such as Katuba. Under the colonial administration, this law was strictly enforced by the police and consequently one saw few Africans in either the European residential or commercial areas of Elisabethville. Only employed Africans and their families had the privilege of permanent residence in a *cité*. The practice was to separate the African and the European parts of town by a "green belt." This was formed, from east to west, by the railway yards, the Camp Massart military base, a string of churches, hospitals, and schools, the *Union Miniere* works, the Lubumbashi River Valley and the golf course. As a result, one had the impression that Elisabethville, with its white population of 14,000, was largely a white city. Unless one made a special trip to Katuba or Kenya or Albert, one was scarcely aware of the 170,000 Africans. This was a common psychological phenomenon one used to find all over Africa: a small European community, aware of its numerical inferiority, isolating itself and attempting to build a community identical to that of the homeland, admitting the African only as far as his presence as a laborer was necessary and desirable. Now, of course, the situation has changed, although not as much as one would think: a few African politicians and wealthy businessmen live in the comfortable burnt-brick bungalows surrounded by bougainvillaea and hibiscus in the shady, white residential district in the northern part of the city. But it is still fundamentally and obviously a white section. The great mass of the Africans, both from personal choice and from economic necessity, still confine themselves largely to their *cité indigène*.

The growth of Elisabethville has been nothing short of phenomenal. As recently as 1935, the town had a population of only 2,400 whites and 25,000 Africans. Since then, both groups have increased sixfold, the Africans attracted by the work, the whites by the high standard of living and excellent climate. The contrast in climate between Elisabethville and a Congolese town like Stanleyville can scarcely be exaggerated. In Elisabethville, the average temperature is 68° F. (hoarfrost is frequent on the Katangan plateaus during the dry season which stretches from April to October), the annual rainfall is 37 inches, and there are 2,723 hours of sunlight per year; the comparable figures for Stanleyville are 77° F., 68 inches, and 1,991 hours of sunlight. In the one, life for a white man is possible; in the other, it is pleasant. As a consequence, Katanga's pre-independence total of 35,000 whites gave it 29.4 per cent of the European population of the Congo, or only about 1,000 less than Leopoldville Province, the seat of the colonial capital.

By no means all of Katanga's whites are either Belgians or settlers. In addition to whites of Belgian nationality, Katanga has about 1,500 Italian Jews who have come mostly from Rhodes and Egypt (Elisabethville has had a synagogue since 1921), more than 1,000 Portuguese, a slightly smaller number of Britons, South Africans, and Rhodesians, and communities numbering several hundred each of French, Dutch, Indians, and Americans (the U.S. citizens are mostly Protestant missionaries). There is also a sprinkling of Swiss, Germans, Poles, and—of all things—Luxembourgers. In the field of small business, there are actually twice as many "aliens" as Belgians, although Belgians are in the majority in all other fields.

Before independence, Katanga was administered by 3,000 white colonial officials. Most of them have now gone. Of the remaining 12,000 white heads of families, about 7,000 were employees of large firms, 3,000 were settlers, and the remainder were missionaries. Of the 3,000 settlers—slightly less than half of whom were "alien" whites—41 per cent were small businessmen and storekeepers, 31 per cent artisans and craftsmen, 20 per cent farmers and ranchers, and 8 per cent professional men—lawyers, doctors, teachers, and the like.

In contrast, then, to the settlers of Kenya and Rhodesia, the average white Katangan is not an agriculturalist but an urban dweller as likely to be a foreigner as a Belgian, deriving his income from the fringes of the mining industry. The Katangan soil is just too poor to provide a living for more than a few people. To ranch each of Katanga's 180,-000 white-owned cattle, for instance, requires about 18 acres of grazing, despite the fact that the foundation strain of the herds is Afrikander, the hearty indigenous cattle (10,000 of these have been interbred with Frieslands, Jerseys, and Brown Swiss to produce a dairy herd). There are also about 18,000 pigs and 6,000 sheep kept by Europeans in Katanga.

The same is true of the African population: Because the soil is so poor, it is fundamentally an urban and semi-urban population. An astounding (for Africa) 56 per cent of Katanga's adult males are salaried employees. There are less than 10,000 African-owned cattle in the entire country. There are, however, 185,000 goats, 140,000 sheep, and 18,000 pigs kept by Africans. The acreage figures of African-owned perennial cropland are even more startling: of the 130,000 acres of perennial cropland tilled by African farmers in the entire Congo, only 3,450 (or less than 3 per cent) are in Katanga. Katanga has no African rubber, cacao, or tea, and only 1,000 acres of coffee and 2,500 of oil palms. Among the annual crops, of course, Africans own thousands of acres of cotton, manioc, tobacco, and potatoes. The consequence of this has been a movement of Africans to the cities. Of the 24 Congolese cities with populations of more than 10,000, seven of them—Elisabethville, Jadotville, Kolwezi, Albertville, Kipushi, Kamina, and Manono—are in Katanga. More than 34 per cent of Katanga's African population has left its tribal communities to seek a new life in the cities, by far the highest percentage of any of the Congo's six provinces. The percentage for the other five provinces is only 20.5 per cent. This has had important social and political consequences. It has made the Katangans easier to educate and Christianize (37 Catholic orders and six Protestant sects work in Katanga), hence has brought them, in a comparatively short time, a degree of civilization far higher than that obtaining elsewhere in the Congo, with the possible exception of the immediate environs of Leopoldville. This, however, has taken place only among those Katangans who have become urbanized. One of the most striking features about Katanga is the contrast between city and country: One minute you are in a city almost as developed as a comparable mining town in Europe or America; but the city ends as abruptly as it began and, within the wink of an eye, you are back in the bitter, monotonous, endless bush where the Africans still live as their ancestors did. This imbalance between city and country creates serious psychological and social problems. There is no transition stage for the Katangan African: He either lives as his grandfather did in M'Siri's day, or he moves into a highly complex twentieth century industrial society. The answer, of course, is that the transition is not as complete as it appears to be on the surface. The paternalism of *Union Miniere* glosses over the tensions and the conflicts which occur within its African workers, both individually and collectively. That this is so was indicated in 1961 when Chokwe and Lunda miners mutilated several Balubas who had been living and working with them for years, presumably in amity, as fellow employees of the mining company. Working, living, and going to school together has tended to break down the tribal barriers between associated tribes and to make common political action possible. By the same token, this eradication of the more impermanent tribal barriers has served to intensify the hatred of the Balubas, who have not been admitted to this new fraternity.

On the subject of education, it is worth noting that Elisabethville contains the Congo's state university, one of two in the entire country (the other being Lovanium, the Catholic university outside Leopoldville). The university, which has a faculty of forty professors and lecturers, opened its doors in September, 1956, under the chairmanship of a gentleman with an appropriately academic name: Professor Campus, Vice-Chancellor of the University of Liège. The well-known American expert on African anthropology Professor Melville Herskovits, inaugurated its university lecture forum. Eventually—assuming that normal life returns to Elisabethville—the university's campus will be located on a 1,250-acre site four miles north of the center of the city on the old airport and near the SABENA guest house. There was fighting there last December and, for the moment, the students are scattered around town in temporary classrooms. During the academic year that ended in 1959, the university, which has a 60,000-volume library, had 168 students. Of these, 144 were white and 24 were

African. In addition, another 18 Africans were attending a special year-long preparatory session designed to bridge the academic gap that kept them from gaining admission to the university. The four most popular departments were Science (sixty-one white and three African students), Education (thirty-four whites and four Africans), Law (twenty-four whites and twelve Africans) and Philosophy (twenty-one whites and one African). Thirty-seven of the students were women but none of these was African. A medical school, racially integrated in all respects, was established in the fall of 1959. Many of the students have left because of the state of war that broke out twice last year in Elisabethville, and all the faculty families were evacuated to Salisbury in December. But the university continues to function, and some of its staff members have considerable influence with Tshombe. One of them is reputed to have been influential in persuading him to accept a cease-fire in September of last year.

Elisabethville is a city in a sense that none of the other Katangan towns are: It has dial telephones, two daily and three weekly newspapers (the Congo's first newspaper *L'Etoile du Congo* was published in Elisabethville in 1911), 23 hotels with a total of 377 rooms, a public library, a museum (containing a chunk of uranium and some rather bedraggled looking animal heads), a zoo, restaurants, night spots, an academy of music, two moving picture theaters, several clubs, a Byzantine cathedral with a dome of brass, a publishing house, art galleries, four banks, a sports stadium, and nearly a dozen foreign consulates. But despite the quiet dignity of its broad jacaranda-lined cobbled streets, Elisabethville is still the city that copper built: Sandburg's Big Shoulders are there, even if they are covered by a well-draped and expensive suit. Mining made Elisabethville, as it made Katanga, and mining means *Union Miniere*. Let us take a minute to examine this extraordinary corporation.

III

A SCANDAL OF RICHES

> "The policy of *Union Miniere*
> is to produce copper."
>
> —HERMAN ROBILIART, President of
> *Union Miniere*, replying to
> accusations that his company
> was meddling in Katanga's
> politics—*New York, November
> 23, 1961.*

To GET a firm grasp of the anatomy of the mining interests which dominate the economic life of Katanga, it is necessary to retrace briefly the financial negotiations which took place immediately before and after the annexation of Katanga by the Congo Free State.

It will be remembered that Leopold II called on the *Societé Generale de Belgique* when he was looking for funds to pay for expeditions to Katanga. The *Societé Generale* is a gigantic company, formed in 1822 with the personal financial participation of the Belgian royal family. Its arms stretch into a dozen industries. The *Societé Generale's* American equivalent would be a combine of the Bank of America, U.S. Steel, General Motors, TWA, the B&O Railroad, and the Mutual Life Insurance Corporation of New York. It has capital reserves of more than $40 million. The financiers of the *Societé Generale* agreed to assist Leopold II in the development of the Congo in

43

general and in the annexation of Katanga in particular. To this end, the *Compagnie du Congo pour le Commerce et l'Industrie* was created. Between the Delcommune and the Stairs expeditions, it was decided that the problems of acquiring and developing Katanga were sufficiently different from those obtaining in the remainder of the Congo to justify the formation of a subsidiary company of CCCI to deal exclusively with Katanga. Thus the *Compagnie du Katanga* was formed.

It was to the *Compagnie du Katanga* that Leopold II made his concession grant in 1891: full property rights to one-third of the unoccupied land annexed by the company and a 99-year renewable concession for exploiting all the minerals in Katanga. At the successful conclusion of the Katanga operation, the *Compagnie du Katanga* and the King agreed in 1900 to the creation of yet another organization, the *Comité Special du Katanga*, to develop their mutual interests. This committee consisted of six representatives, four (including the president) chosen by the King and two by the *Compagnie du Katanga*. Two-thirds of all profits deriving from CSK's operations were to go to the King and one-third to the *Compagnie du Katanga*.

A year before the creation of CSK, a company called Tanganyika Concessions Ltd. was formed in London under the management of Sir Robert Williams (1860–1938), one of Cecil Rhodes' lieutenants. Rhodes, despite the Belgian annexation of the territory, was determined to play a role in Katanga. Without further delay, Tanganyika Concessions sent an expedition into Katanga. Fearing an international incident and anxious to placate Rhodes, CSK agreed to share Katanga's wealth with the Williams group. An agreement was concluded whereby Williams was granted prospecting rights in Katanga. Any discoveries were to be jointly operated, with CSK providing 60 per cent of the capital (and reaping an equal percentage of the profits) and Tanganyika Concessions 40 per cent. Tanganyika Concessions, incidentally, is tied in with the great British and South African mining interests.

The agonizing year-long wait while the first mining equipment was brought in by oxcart from the Angolan port of Benguela soon demonstrated the urgent need for transport. Katanga was 1,300 miles from the coast and 450 miles from the nearest railhead. Williams agreed to arrange the financing of a 1,145-mile railroad through Angola to Katanga and to see to the extension of the Rhodesian railway. For his part, Leopold laid the groundwork for the creation of the *Chemin de Fer du Bas-Congo au Katanga* (BCK), providing an all-Congolese route to the sea.

In an effort to keep the mining side of the operation separate, yet another corporation was founded by the interested parties in 1906. This was the *Union Miniere du Haut-Katanga* (UMHK). Its first chairman, furnished by the *Societé Generale de Belgique*, was the engineer Jean Jadot (1862–1932), builder of the Peking-Hankow railway, after whom the Katangan mining center of Jadotville is named. Williams was UMHK's first vice-chairman.

Union Miniere's initial capitalization was set at 10 million Belgian francs (in 1906 the rate of exchange was 5 Belgian francs to the dollar—today it is 50 to the dollar), represented by 100,000 shares, half held by *Societé Generale* and half by Tanganyika Concessions. Another 60,000 shares were issued to CSK in consideration of its special role in the development of Katanga; Tanganyika Concessions received 40,000 additional shares for the same reason (present number of UMHK shares: 1,242,000, about 25 per cent of which are French-owned). Leopold's interest in *Union Miniere* eventually was acquired by the government of the Belgian Congo to be held in trust for the people of the Congo.

This is the present percentile division of capital and voting rights in *Union Miniere:*

	capital	voting rights
Congolese Government	18.14%	23.82%
Tanganyika Concessions	14.47%	20.21%
Compagnie du Katanga	8.77%	13.40%
Societé Generale	4.64%	6.94%
Private Shareholders	53.98%	35.63%

The shares belonging to the Congolese Government have not as yet been turned over to Leopoldville. Neither have they been placed at the disposal of the government of Katanga. Tshombe has, however, been receiving the royalties, dividends, and taxes accruing from these shares. It is estimated that 80 per cent of Katanga's annual revenue of $84 million comes from *Union Miniere*. In short, Tshombe has been financing his secession from the Congo by profits from the shares technically owned by the Leopoldville government. *Union Miniere* could, of course, have refused to pay Tshombe dividends from the shares. Had the company done so, Tshombe would have closed or nationalized the mines. Bearing this in mind, it is difficult to blame *Union Miniere* for keeping the Congolese shares intact pending a political solution to the problem of Katanga, while paying Tshombe the dividends as the price of staying in business.

Examination of the events leading up to the creation of *Union Miniere* and scrutiny of the share distribution explains the intense British interest in what is going on in the Congo today. British financiers historically have been intimately associated with the development of Katanga. Today, British (and American) interests directly own 14.47 per cent of *Union Miniere*'s capital shares in the form of the Tanganyika Concessions holdings (and the Belgians have a cross-holding of a million-odd shares in Tanganyika Concessions). In addition to this, the British-owned Benguela Railway from Elisabethville to the Angolan coast is largely dependent on *Union Miniere* for its freight traffic. With the BCK railway through the Congo to Matadi cut, all of *Union Miniere*'s copper now goes out either through Angola or Rhodesia (under normal circumstances, more than half of *Union Miniere*'s production went out through the Congo while the Angolan and Rhodesian routes divided the remainder of the traffic about equally). Consequently, the Benguela Railway should be able to pay its British stockholders a considerable dividend this year. British members of *Union Miniere*'s Board of Directors include Captain Charles Waterhouse (who is also chairman of the board of Tanganyika Concessions), Sir Ulick Alexander, and Lord Selbourne. Lord Clitheroe has also declared his financial interest in companies associated with *Union Miniere*. These men find political allies for their support of the Tshombe regime in backbench Conservative MP's of the Suez Rebel sort and in Sir Roy Welensky's Central African Federation.

This does not mean, as some observers have implied, that British and Belgian financiers are united in a secret plot to maintain Tshombe and to defeat the ends of the Leopoldville government and the United Nations. Obviously, these men have a stake in Katanga. But most of them have interests elsewhere that are equally if not more important. The *Societé Generale de Belgique*, for instance, owns 4.64 per cent of *Union Miniere*'s stock. But it also has vast holdings in the rest of the Congo. These include the *Compagnie du Congo pour le Commerce et l'Industrie* (the oldest Belgian enterprise in the Congo, active in agriculture, manufacturing, and commerce), *Societé Miniere de Beceka* (which produces from its Kasai mines more than 60 per cent of the world's industrial diamonds), *Banque du Congo* (a commercial banking company with branches throughout the Congo), *Compagnie Maritime Belge* (a shipping company which operates between the U.S.A., Belgium, the Congo, and other African ports), and *Societé de Traction et d'Electricté* (which manufactures and distributes electric power in Belgium and advises Congolese enterprises on these subjects).

These are not fly-by-night organizations. CCCI alone has eleven major subsidiary companies with a combined capital of $57.8 million. These companies grow palm products, cacao, rubber, sugar, coffee, and cotton, raise cattle, manufacture cement, import and sell automobiles, agricultural machinery, pharmaceutical supplies, medical supplies, optical instruments, and petroleum products, build boats, and manage service firms.

Societé Miniere de Beceka has a capital of $24 million and owns shares in a manganese mining company. The *Banque du Congo*, with capital and reserves of $12.4 million and total resources of $180 million, has 21 branches and 1,713 employees. The *Compagnie Maritime Belge* operates a fleet of 36 ships.

These investments are all in the Congo proper, not in Katanga. Hence it is patently obvious that even if, as some people would have us believe, capitalists think and act only from their pocketbooks rather than from their hearts and minds, *Societé Generale*'s major interest lies in the Congo proper. If it or its stockholders support Tshombe, they do so because they think that an autonomous Katanga is the only just and workable solution. Their point of view deserves careful consideration if only because, in contrast to most of Tshombe's detractors, who wouldn't know a Bayeke from a Bakongo, they have an intimate knowledge of the Congo and its people dating back more than seventy-five years.

The same thing goes for Tanganyika Concessions, *Compagnie du Katanga* and the private shareholders, who among them account for 78.41 per cent of *Union Miniere*'s capital. Most of the 120,000 private shareholders, no one of whom holds more than 0.5 per cent of *Union Miniere*'s voting rights, probably own stock in companies outside Katanga. Tanganyika Concessions obviously does. As Herman Robiliart, President of *Union Miniere*, put it when he addressed a press conference in New York on November 23, 1961:

"Like any private enterprise anywhere, we need peace and order, not war and strife, to conduct our operations smoothly. Those who accuse us of military adventuring assume that we are ignorant of our own self-interest. It is preposterous to suppose that a private company would engage in activities that would invite harm to its personnel or its properties." That is the voice of logic.

That is not to say, however, that *Union Miniere*'s employees in Katanga support either the Central Government or the United Nations operations in Katanga. The great majority of them do not. They fear the neo-Communism of the Gizengist group in the Congo. They hate the local United Nations forces as the instrument that would, they believe, put them at the mercy of the Gizengists. And they despise the Blue Helmets because they have killed their friends or families, both in their offices and in their homes. Almost all of them, for these reasons, support Tshombe. But they do this as individuals, not as employees of *Union Miniere*. And they are just as entitled to their political opinions as those equally opinionated and largely misinformed people who oppose the Katangan leader from comfortably insulated positions in Washington and New Delhi.

At any rate, it contributes nothing to the solution of the Katangan problem to assume that any company doing business in Katanga, any individual owning stock in such a company, or any white man living there automatically acts from evil motives. It just isn't true. Nor should the hostage nature of the situation be forgotten: Companies which operate in Katanga and whites who live there are subject to the laws of the state and wholly dependent for their lives and livelihoods upon the good-will of Katanga's government and people. Even if they did not believe in the cause of Katangan independence, it would be both foolish and dangerous for them to adopt an anti-Tshombe position. These are considerations that should not be forgotten.

Back to *Union Miniere*. We have seen that the company was established with British, Belgian, and South African capital in 1906. Elisabethville, Katanga's capital, was founded in 1910, and the railhead reached it the same year. The first copper ingot was smelted at Elisabethville's Lubumbashi plant in the middle of 1911. But there were many problems yet to be solved. Katanga was so lightly populated that little African labor was available for the mines. This meant that *Union Miniere* officials had to go as far afield as Mozambique and Nyasaland to recruit labor. Coke for the smelters had to be imported from Europe. As a result, it cost exactly twice as much to produce a ton of copper in Katanga as it could sell for in Europe. These problems were temporarily overcome by the development of an efficient recruiting system and the exploitation of collieries at Wankie in Southern Rhodesia.

The outbreak of World War I had two important effects on *Union Miniere:* It forced the company into an all-out productive effort and it necessitated the use of African personnel as engine drivers and in other semi-skilled posts. This was a step never to be reversed. In contrast to the situation in South Africa and the Rhodesias, where certain jobs were reserved for whites, an African employee of *Union Miniere* was free to progress as far as his brains, skill, and initiative would take him. By 1917, *Union Miniere* was producing more than 25,000 tons of copper per year. It was not, however, until two years later, after thirteen years of existence, that *Union Miniere* was able to pay its first dividend. There were dark days ahead: the collapse of copper prices in 1920, the depression of the 1930's (when the price of copper tumbled from its ten-year level of 14 gold cents to four cents and *Union Miniere*'s production fell in a single year from 139,000 tons to 54,000 tons), the collapse of Belgium in World War II. But there were moments of triumph, too: Although Belgium was defeated, *Union Miniere* shipped 800,000 tons of copper to Britain during World War II, 6,000 tons of cobalt to the U.S., and provided the uranium which built the first American atomic bombs. America did not forget *Union Miniere*'s contribution to the war effort. In 1946, Jules Cousin, chairman of the company's Elisabethville management committee, was awarded the Medal of Freedom. He returned the medal to President Kennedy last December in protest against United States support for the "mercenary killers" of the United Nations.

Today, *Union Miniere* is one of the great mining companies of the world. It ranks third (after Anaconda and Kennecot) among the world's copper producers, accounting for about 8 per cent of the world's supply. *Union Miniere*'s production ranks Katanga as the world's fifth largest copper producer, after the U.S., Chile, Northern Rhodesia, and Canada. In 1960, its record year, *Union Miniere* produced 300,675 tons of copper, despite a 10 per cent cutback in production during the last three months of the year in an attempt to stabilize copper prices. (In 1961, it dropped to 293,000 tons.) And remember that this took place during 1960, for half of which the rest of the Congo was in a state of near-chaos. To put *Union Miniere*'s copper production another way: For every 11 tons of copper produced by the entire Communist bloc, *Union Miniere* produced 6 tons. This may help to explain Russian interest in the Katangan problem. Tshombe's country is a rich prize, indeed.

And this is not the extent of Katanga's mineral wealth, which Jules Cornet described as "a geological scandal." In 1960, *Union Miniere* exported—mainly to the U.S.—8,222 tons of cobalt, or more than 60 per cent of the world's supply of this strategic metal (and this was increased to 8,400 tons in 1961.) It also produced 16 per cent (25,101 kilograms) of the world's germanium (useful in the construction of Sputniks and transistor radios), 5 per cent of its manganese, and virtually all of the world's radium (27.6 grams), used in the treatment of cancer. *Union Miniere*, which registered a profit of $47.3 million in 1960 (down from $70.7 million in 1959 but in line with 1958's $48.2 million and 1957's $49.8 million), also produced 193,004 tons (4 per cent of the world's production) of zinc concentrates, 208,959 kilograms of cadmium (3.5 per cent of the world's production), and 45 kilograms of gold. *Union Miniere* ranks sixth among the world's silver producers and, in 1960, exported 123,258 kilograms, or 1.6 per cent of the world's production.

Katanga is also rich in iron, which is virtually unexploited, and has coal reserves of 8 million tons. The coal is of low quality with a 30 per cent ash content, which makes it difficult to coke. The discovery of new coking techniques, however, could result in the establishment of a steel industry in Katanga. Everything else is there: coal, iron, and abundant electrical power.

Uranium was discovered at Shinkolobwe near Jadotville, 87 miles northwest of Elisabethville, in 1915, by Major R. R. Sharpe, a Rhodesian. Sharpe returned to England to serve in the war and one of the richest radium mines in the world went unregistered until his return in 1922. Shinkolobwe, like the Prince Leopold copper mine at Kipushi and unlike all the other *Union Miniere* workings, is an underground mine. It was originally used for the extraction of radium. Shinkolobwe was closed in 1938 and reopened in 1943, when its ore was required for the construction of the Hiroshima and Nagasaki atomic bombs. The Belgians maintained the tightest security precautions at Shinkolobwe, refused to admit visitors, and never released production figures, even when the rest of the world's uranium producers were doing so. It is believed, however, that Shinkolobwe's annual uranium production ranged between 850 and 1,100 tons. As the wind of change blew in hurricane force through the Congo, *Union Miniere* announced (in 1958) that Shinkolobwe's reserves were dwindling fast. Two months before independence, the company said that the mine was exhausted and had been closed down, its machinery dismantled. In most cases relative to economic affairs, one would be inclined to accept *Union Miniere*'s word. But the Belgian mania in regard to atomic matters, the obvious fear that uranium will make Katanga attractive prey for both Russia and America, makes one wonder whether the country's uranium is exhausted.

Finally, tin mined at the northern Katangan town of Manono by a firm called *Compagnie Geologique et Miniere des Ingenieurs et Industriels Belges* (through the Belgian penchant for contraction of corporate titles mercifully reduced to GEOMINES) accounts for 2.5 per cent of the world's production.

The mineral wealth of Katanga staggers the imagination. Before independence mining accounted for one-third of the tonnage and two-thirds of the value of all the Congo's exports. Katanga was responsible for about 80 per cent of this, with copper alone accounting for 56 per cent of the value of all minerals. *Union Miniere* itself accounted for 20 per cent of the Congo's gross national product and provided 45 per cent (*not* 65 per cent, as has been stated so frequently) of the Congo's revenues. Nearly half of the latter percentage was returned to Katanga for its local budget. Consequently, Katanga's actual contribution to the budgets of the other five provinces was more on the order of 25 per cent. *Union Miniere* produces enough copper to fill all Belgium's requirements and much of France's —70 per cent of its production going to these two countries. The result of this mineral wealth has been to change the face of Katanga, to make it into a Central African Ruhr containing 20 per cent of all private investment in the Congo, nine of the country's 35 water purification plants, more than half of its railway mileage, 83 per cent of the country's hydroelectric power, 57 per cent of its steam power, and 52 per cent of its diesel power (or 80 per cent of all forms of power). Katanga, the biggest energy-producing center in Africa, has so much electricity that it can afford to export power to the Northern Rhodesian mines 260 miles away from the Le Marinel hydroelectric scheme, for the moment probably the largest single producer in Africa. The lines that transmit the power are reputed to be the longest and have the highest voltage (220,000 volts) on the continent. Katanga itself contains more than 650 miles of high tension wires feeding *Union Miniere*'s mines and the cities that have grown up around them.

CSK, as we have seen, inherited Leopold's original concession to the *Compagnie du Katanga* of about 20,000 square miles. From CSK, for an annual ground-rent of about $4 million, *Union Miniere* obtained the mining concession over approximately 13,100 square miles, an area larger than Belgium itself, the equivalent of about the states of Maryland and Delaware combined. Roughly 7,700 square miles of this, lying in Upper Katanga (south of the 10th Parallel), contains almost all of Katanga's known copper reserves. The remainder, in the Baluba areas to the north, is the less valuable tin-mining concession, which has not been worked since 1946. The actual area in which most of the copper is mined lies in a belt 200 miles long and from 15 to 60 miles wide, containing 150 known mineral deposits. It is an old (and true) joke that *Union Miniere* sends out its prospectors to search for areas within this belt where there are *no* minerals so that sites can be found for its housing developments.

Katanga's copper is almost embarrassingly easy to mine and the lode is the richest in the world. The great majority of the ore is located close to the surface and is "mined" by the open-cast method, which means that the thin surface layer of dirt is dug away and the ore excavated in terraces or benches from a great hole. Most of this sort of mining is heavily mechanized, the ore being torn from the earth in huge mouthfuls by ten-ton buckets and dumped into twenty-ton trucks that haul it to the treatment plants. As a result, the productivity of the average miner has increased from 2.5 to 32 cubic yards per day. To relieve a local unemployment situation, however, some mines worked by hand labor are still kept open.

Of all *Union Miniere*'s ten workings, however, its one underground mine, the Prince Leopold mine at Kipushi (a town with a population of 1,000 whites and 16,000 Africans), is the most spectacular. The Prince Leopold mine, the world's richest, which burrows 1,600 feet into the earth not more than 650 yards from the Northern Rhodesia border, produces ore that sometimes reaches 16 per cent copper content and averages 10 per cent—twice that achieved in the other Katangan mines and three times the purity of the Northern Rhodesian ore (the richest American copper mine, in contrast, produces ore of only 1.5 per cent copper content). Production began at Prince Leopold in 1926, and it is believed that the vein, which is 200 feet thick and 2,000 feet long, will be exhausted by 1978. *Union Miniere*'s ten mines include Musonoi and Kamoto (which produce copper and cobalt), Kinganiyembo, Ruwe, and Kolwezi (which produce only copper). These constitute the so-called Western Group, by far the most important: It accounts for 77 per cent of all the copper produced by *Union Miniere*. The Southern Group, which includes Prince Leopold (which produces zinc and germanium in addition to copper), is made up of Ruashi, *Etoile du Congo*, and Karavia, all producing only copper. The Central Group consists of the Kambove mine, which also produces only copper.

About half of the ore gouged from the earth at these mines is treated electrolytically at *Union Miniere*'s Shituru (Jadotville) and Luilu (Kolwezi) plants until, like Ivory

Soap, it is 99.95 per cent pure. Shituru can handle 135,000 tons of electrolytic copper and 6,000 tons of cobalt per year. The new Luilu plant can treat 100,000 tons of copper and 3,500 tons of cobalt per year. The balance of the cobalt and all of the zinc are treated at Jadotville. The remainder of the copper production is refined by the blister method (producing ingots 98.5 per cent pure) at *Union Miniere*'s Lubumbashi plant in Elisabethville, which has the capacity to produce 125,000 tons of blister copper per year.

In its fifty-five years of existence and half a century of mining, *Union Miniere* has produced 6.3 million tons of copper, 116,000 tons of cobalt, and 2.4 million tons of zinc concentrates. This has been accomplished through one of the closest intermeshings of the state and private industry that exists today outside of the Communist bloc. If *Union Miniere* is rampant capitalism, it is also socialism with a vengeance: Through its ownership of two-thirds of the stock of the now defunct CSK, the Congolese nation has become the largest shareholder in UMHK. Since the state receives not only taxes and royalties but also dividends from *Union Miniere*, the Congo, when the political problem of Katanga is settled, will milk the UMHK cow from both ends and have a doubly vested interest in its well-being.

Union Miniere's activities go far beyond those of most mining companies. Its wholly owned subsidiaries and companies in which it has important holdings represent an endlessly proliferating network of tier after tier of interlocking corporations. A few examples follow.

Compagnie Foncière du Katanga (COFOKA) builds and maintains apartments, office buildings, and residences both for *Union Miniere* and for private individuals. As of last year, COFOKA (which had built in 1952 and maintained until the U.N. take-over the enormous multimillion dollar Kamina military base in northern Katanga), owned

1,720 buildings covering more than 600 acres in Katanga and maintained 2,000 others.

Societé Generale des Forces Hydro-Electriques du Katanga (SOGEFOR) owns the Franqui Power Plant at Mwadingusha beneath the 380-foot-high Cornet Falls on the Lufira River 40 miles from Jadotville. The dam above the falls, built in 1930, is 39 feet high and 1,640 feet long. It creates an 111,000-acre lake that stores more than 320 billion gallons of water. SOGEFOR also operates for *Union Miniere* the Bia Power Plant at Koni Falls five miles below Cornet Falls on the Lufira River (completed in 1950), the Delcommune Power Plant, built in 1953 at N'Zilo Gorge on the Lualaba River (the dam of which holds some 475 billion gallons of water), and the mammoth Le Marinel Power Plant at Lukuga Falls 20 miles downstream from the Delcommune Plant. Le Marinel, which went into action in 1956, alone has an annual productive capacity of 1.4 million kilowatt hours. Taken together, the four plants can produce 2.5 billion kilowatt hours in an average year, 25 per cent of highly industrialized Belgium's power production. In 1960, a little over 2 billion kilowatt hours were actually produced.

Another *Union Miniere* subsidiary, *Societé Generale Africaine d'Electricité* (SOGELEC) owns part of the system that distributes this power. It has the concession for supplying power to Elisabethville and Jadotville, which consumed 73.6 million kilowatt hours in 1960.

The zinc concentrates produced by *Union Miniere* are bought by yet another subsidiary, *Societé Metallurgique du Katanga* (METALKAT), which treats them by electrolysis and recovers their zinc, cadmium, and copper content. In 1960, METALKAT produced 53,358 tons of electrolytic zinc. The company also operates for *Union Miniere* a plant that treats metallurgical dusts recovered at UMHK's Lubumbashi plant in Elisabethville.

When *Union Miniere* or METALKAT need industrial

chemicals for their operations, they buy them from another *Union Miniere* subsidiary, *Societé Generale Industrielle et Chimique du Katanga* (SOGECHIM). In 1960, SOGE-CHIM produced 119,010 tons of sulphuric acid, 1,863 tons of sodium chlorate, and 134 tons of glycerine. The last two products are used in the manufacture of explosives, which is handled by another *Union Miniere* subsidiary, *Societé Africaine d'Explosifs* (AFRIDEX). Although—contrary to some reports—there is nothing to indicate that AFRI-DEX (which produced 2,955 tons of explosives in 1960) has supplied Tshombe's gendarmes with munitions of any sort, the potential is there. SOGECHIM also supplies Jadot-ville with drinking water.

When *Union Miniere* needs coal, it gets it from its *Charbonnages de la Luena* (CHARLUENA) subsidiary, which operates coal mines 280 miles north of Elisabethville at Luena, in the heart of the Baluba country. In 1959, CHAR-LUENA produced 247,000 tons of coal. Because of un-settled conditions (the Balubas, as we have seen, are the historic foes of Tshombe's Lunda tribe and Munongo's Bayeke), production fell to 163,000 tons in 1960. On January 15, 1961, a *Union Miniere* physician, Dr. Leo-pold Mottoulle, was murdered in the company's hospital at Luena while making his rounds. UMHK then ordered the collieries abandoned. They were reopened late in Feb-ruary, but the situation has progressively deteriorated, and this source of coal appears lost to *Union Miniere*. Under such circumstances, UMHK simply turns to the Wankie Colliery Company Ltd. of Southern Rhodesia, in which it has substantial holdings and which acts as an alternate source of supply.

To mill the corn, wheat, and manioc that it sells to its employees at heavily subsidized prices, *Union Miniere* re-lies on another subsidiary company, *Minoteries du Katanga* (MINOKAT). Since independence, MINOKAT has had difficulties in obtaining steady supplies of food. Drawing largely on reserve stocks during the last half of the year, it milled 36,000 tons of flour and meal during 1960.

When *Union Miniere* needs lead or manganese, it calls on its *Societé de Recherche Miniere du Sud-Katanga* (SUD-KAT) subsidiary, which in 1960 produced 23,863 tons of manganese from its Kasekelesa mine. SUDKAT also sells some manganese, lead, and zinc (the last two mined at Kengere) abroad.

Ciments Metallurgiques de Jadotville (CMJ), another arm of *Union Miniere*, produced 14,579 tons of cement in 1960, most of which was sold to its cousin firm, COFOKA, for construction purposes. That completes the list of *Union Miniere*'s major subsidiaries operating in Katanga.

The newest member of the *Union Miniere* family, established in January of 1960, is *Societé de Recherche et d'Exploitation Bauxicongo*, which is developing bauxite deposits in the Lower Congo near Matadi, *outside* of Katanga.

Union Miniere has an electrolytic copper refinery at Limoges in France and, until recently, was a large stockholder in SABENA, the Belgian airline. Although it transferred 80 per cent of its SABENA stock, Union Miniere still owns 26,313 SABENA shares with a par value of $10 each. Another of UMHK's Belgian subsidiaries is the *Societé Belge pour l'Industrie Nucleaire* (BELGONUCLE-AIRE), which shares in the operation of two Belgian nuclear reactors and is participating in the construction of the Enrico Fermi Atomic Power Station near Detroit. The mining company also owns two subsidiary research and information companies that seek and publicize new uses for copper and cobalt. But *Union Miniere*'s principal associate outside of Africa is the *Societé Generale Metallurgique de Hoboken* (SOHOBO), which owns a group of plants at Hoboken (near Antwerp), and at Olen and Reppel, in the Campenine (Limburg Province, where the smelly cheese comes from). These plants treat that portion of *Union Miniere*'s production which is not fully refined in

Katanga. The Hoboken plant, five miles north of Antwerp on the right bank of the Scheldt, mills, roasts, and sinters copper-lead ores and other raw materials containing lead, tin, and precious metals. The Olen plant, located on the canal that links the Scheldt and Maas rivers 13 miles from Turnhout, has copper, cobalt, and radium refining facilities. It can produce 120,000 tons of copper and 2,000 tons of cobalt per year. The Reppel plant produces arsenic salts from the by-products of the Olen and Hoboken plants.

Union Miniere also owns shares in the railways that crisscross Katanga, in a ranching firm that breeds livestock near Kolwezi, in Congolese insurance and shipping companies, in a lumbering firm operating in Kasai, and in COBELKAT, a company whose purpose it is to encourage white settlement in Katanga.

That, roughly, is the industrial anatomy of the *Union Miniere* complex. It performs other functions too numerous to mention, from workshops to garbage collection. In addition, its presence and the presence of its 1,755 white and 19,731 African employees (their dependents number 4,000 whites and 80,000 Africans), has triggered the development of industries not associated with *Union Miniere* by subcontracting and purchasing worth more than $6 million per year to independent firms. These include a cement factory (in 1959 three of the Congo's four cement factories were located in Katanga), two breweries, vegetable oil refineries, flour mills, a dairy, salt works, fisheries, textile factories, soft-drink plants, a paint factory, printing firms, two cigarette factories, machine shops, automobile agencies, a lumber industry, department stores, hotels, restaurants, and literally scores of small businesses of a similar nature. Of all the Congo's 12,815 manufacturing firms, 4,141 (or nearly a third) are located in Katanga. Nor has the white man been the only one to benefit from this fact. Almost half of the Congo's 4,871 African-owned manufacturing firms are in Katanga, which has only a little more than a quarter of all the Congo's white-owned firms.

It is probably fair to say that *Union Miniere* and its subsidiaries are directly responsible for 75 per cent of Katanga's industrial and commercial activity, and indirectly responsible for another 20 per cent. If this huge enterprise did not exist, Katanga would be just an expanse of lightly populated arid bush, presenting no international problem and no political or economic prospects. That is why it is accurate to say that *Union Miniere*, in an economic sense, *is* Katanga. If cartels and profits are wrong, then *Union Miniere* is wrong. But even the most superficial scrutiny of the company's record demonstrates that it has used its tremendous power and borne its enormous responsibility in most cases with both justice and charity. In fairness, however, it must be admitted that the great triumvirate that before independence ran not only Katanga but all the Congo—big business, the church, and the state—cracked down hard on all those who did not happen to share their vision of what was good for man and society. Those who either shared that vision or did not care one way or another, those who were willing to play according to the rules of the triumvirate (and that meant no political activity for white or black) prospered. "Agitators"—and this could include anyone from a Jeffersonian democrat to a Communist—were dealt with immediately and severely. Those with ideas about trade unionism came in for particularly close scrutiny. Since man by essence seems to be a political animal, this was not only unfair but unwise. The treatment of dissenters was a sin that arose from the triumvirate's assumption that it was not only omnipotent but perfect. Criticism struck not only at the business interests but at the foundations of church and state, hence was heretical, treasonous, and not to be tolerated. It was not tolerated and, in the process, freedom of thought, the liberty of the individual, and human dignity were violated. It should be remembered, however, that *Union Miniere* was dealing with a people only two generations removed from M'Siri's collection of human skulls. Although it is easy to criticize the company, it is more difficult to propose an alternative workable approach.

On the whole, *Union Miniere*'s record was and is good in the social sphere. In contrast to the conditions obtaining in many other African mining industries, *Union Miniere* for the past thirty years has encouraged its African workers to bring their families with them to the mines. It has not done this entirely out of the goodness of its heart: Its business is to mine copper, and studies show that a married man accompanied by his family is a more stable, teachable, productive worker than a lone male who inevitably and frequently must leave the mines to return to his family. But whatever the motives, the effect has been good. In 1926, when *Union Miniere* was still recruiting its labor outside of Katanga, there were 22 women and 32 children for every 100 male workers living in UMHK's housing quarters. Today, the corresponding figures are 84 and 293.

As of March, 1961, 22,324 children were attending schools either directly managed by *Union Miniere* or financially supported by it. UMHK has 70 schools of its own, including 15 kindergartens, 33 primary schools, and 22 professional, technical, and teacher-training schools. Sixteen high schools attended by 750 boys and girls from workers' families receive *Union Miniere* subsidies. The teaching staffs of these schools include more than 100 whites and 700 Africans trained in *Union Miniere*'s specialized schools. Adult education classes (including one for African women that had 3,335 students in 1960) and 70 on-the-job training courses attended by about 1,000 workers this year, also exist. The company runs pre-vocational schools attended by 643 boys, and domestic science classes for 623 girls. Forty special courses for 363 Africans tabbed for managerial posts are also run. Three hundred and eighty-nine

Africans already hold executive or supervisory posts in the company—18 per cent of the total managerial staff. Most of these, however, are junior posts.

In the field of health, *Union Miniere* operates five general hospitals and five maternity hospitals (in which 5,000 babies are born per year) in addition to scores of dispensaries. These institutions are staffed by 32 white doctors, 96 white nurses and medical assistants, and 638 African medical assistants, nurses, and attendants. Free medical facilities are available, not only to workers and their families but to all those who care to use them. In one recent year, nearly a third of 602,077 hospitalization days were taken up by patients other than *Union Miniere* personnel and their dependents. The excellence of this care, which many an American would be lucky to have, is not open to question: Over the last twenty years, the birth rate of *Union Miniere* employees and their families has risen from 37 to 71 per thousand, while the death rate has fallen from 12 to 5. The death rate among children has fallen from 102 to 9 per thousand. In one five-year period—from 1950 to 1955—infant mortality in Elisabethville fell from 20 per cent to 6 per cent.

Union Miniere's Swahili house organ for its African workers has the largest circulation (50,000) of any newspaper in Katanga. The company maintains a radio network that broadcasts daily to its townships.

Union Miniere provides excellent free housing for all its employees. It has built more than 20,000 homes for its African employees alone, thus providing housing for more than 100,000 people, or 7½ per cent of Katanga's total population. To house this percentage of the population, a U.S. firm would have to provide homes for twelve million people. These are permanent homes with electricity and inside plumbing, each with its own fenced yard. For those who wish to build or buy their own homes outside the company's townships, *Union Miniere* provides financial assistance. In addition to the homes themselves, *Union Miniere* has built roads, churches, clubs, stores, playing fields, and social centers for its employees, black and white. To service these, it pays the salaries of eighty-two nuns, chaplains, and social workers.

When I first visited Katanga in 1958, 45 per cent of the African labor force was receiving all of its wages, reputed to be the highest in Africa, in cash. The remainder, the newer employees who had not yet demonstrated sufficient responsibility to be entrusted with their own or their families' health, received part of their wages in cash and the rest in kind. Their weekly rations included one pound of sugar, seven pounds of corn meal, five pounds of cassava, one pound of peanuts, half a pound of beans, twelve ounces of palm oil, three pounds of sweet potatoes, one pound of green vegetables, one-and-a-half pounds of bread, four ounces of suet, one-and-a-half pounds of meat, one-and-a-half pounds of fish, and one pound of rice per person. Pregnant women and nursing mothers received double rations. Children, in addition to their regular rations, received cod-liver oil, milk, and hot meals at school. This, coupled with the fine medical care, unquestionably made the Katangan mineworker the healthiest African on the continent. After three years with the company, the average miner's weight increased from 120 to 160 pounds. But the Africans never liked the system. Certainly it reduced the amount of money available to them for luxuries; obviously it was paternalistic. At any rate, all workers now receive their full wages in cash. Food is available at a low, subsidized cost as a fringe benefit, and free seed, fertilizer, and tools are provided for workers who want to have their own vegetable gardens. Other benefits include family allowances, free medical care, health and disability insurance, paid vacations, and old-age pensions. *Union Miniere*'s total investment in social welfare benefits to date exceeds $80 million.

Anyone who doubts the veracity of these statements has

only to consult the company's employment records. When *Union Miniere* came to Katanga, the labor force was so small that it had to import workers from Mozambique and Nyasaland. After World War I, when Belgium acquired heavily populated Ruanda-Urundi—largely as a source of labor—it was able to draw for most of its needs there and among the Balubas of the Lomami River Valley (UMHK stopped all foreign recruiting in 1928). Recruiting on the Lomami, incidentally, created one of the worst political and human problems in southern Katanga by introducing the hated Balubas into the heart of Upper Katanga. Now 35,000 of them are huddled in United Nations-protected refugee camps. Because it offered good pay (up to $250 per month for a few highly qualified Africans as long ago as 1958; the company's annual wage bill amounts to more than $30 million) and encouraged its laborers to bring their families, *Union Miniere* quickly stabilized its labor force. The average annual turnover now is only 10 per cent; half the company's African employees have been with it for more than ten years, and a quarter for more than sixteen years. There are second generation *Union Miniere* workers, and all but 7 per cent of the company's labor force is made up of local people.

Nor should anyone delude himself into thinking that *Union Miniere* intends to leave Katanga. Its capitalization is too heavy ($160 million) and its prospects are too good for that. At the present rate of production, Katanga's copper and cobalt reserves will last 200 years. Its renewable concession does not expire until March 11, 1990. The company's total disbursements for 1960 (the net dividend, the statutory royalty, and various taxes and duties) amounted to $85.9 million. Sixty-one per cent of this amount went to the Congolese Government, the Katangan Government, and the Belgian Government (the Belgian Government's share was a modest $1.8 million). *Union Miniere* is also a creditor of the Congolese Government, to the extent of state securities with a par value of $21 million.

There is no question of *Union Miniere*'s attempting to cut its losses in Katanga. Every indication points the other way. Production of copper has risen (between 1957 and 1960) from 240,280 tons to 300,675, cobalt from 8,115 tons to 8,222 tons, zinc concentrates from 188,183 tons to 193,-004 tons, germanium from 9,065 kilograms to 25,101 kilograms. Only last year, *Union Miniere* doubled the annual productive capacity (to 100,000 tons of copper and 3,500 tons of cobalt) of its new automated $50 million Luilu treatment plant at Kolwezi. The West Kambove Concentration Plant, equipped to deal with one million tons of mixed oxide and sulphide ores annually, was placed in operation only two months before the Congo's independence. Work is now underway on another concentrator at Kakanda, which is expected to come into operation late this year. Another one-million-ton-per-year concentrator and full scale underground works are planned for Kamoto by 1965. Altogether, *Union Miniere* has invested approximately $300 million in plants and social installations in Katanga. An additional capital construction program of $20 million per year is planned, and work is going ahead. These are not the actions of a company that intends to close up shop.

Those who make foreign policy must make it on the assumption that *Union Miniere* will remain in Katanga. The company dominates Katanga's economy and unquestionably will continue to do so until it is either destroyed or nationalized. Neither of these alternatives would be good for Katanga, the Congo, or the West. It is in the nature of things that, because of *Union Miniere*'s economic position, its officials will have political influence in Katanga. By definition, this need not necessarily be a bad thing. And it is not accurate—as has already been implied and will be shown later—to equate political influence with political domination: Tshombe is neither the creature nor the puppet of *Union Miniere.*

Union Miniere, like the great chartered companies of the past (such as the Hudson Bay Company, the Virginia Company, and the East India Company), which opened up continents to trade and commerce, has had heavy responsibilities from the moment of its inception. In the main, it has performed these functions with justice, foresight, and generosity. With its system of interlocking companies and directorates, it is certainly capitalism with a vengeance. It is also capitalism with a conscience. It needs to make no apologies for its record. It runs a good shop. It may be something of an anachronism, and it may suffer from the curse of bigness: impersonality, corporate smugness, and arrogance. But it is the economic foundation of Katanga, and most of that which is good in the country stems from it. *Union Miniere* is certainly all-pervasive and ubiquitous; but it is essentially no more evil than the Ford Motor Company. If giant corporations have made Katanga in the economic sense, its politics are largely personal. It is time now for a quick look at the men who have influenced events in Katanga.

IV

DRAMATIS PERSONAE

"Tshombe is a turncoat, a traitor
to the interests of the Congolese people."
—Nikita Khrushchev

"Tshombe is one of the most impressive men
I have ever met and one of the most maligned
men in history."
—Senator Thomas J. Dodd

In Katanga and the Congo, as in the rest of Africa,
politics is a highly personal art. What counts is men,
not issues. It is not so much what a man stands for that is
important, as what he is and to what tribe he belongs. Plat-
forms betray a bewildering similarity, issues become grey
and blurred at the edges. In the end, one comes back inevitably to the men who are at once the leaders and the
hostages of the people they represent. The cast of principal African characters in the Katangan drama includes
four Katangans and two Congolese. All of them influenced,
for good or evil, the course of events in Katanga. The
interplay between these characters was constant, sometimes
obscure, and frequently sharp. Had the personalities of
some of them been a little different, much blood and gold
might not have been wasted, much suffering might have
been averted. This is not to say that these men were the
sole architects of the Katangan tragedy; they were not. As

in any drama, unseen forces were at work, acting often through minor characters: a telephone call in Brussels, a hurried conference in Paris, a luncheon in London, a visit to the President in Washington shaped events thousands of miles away in Elisabethville. At times, the principal actors in Elisabethville seemed to lose control, to become puppets dancing on international strings, incapable of initiating action. Most of the time, however, the principal actors left their personal stamp on the small slice of history being acted out in Katanga. Had they not been the men they were, the play itself would not only have had a different character but, perhaps, a different ending. While noting the existence of external forces, one must come back to the men on the scene to understand the events of the last two years.

One must start with Tshombe. Moise Kapenda Tshombe was born in November, 1919, at Masumba, the royal capital of the Lunda paramount chief Mwata Yamo, to whom he is related both by blood and by marriage. Masumba is six miles northeast of Kapanga, administrative headquarters of the department of the same name, one of the four departments of Lulua Province. Kapanga is the northernmost department of Lulua, bordered on the north by Kasai and on the west by Portuguese Angola. It is at once the Lunda heartland and an area of contact with the northern Balubas of Kasai.

The future Katangan leader was the eldest of more than half a dozen sons of Joseph Kapenda Tshombe, a wealthy merchant who owned a string of sixteen village stores, a sawmill, a hotel, a fleet of trucks, and several cotton plantations. The elder Tshombe employed a natural shrewdness and his blood relationship to the Lunda royal house to become the Congo's first African franc millionaire. It was up to young Moise, as the eldest son, to take over the family business of *J. Kapenda Tshombe et Fils*. To this end, young Tshombe was sent by his father to American

Methodist missionary schools. After completing his primary and junior secondary work at local schools, Tshombe went on to the Methodist teacher-training institute at Kanene, 90 miles southwest of the military base of Kamina, in what is today Grands Lacs Province of Katanga. A correspondence course in accounting completed his formal education, and young Tshombe was off to Elisabethville to take charge of the family's businesses there.

Tshombe's reaction to Elisabethville was similar to that of many a young country boy (with too much money) to New York: he was dazzled. After years in the remote bush country of the hot Lulua and Lubudi river valleys, Elisabethville's broad avenues and gay nightclubs were too much for him. He spent most of his time sporting around town in a large Ford, and soon became well-known in Elisabethville's version of café society. His irate father, like many another self-made capitalist dealing with a spendthrift son, reckoning that the young man's salvation lay in hard work far from the bright lights, set him up with a string of rural stores of his own and shipped him off to the bush to manage them.

But Tshombe, who by then had married the favorite daughter of Chief Bako Ditende (later to become Mwata Yamo Ditende Yawa Nawezi III, ruler of all the Lundas), was not to share his father's success in business. Three times the younger Tshombe went bankrupt and each time his father bailed him out. The paternal prop was removed in 1951 with the death of the elder Tshombe. Moise, who had returned to Elisabethville four years before, took over his father's interests. Although this second Elisabethville period was as disastrous financially for Tshombe as the first, it was important both for him and for Katanga in a political sense. Tshombe, who had always been a gay, gregarious, and personable individual, now was the head of the largest African business concern in Katanga. He quickly was granted the status of an *evolue* (which gave him the same privileges and responsibilities as a white man) and elected president of Elisabethville's African Chamber of Commerce. His tribal political connections were silver-plated, his manners were good, and his French excellent. He had always gotten along well with whites and now he found all doors open to him. When his business ventures began to falter again, Tshombe made a crucial decision: He handed over the management of his commercial affairs to a brother (he has seven brothers, all of them prominent in Katangan affairs) and went into politics. In 1947, he stood for and won a seat on Elisabethville's multiracial city council. Four years later, on the death of his father, he took the elder Tshombe's seat on the advisory Provincial Council, where he served until 1953.

Tshombe was as great a success in politics as he had been a failure in commerce. He was in solidly with the Lundas. The years spent managing his string of bush stores had given him contacts with other tribal leaders. His well-tailored suits, American button-down shirts, and ubiquitous black homburg were familiar sights in the mining centers of Elisabethville, Jadotville, and Kolwezi. Behind the wide grin and the flashy clothes something else had been added: Tshombe, a man who had wasted much of his life, now saw what he wanted and went for it with a drive and tenacity few had realized he possessed. He had always been intelligent; but he had lacked purpose. He found that purpose in politics and the acquisition of power. Tshombe, now a family man with ten children, was no longer seen in his familiar after-dark haunts. While others played, he maneuvered for leadership.

In 1956, he founded the Lunda Tribal Association. The Belgians gave it their approval: after all, Tshombe was known to be "safe" and the association was a nonpolitical debating club and welfare organization. By 1959, this inevitably grew into Katanga's first political party, the

Confederation des Associations du Katanga, popularly called CONAKAT.

The hard core of CONAKAT, although seventeen tribes are grouped under its banner, was and is Tshombe's own Lunda tribe. The fact that he is not only a Lunda but a member of the royal house and the son-in-law of the Lunda paramount chief assures Tshombe of the total support of one of the largest tribes in Central Africa, one that remembers its great days under Tshombe's royal ancestors. But CONAKAT also drew to it the majority of Katanga's smaller tribes. The word "confederation" in CONAKAT's name is significant. Tshombe, like other African nationalists—such as Chief Obafemi Awolowo, the Nigerian Yoruba leader—believes that the tribe should be the firm foundation of the nationalist movement. The majority of African nationalists, however, look on the tribe as a rival focal center of political power and wish to sweep it away. Because he is a tribal nationalist, Tshombe had no desire to submerge Katanga's other tribes. By adopting a confederal form of organization for CONAKAT, he imitated the structure of the old Lunda empire, which was no more than a confederation of tribes that accepted the Lunda paramount chief as the first among equals. Consequently, it was logical and inevitable that Tshombe should resist the centralist drive of Patrice Lumumba, aiming instead for a confederal Congo, solidly based on tribal pillars.

That this tribalism is not exclusive to the point of denying authority to members of other tribes is demonstrated by Tshombe's selection of his top CONAKAT lieutenant. Rather than naming one of his own Lundas, Tshombe turned to Godefroid Munongo. Munongo, born at Bunkeya in 1925, occupies relatively the same position in the Bayeke tribe that Tshombe does among the Lundas: His grandfather was M'Siri, the great Bayeke Chief who conquered most of southern Katanga in the nineteenth century, and his brother Antoine Mwenda, is paramount chief of the Bayekes.

Munongo, who is the twelfth of M'Siri's successor's thirteen children, was educated at Catholic mission schools in Bunkeya and Elisabethville before spending two years at a Thomist seminary at Baudouinville on Lake Tanganyika. Leaving the seminary in 1949, the stocky Bayeke spent the next four years at the Kisantu University Center (a sort of junior college) near Leopoldville, where he studied administration. Upon graduation he entered the Belgian colonial administration. Starting as a police-court judge, he worked his way up through the colonial hierarchy, until, in December, 1959, he became one of the key figures in the administration of the vast Inga hydroelectric scheme which, if finances and political conditions ever permit its completion, will harness the tremendous power of the Congo River.

In July, 1959, before going to Inga, the thirty-seven-year-old Bayeke leader had participated in the founding of CONAKAT. He had, in fact, been elected first President-General of the party, but had to relinquish the post in favor of Tshombe because his civil service status precluded participation in politics. In May, 1960, he was elected to the Katangan Provincial Assembly from Elisabethville and, when Tshombe's government was formed, assumed the vital portfolio of Minister of the Interior. In Tshombe's absence, it has been Munongo—who is married and has three children—who has acted for him, as he did when the Katangan President was arrested in Coquilhatville on April 26, 1961, and held prisoner for nearly two months. Had it not been for two quirks of fate—Tshombe's business failure and Munongo's civil service status—Tshombe might not be President of Katanga today.

After Tshombe and Munongo, the third most important man in CONAKAT and in the Katanga Government is thirty-seven-year-old Jean Baptiste Kibwe, who repre-

sents yet a third tribe. Kibwe was born in Elisabethville
and is a member of the Batabwa tribe, which inhabits the
Marungu highlands between Baudouinville and Albertville
overlooking Lake Tanganyika. Kibwe's father, although he
was a chief, came to Elisabethville to find employment
many years ago and worked as a messenger in the office
that his son now occupies, as Vice President of Katanga. As
a child, Kibwe performed the rather astounding feat of
attending kindergarten for five years, a longevity record
difficult to match even in Africa. He was a choir boy (he
later led the choir's drum section), a wolf cub, a noted
soccer player, and, eventually, a scout master. After completing high school (his teacher in his sophomore year
was the late Joseph Kiwele, Tshombe's first Minister of
Education and composer of the music for "La Katangaise,"
Katanga's national anthem), Kibwe worked for *Union
Miniere*, for a bank, and finally for the Belgian colonial
government. He later studied law, became a judge, and
eventually practised as an attorney. On the formation of
CONAKAT, he became its vice president. Like Tshombe
and Munongo, he was elected to the Provincial Assembly
in May, 1960, after which Tshombe named him Katanga's
Finance Minister and Vice President. It is he who has seen
to it that sufficient funds have been extracted from *Union
Miniere* to finance Katanga's secession.

Not all of Katanga's tribes, of course, share the en-
thusiasm of the Lundas, Bayekes, and Batabwas for
Tshombe's government. We have seen how, in the middle
years of its operations, *Union Miniere* brought Balubas
from the Lomami Plains to work in the mines. The Balubas, like Kenya's Kikuyus and the Bassas of Cameroun, are
an intelligent and industrious people. Also like these two
tribes—perhaps to some degree because of this intelligence
and industry—they are generally detested by the other
tribes with whom they come in contact. We have seen
also that the Balubas once had a great empire and have

been, for five hundred years, the bitter rivals and implacable enemies of the Lundas. Over the course of the years, more than 100,000 Balubas moved south into the country of their enemies to work in the white man's mines, in commerce, and in the administration. Because of their brains and perseverance, they gradually secured for themselves the most important and best-paying jobs in these fields. It is estimated that before independence the Balubas outnumbered all other tribes in Katanga's three major cities of Elisabethville, Jadotville, and Kolwezi. Such a situation never makes for harmonious relations. The lid was kept on by two factors: the Belgian security forces and prosperity, which meant that there were jobs for everybody.

The situation began to worsen in December, 1957, when municipal elections were held in Elisabethville. CONA-KAT had not yet been formed, and consequently, the voting of the local people was fractionalized among the competing tribes. The Kasai Balubas and other "alien" Africans, however, voted as a bloc. As a result, three of the capital of Katanga's four burgomasters were Kasai Balubas and the fourth was a Bakisu from Kivu. This situation became exacerbated in 1958 and 1959, as falling copper prices and failing confidence on the part of local Belgians produced a serious recession in Katanga. As more and more Africans found themselves out of work, they turned in their misery, anger, and frustration against the Balubas, who now were not only competing with them but depriving them of their bread. CONAKAT's principal plank became the repatriation of 160,000 "alien" Balubas to Kasai (there are 600,000 Katangan Balubas in addition to these, the Balubas being Katanga's largest tribe, followed closely by the Lundas). Here began Tshombe's first active cooperation with the *Union Katangaise*, the association of Katanga's whites, and the forty-three-year-old leader's first thoughts of secession. The whites, of course, wanted secession—or at least federation—for entirely different reasons than Tshombe: The whites were fearful of their future under the radical African leaders of the northern Congo and felt they could best preserve their way of life (their privileged status, if you will) if Katanga were autonomous and under the control of a man they knew, a man obviously moderate in racial matters and favorably disposed toward private enterprise. On Tshombe's part, the idea of secession arose almost completely out of the recession and tribal hatred for the Balubas. Only an independent or autonomous Katanga, Tshombe reasoned, could keep the majority of its mineral revenues for its own development; only a state in charge of its own immigration affairs could halt the flow of Kasai Balubas into the southern heartland of Katanga and repatriate those who not only threatened to become the dominant political force in the country and the most prosperous community, but to lead the rest of the tribes to the brink of starvation in the competition for jobs during hard times.

At any rate, CONAKAT adopted "Baluba, go home!" as its principal article of political faith. As in physics, any political action produces an equal reaction. In this case, the reaction to CONAKAT's belligerent action was the formation of the BALUBAKAT CARTEL (sometimes called the *Parti Progressiste Katangais*) under the leadership of Jason Sendwe. The CARTEL was an amalgamation of three tribal organizations. The first of these (and the most important) was Sendwe's BALUBAKAT, composed of those Balubas indigenous to Katanga. The second was FEDEKA, an organization representing the "alien" Balubas from Kasai. The third was ATCAR, the political spearhead of 100,000 Chokwe tribesmen whose ancestors broke the Lunda empire in 1887.

Sendwe was born in 1917, at Kabongo, a railway town in Grands Lacs Province of Katanga, on the Lomami Plains in the heart of Balubaland. Although his blood is not as blue as Tshombe's, he is related to one of the Baluba chiefly families. Like Tshombe, he grew up a Methodist and was educated by American missionaries. For five years he studied medicine, finally becoming a medical assistant. He worked for a time among lepers until qualifying as a pastor and teacher. In 1942, he went to work for the Belgian colonial government. He served on the Protestant Council for the Congo and played a leading role in the founding of a multiracial fraternal organization called the *Amitiés Belgo-Congolais*. In 1957, he moved to Elisabethville and founded a Baluba cultural organization. Although he was one of CONAKAT's first members, he left it in November of 1959 to found BALUBAKAT. Later, as we have seen, he became leader of the BALUBAKAT CARTEL and focal point of the anti-Tshombe movement. Sendwe, who has ten children and claims to speak fourteen languages (including English, which Tshombe does not), is an intelligent (he has written a book called *The Traditions and Ancestry of the Balubas*), dynamic man. He is less suave than Tshombe, has strong moral convictions, and suffers from just a strain of authoritarianism in his make-up. He shows his emotions and capitalizes on those of others. In short, he is a demagogue with a conscience.

Sendwe's policies were more or less dictated by the posture assumed by Tshombe. If CONAKAT stood for the expulsion of "alien" Africans and a loose confederal relationship with Leopoldville, it was inevitable that the BALU-BAKAT CARTEL should espouse the cause of the "aliens" and demand a unitary form of government for the Congo. Thus Sendwe lined up with Lumumba.

Nor should the clash of personalities between the two men be forgotten. Tshombe, the rich man's son and the paramount chief's son-in-law, is sophisticated, smooth, complex, and opportunistic—a bonvivant; Sendwe, lacking in both connections and money, is brusque, simple, and idealistic—an ascetic. The traditional Lunda-Baluba rivalry, the conflict of interest and philosophy between CONAKAT and BALUBAKAT, the differing personalities of the two men, all combined to preclude the possibility of fruitful collaboration within Katanga.

So much for men and motives within the breakaway province. The events outside Katanga that led to its secession is largely the story of the clash of personalities, ambitions, and political philosophies among three men: Tshombe, Joseph Kasavubu, and Patrice Lumumba.

The political philosophies of Tshombe and Kasavubu are curiously similar, although the two men personally have little in common. Kasavubu was born at Tshela, near the coast in Leopoldville Province. Although the rest of his family belongs to the progressive Bakongo tribe which lives along both banks of the Congo, Kasavubu has one unique ethnic distinction: He is the only African leader with a Chinese grandfather—that gentleman having come to the Congo to help Stanley build his railway into the interior. Kasavubu was educated by the Roman Catholic Fathers of Scheut, and later attended a seminary at Mbata Keila. He then went on to the big Catholic higher seminary at Kabwe, near Luluabourg in Kasai, where he studied for the priesthood for three years. He decided against the priesthood, however, and returned to Leopoldville Province, studying for a year at Kangu, 25 miles from his home. After a year at Kangu (also run by the Fathers of Scheut), he was certified as a teacher in 1940. He taught for two years, and then (like Munongo and Kibwe), entered the colonial government, where he served in the treasury until his entry into active politics in 1958.

Like Tshombe, Kasavubu laid his political foundations on the tribe. He was active in cultural and educational organizations, playing an important part in a society dedicated to the purification of the Kikongo language.

A word should be said here about Kasavubu's Bakongo tribe. Like the Lundas, the Bakongos have a great imperial tradition. The Bakongos came to their present lands from the southeast some time toward the end of the thirteenth century. When the Portuguese reached the Congo two hundred years later, they found the Bakongos living on both sides of the river and far into what are today Angola (as far as Luanda) and former French Congo (to Pointe-Noire). To the east, the Bakongo empire stretched as far as the Kwango River, which today forms the eastern boundary between Angola and the Congo. The center of gravity of the Bakongo empire was on the south bank of the river, and the king had his capital at Mbanza, the San Salvador of today (in Angola near the southern frontier of the Congo). The political structure of the Bakongo kingdom was similar to that which existed in Europe in the Middle Ages. The country was divided into districts ruled by vassal princes. Society was rigidly organized. The Bakongos were familiar with copper and iron casting, they manufactured pottery and made cloth (from bark) so strong that the Portuguese sailors used it for their sails. The natives had a few domestic animals (pigs, sheep, and goats but no cattle) and they cultivated millet, bananas, peas, squash, and yams.

The balding Portuguese mariner Diego Cao reached the Congo a decade before America was discovered. In 1484, the Bakongo monarch Nzinga Ntinu received a delegation from the King of Portugal and sent ambassadors to Lisbon to request the first African technical assistance program. Portugal complied, sending masons, carpenters, and missionaries to Nzinga Ntinu. The Bakongo king was converted to Catholicism in 1491, and his son and successor, Don Affonso, was consecrated Bishop of the Congo in 1520. Don Affonso's son also became a bishop, the Bakongos sent ambassadors to Spain and the Vatican, and a Papal Nuncio took up residence at Mbanza. Churches were built, and baptisms took place at the rate of 2,000 a day. But the Portuguese had also introduced the slave trade and, although Don Affonso had been one of their principal suppliers in the early days of the trade, he later became alarmed at its volume, and relations between Lisbon and Mbanza became strained. At about that time, the Huns of Africa, the Jaga tribe, were threatening the Bakongo empire. Don Affonso's successor, Don Alvaro, appealed for help from the Portuguese as his kingdom was overrun and Mbanza put to the torch. The Portuguese sent an expedition in 1580 which, after three years of heavy fighting, expelled the Jagas from the Bakongo kingdom.

But good relations were never again established with Lisbon. In 1590, Don Alvaro II declared war against Portugal, tried to put his kingdom under Papal trusteeship, and encouraged the Dutch in their forays against Portuguese Angola. After the capture of Luanda by the Dutch in 1641, the Bakongo kings established embassies in Holland and received Dutch delegations at their capital. The Portuguese recovered, however, and expelled the Dutch from Angola. They then turned upon the Bakongo king, Don Antonio, and crushed the Bakongos at the battle of Mpila in 1665. From that day forward, the Bakongo kingdom's decline was swift and terrible. Defeated in war, weakened by the slave trade, and cut off from European commerce by the shift of Portuguese interest to Angola, the Bakongos never succeeded in recapturing their past eminence. At the same time, Portugal, exhausted by her imperial ventures, went into a slow decline. The missionaries and traders left the Congo, the churches crumbled into dust, Christianity was forgotten, and the Bakongo kingdom reverted to its darkness—spiritual and temporal. The final humiliation came in 1885, when the kingdom was divided among the French, Belgians, and Portuguese.

But the fact remains that the Bakongo kingdom was once one of Africa's greatest empires. It had opened its frontiers to European trade, culture, and religion. It had established diplomatic relations on a basis of equality with several European states. Its kings and their courts were Christian and literate in Portuguese. In short, the kingdom of the Bakongos was one of the few African states to play a part in world history from medieval times almost to the present. This was the heritage of Kasavubu and it captivated him. The squat, pudgy little man with the glasses, somewhat mongoloid in appearance, dreamed of the resuscitation of the Bakongo kingdom. In 1955, he became president of *Association des Bakongo pour l'Unification, l'Expansion et la Defense de la Langue Kikongo*, commonly called ABAKO. Like the tribes of southern Katanga, the 800,000 Bakongos feared that they would be swamped by the influx of "alien" Africans (principally the Bangala tribe) attracted to their homeland by the job opportunities and bright lights of Leopoldville. So when Kasavubu stood stripped to the waist upon a leopard skin, whirling above his head the ancient sword of the Bakongo kings and proclaiming in his squeaky voice that the ancient empire should be reconstituted, the Bakongos flocked in from the villages to kiss his feet and proclaim their loyalty to "King Kasa."

In December, 1957, Kasavubu's organizational skill and the natural and monolithic unity of the Bakongos combined to give ABAKO a sweep of the municipal elections, the first ever to be held in the Congo. Kasavubu became Mayor of Dendale, one of Leopoldville's communes, and he and ABAKO were on their way. The following year, Kasavubu made plans to attend the All-African Peoples Congress in Accra, but was unable to do so because his papers were not in order. Patrice Lumumba did go and there gained the unqualified personal support of Kwame Nkrumah. Had it not been for the lack of a smallpox certificate, Kasavubu might have outshone Lumumba at Accra, and the course of the Congo's history might have been entirely different.

But it was Kasavubu, not Lumumba, who spearheaded the nationalist thrust in the Congo. Paradoxically, he cared little about what happened to the rest of the Congo. His one dream was to secure independence for the Bakongos and to link them with their tribal brothers in Angola and the former French Congo. But the effect of his actions was to lead the entire Congo both to independence and to chaos.

In January, 1959, the Bakongos rioted in Leopoldville. As a result, the Belgians instituted sweeping constitutional reforms, including the promise of territorial elections by the end of the year. Kasavubu and his top aides were arrested and exiled to Belgium, and ABAKO was banned. In May, Kasavubu was released. He returned to the Congo and rebuilt his party under the new name of the *Alliance des Bakongo*, contracted like that of its organizational predecessor to ABAKO. The disorders among the Bakongos continued and it was this more than anything else that led the Belgians to call the 1960 Round Table Conference in Brussels which resulted in Congolese independence. At this conference, which will be discussed in fuller detail in the following chapter, Kasavubu argued strongly first for Bakongo independence, later for autonomy under a confederal alliance, and finally for federalism.

Perhaps the most striking thing about Kasavubu is his enigmatic character. Slow-thinking, unwilling to move until sure of victory, hesitant to act, he has a capacity for action when finally aroused, and a stubborn streak coupled with a cunning mind, which makes him a formidable opponent.

It is clear that Tshombe and Kasavubu have much in common. Both are tribal nationalists who seek to preserve, not to destroy, the fabric of the society that has produced them. Both of them come from tribes with great imperial traditions. Both have seen the dominance of their tribes threatened within their own homelands by an influx of "alien" Africans. Both control areas of comparatively great wealth (while Leopoldville Province lacks Katanga's minerals, it contains rich plantations, good communications, and much secondary industry). Both have demanded autonomy for their homelands and the reconstitution of their ancient empires. Both are pro-Western and non-racial in their political philosophies. Both lost at the Brussels Conference. The difference between the two has been that Tshombe acted on his secessionist ideas, while Kasavubu has been content to bide his time. The presence of Kasavubu in the president's office in Leopoldville is one of the few encouraging aspects of the present situation in the Congo, for he, above all men, has the capacity and the personality to negotiate with Tshombe. Had he been able to capture the Prime Ministership in 1960, Tshombe might not have seceded. If he takes an active role now, it is possible that a confederal or federal Congo, in which both Lundas and Bakongos can live, may emerge.

The fly in the ointment—as far as both Kasavubu and Tshombe were concerned—was always Patrice Emery Lumumba. Lumumba was born on July 2, 1925, in the mud-hut village of Katako-Kombe, in the Sankuru district of northern Kasai Province. Lumumba was a member of the small but war-like Batetela tribe, which enjoys no imperial tradition but is famed for its savagery in war (and for many years has provided the *Force Publique* with recruits). His parents were Catholics, and Lumumba attended Catholic mission schools for a couple of years before transferring, against the wishes of his parents, to a Protestant school. His formal education ended with primary school but he kept on reading and learning while working as servant to a Protestant missionary. His few years in a Protestant school, and those more important ones as the servant and protégé of the missionary, left Lumumba antagonistic toward Christianity as a whole and Catholicism in particular. His hate of Catholicism apparently grew out of the association of the Catholic Church with the state in the Congo and the feeling of persecution which Lumumba, as a nominal Protestant, experienced in a Catholic-oriented society.

Early in life, Lumumba displayed both his nervous energy and his lack of moral principles in repaying the missionary for his kindness by stealing his watch and a sum of money, which he used to pay his fare to Stanleyville in Orientale Province, the Mecca of young men from impoverished northern Kasai. He then wrote to the pastor for a character reference! As evidence both of Lumumba's mesmeric qualities and of the pastor's Christian forgiveness, he got the reference and used it to obtain a clerical job in the Stanleyville post office. He married, and, at the time of his death in 1961, had at least eight children.

While working in the post office, Lumumba was a frequent contributor to Stanleyville's broadsheets and president of the local Civil Servants Union. His post office career came to a rather abrupt halt in 1956, after eleven years of service. Belgian administrators had noted that Lumumba, who owned a car, was living at a standard above that of the average clerk. A perusal of the books revealed that the post office was $2,200 short. He was arrested, charged with embezzlement, and sentenced to two years in Jadotville prison. Until his death, Lumumba maintained that he was innocent, that he had taken the rap for his subordinates. He appealed his sentence—which was reduced to eighteen months—and got an additional six months off for good behavior. He was back in Stanleyville a year after his conviction.

Lumumba stayed in Stanleyville only long enough to found a tribal organization among his fellow Batetelas there before moving on to Leopoldville, where he got a job as a salesman with BRACONGO, brewers of "Polar" beer. Company officials remember him as one of their most industrious employees. Meanwhile, Lumumba was making a name for himself with his writings and oratory among Leopoldville's *evolue* group. The tall, thin, mercurial man with the small head, the smooth talk, the bright smile, and the constantly fluttering hands was soon a well-known figure in the bars of the native quarter. There he met (and took an instant dislike to) Kasavubu.

He joined a Christian Democratic study group that included among its members Joseph Ileo, editor of the bi-monthly *Conscience Africaine* and the man who was to succeed Lumumba as Prime Minister of the Congo two years later. Two years before, Ileo had published a thirty-year plan for the emancipation of the Congo and followed this up with the formation of an action group called the *Mouvement National Congolais* (MNC). Into this organization he welcomed both Lumumba and Cyrille Adoula (who was later destined to succeed Ileo in the Prime Minister's office), a trade unionist. Lumumba quickly gained control of the MNC, which by then also numbered among its members the Kasai Baluba leader Albert Kalonji and the soldier-journalist Joseph Mobutu; both were to play fateful roles in Lumumba's brief but stormy career.

In August, 1958, General de Gaulle came to Brazzaville, across the Congo River from Leopoldville, to offer the French Congolese the choice between autonomy within the French Community, or complete independence (they chose the former). This encouraged Lumumba and the other members of the MNC to sign a petition demanding independence for the Congo. In December of the same year, as has been mentioned, Lumumba attended the All-African Peoples Conference in Accra, where he obtained for his faction the financial and psychological backing of Nkrumah. The Bakongo riots of 1959 introduced a new element of urgency into the race for political power, and Lumumba pulled out all the stops in his attempt to build the MNC into a national political party.

In fact, he pulled out a few stops too many, and the MNC Central Committee, accusing him of dictatorial methods, demanded his resignation on July 16, 1959. The MNC split down the middle, the smaller moderate group mustering under the leadership of Kalonji, Adoula, and Ileo, and calling itself the MNC (Kalonji), and the larger, radical group (totalling about 450,000 members) retaining the name MNC, remaining loyal to Lumumba.

The MNC had been the one Congolese political party with some national backing. It had supporters in every province and its leadership contained the best brains in the Congo. It had at least a slight chance of being able to form a national government after the elections. With the split in the MNC, all chance of a stable Congolese government was lost.

This blow to his power infuriated Lumumba—at best a not very stable individual—and his speeches became even more incendiary and racist in character. In November, 1959, he was arrested, charged with sedition, and sentenced to six months in jail but released two days later on the order of the Belgian cabinet so that he could attend the Round Table Conference in Brussels, to be held in January, 1960. Meanwhile, his MNC had won fifty-five out of seventy-three seats in Orientale Province's provincial elections held in December.

Here again, a quirk of fate influenced the tragic history of the Congo and of Katanga: Had Lumumba served his six-month sentence, the Round Table Conference would have been dominated by Kasavubu, Tshombe, and Kalonji, all of whom wanted, as a minimum demand, a federal constitution for the Congo. They probably would have gotten it, and that would have lessened the secessionist pressure in Katanga. In addition, Lumumba's absence from the scene during the crucial last six months before independence, while it would not have lessened his hold on Orientale, might well have prevented him from becoming the Congo's first Prime Minister. The attitude of Tshombe and of Katanga's whites toward a government with, say, Kasavubu as President and Kalonji as Prime Minister, would have been considerably different from what it was toward the Lumumba-dominated government that eventually took shape. From start to finish, it was Lumumba's abrasive personality and his domineering policies that insured the secession of Katanga.

This is not to say that Lumumba was not competent. He was an extremely able and energetic man, perhaps the most brilliant and hard-working of the Congolese leaders. What finally defeated him and plunged the Congo into chaos was his intransigence, his lack of tolerance toward other leaders (his relations with Tshombe and Kasavubu were incredibly bad), his dependence on outside help (both Ghanaian and Communist), and his insistence on the eradication of tribalism and the establishment of a unitary form of government. Coming from a small and insignificant tribe and being himself of peasant origin, Lumumba not only failed to understand the importance of the imperial traditions of the Lundas and the Bakongos but adopted an attitude toward such manifestations of tribalism that was plainly antagonistic.

Thus it can be seen that by January, 1960, seven months before the Congo's independence, the lines of conflict were already drawn. In Katanga, the Lundas led by Tshombe, the Bayekes headed by Munongo, and the Batabwas directed by Kibwe had joined together with the majority of the Katangan tribes in an anti-Baluba alliance. Sendwe's Katangan Balubas, desperately in need of allies, had turned to Lumumba, Tshombe's arch foe. Kasavubu had consolidated his control of the Lower Congo. Lumumba, bitterly resentful of the split in the MNC that had robbed him of the chance of national leadership, was politically well dug-in in Orientale and became daily more radical and racist. Only a miracle could have saved the Congo from chaos and prevented Katanga's secession, and that miracle did not come.

In fact, the Belgians added immensely to their difficulties by releasing Lumumba from prison. To have backed the MNC and Lumumba prior to July, 1959, would have made sense. Where the Belgians erred was in continuing to dream of a unified Congo after the split in the MNC, which precluded such an eventuality. It is one of the rather unfunny jokes of history that the Belgian Government, which actively assisted Lumumba and promoted the ideal of a unitary Congo by releasing the Batetela leader from prison so that he could participate in the conference, should be accused less than a year later of causing the Balkanization of the Congo and of plotting to kill Lumumba.

There were other men in addition to these six—Tshombe, Munongo, Kibwe, Sendwe, Kasavubu, and Lumumba—who played important roles, for good or for evil, in the tragedy of Katanga. They will be introduced as they come on stage. But it was these six who played a dominant role from the beginning in the whole sorry affair, the first formal act of which was to take place in Brussels.

On to Brussels.

V

POLITICAL JOCKEYING

"Seventy-five years of collaboration between the
white and black populations have ensured the
Congo's unity."

> —GASTON EYSKENS, Prime Minister
> of Belgium, speaking to the Belgian
> Chamber of Representatives on
> January 13, 1959.

"May God protect the Congo."

> —KING BAUDOUIN, addressing the
> Congolese delegates to the Brussels
> Round Table Conference on
> February 21, 1960.

THE ROUND Table Conference opened in Brussels on
January 20, 1960. On hand were eighty-one Congolese
delegates who shuttled back and forth between their hotels
and the conference hall in chartered streetcars. Of these,
sixty-two represented political parties, while nineteen spoke
for tribal associations or were representatives of chiefs.
More than a hundred other Congolese and several Belgian
settlers were also present in an advisory capacity. As the
conference opened, there was no indication that it would
result in setting a date for independence. Belgium had
agreed to the principle of independence; but the questions
of both terms and timing remained to be decided. From
early statements made by Belgian spokesmen, it is clear

that it was hoped a transition period could be agreed upon, during which the Congo would have a degree of autonomy. Meanwhile, a Belgo-Congolese union, perhaps along the lines of the French Community, would be worked out. It was even thought that it might be possible for King Baudouin—as it had been for his great-great-uncle—to wear the crowns of both Belgium and the Congo. The important thing, from the Belgian point of view, was to safeguard Belgium's vast economic stake in the Congo and to maintain its influence among the new political elite.

This nicely proportioned applecart was upset at the very beginning by the unanimous insistence of the delegates that the Conference should set a date for the Congo's complete and immediate independence. Even "safe" tribal delegates, fearful of being politically outflanked by their radical opponents, voted for the measure. This unexpected development placed the Belgians in a dilemma. They had called the Round Table Conference and approved the delegates as representative. If they refused to accede to a unanimous request of the delegates, the Conference might well collapse on its first day. If that happened, the only alternative would be to rule the Congo by force of arms. Belgium had neither the desire nor the power to do that. It gave in and acceded to the Congolese request.

This proved to be a tragic decision. It would have been a correct and laudable move, had Belgium done anything to prepare the Congo politically for independence. This it had not done. Belgium had accomplished a great deal for the Congo in economic and social terms. It had a record in these spheres of which any colonial power could be proud. But the Congo had never had a national election, nor elections of any sort, for that matter, until three years before the Conference took place. Belgium had done nothing in the political sphere to prepare the Congo for independence, yet, at the Round Table Conference, it acted as if it had done everything. At best it was a long-shot gamble; at worst it was a crime.

This is not to say that the Belgian agreement to grant the Congo independence on June 30, 1960, could not have worked. It could have if everything had gone smoothly. Belgium was banking on order being maintained, on the Congolese leaders accepting political advice, on the Congo continuing to receive Belgian technical and financial assistance, on racial good-will being maintained. Unfortunately, nothing ever goes smoothly in Africa. When the first unexpected and unfortunate event took place (the revolt of the *Force Publique*), the carefully contrived Belgian scheme collapsed like a house of cards.

Having been out-maneuvered by the surprising show of unity on the part of the delegates into agreeing to the Congo's independence on June 30, 1960, the task remained to write a constitution for the country and to agree on terms of Belgo-Congolese cooperation. At that time, the villains of the drama, in Belgian eyes, were Tshombe and Kasavubu, the two men who have often been accused of being puppets of the Belgian Government. Both Kasavubu and Tshombe were still fighting for a loose confederal constitution, as was Kalonji, the Kasai Baluba leader. This Belgium clearly did not want. Every statement by the Belgian delegates to the Conference emphasized the territorial integrity of the Congo and the desirability of a strong central government. Kasavubu was accused of being a Communist, of being in the hands of the French fascists (had he not long advocated the union of the Bakongo areas of the two Congos?), while Tshombe was described as the tool of the industrialists. The heroes of the hour were smiling Patrice Lumumba, flown straight from prison to the conference table (he was met at the Brussels airport and handed a bouquet of roses by his six MNC delegates who had boycotted the Conference until his arrival), his wrists still scarred from handcuffs but his spirit bouyant and his manner affable toward the Belgians, and Paul Bolya, the thirty-six-year-old medical assistant who led the moderate *Parti Nationale de Progrès* (PNP), which was largely Belgian-supported. Both Lumumba and Bolya wanted a unitary constitution.

Kasavubu, glowering and clearly unhappy with the Belgian campaign to discredit him, started the conference from a position of strength. In a series of quick agreements, he forged an alliance between his own ABAKO, the MNC (Kalonji), and, oddly enough, the *Parti Solidaire Africain* (PSA), a left-leaning peasants' party led by Cleophas Kamitatu and Antoine Gizenga. This gave Kasavubu twenty-two of the sixty-two political delegates, only three less than the combined strength of the PNP and Lumumba's MNC. Tshombe's four delegates were playing a lone hand, while the other eleven delegates were split among four minor parties.

By insisting on a federal Congo and the immediate creation of an interim Congolese government (with the clear implication that he should be designated to lead such a government) Kasavubu fell from this position of strength. Not only did the three-party-alliance which he had constructed fly apart but his own ABAKO split down the middle, with his top lieutenant, Daniel Kanza, leading the revolt of ABAKO's Protestant delegates. At this crucial point, Kasavubu withdrew from the conference and disappeared from sight for two weeks.

Lumumba and the other leaders favoring a unitary form of government for the Congo took advantage of Kasavubu's absence (with the obvious support of the Belgians) and the disarray which existed in the federalists' ranks to push through a provisional constitution (referred to hereafter as the *loi fondamentale*) that, although on the surface it provided for some devolution of power to the provinces, essentially assured a strong central government of an independent Congo "within its present frontiers." Luluabourg, headquarters of Kasai Province, was chosen as the new capital of the Congo in a move to further diminish ABAKO's power (the move to Luluabourg was never made, and it is now doubtful that it ever will be). In return for this, whites, lunatics, and prisoners were deprived of the franchise. Lumumba and the other delegates favoring a unitary state quickly agreed to treaties guaranteeing Belgium's interests, providing for technical and economic assistance, and assuring the maintenance of the three Belgian bases (built at a cost of $210 million) in the Congo. When Kasavubu finally returned to the conference, his fight and that of Tshombe and Kalonji for a loose federal constitution was already lost.

The events of the past year would seem to indicate that Belgium backed the wrong horse when she supported those delegates who wanted a unitary state at the expense of the federalists. The Belgian motives were obvious and good. Aware of the centrifugal tendencies within the Congo, Belgium sought to short-circuit them by providing for a strong central government, banking on Lumumba's ability to create a sense of nationalism strong enough to override tribal rivalries. They were taking the chance that by depriving the Congo of a federal or confederal form of government, they were closing the safety valves that might allow tribalism to work off steam and, in the process, to become a positive force for national unity. In fact, the absence of these safety valves was an important contributory factor in the secession not only of Katanga but of Kalonji's "Mining State." In the end, Belgium avoided final responsibility in the matter in that the *loi fondamentale* was both vague and provisional. It had to be confirmed by the Congolese House of Representatives and Senate before it became law. As things worked out, Katanga seceded before the *loi fondamentale* was ratified, and, consequently, in a strictly legal sense, Katanga's secession is lawful because the constitution lacked legal force when the province left the Congo.

Tshombe returned to Katanga a very disappointed man. Lumumba had laughed at him because of the train of white advisers he brought with him to the conference. The Belgian Government had virtually ignored him and his demands for confederation. He soon regained his normal good spirits, however, and set himself to the task of winning the coming provincial elections. So confident was he of the outcome that he flew off to the United States on a State Department Leader Grant, returning only a few weeks before the elections.

That was when I first met the Katangan leader. The rains were over for another six months, and the air in the Katangan capital was cool and sparkling. We arranged to meet late in the morning for a drink on the terrace of the Hotel Elisabeth. Tshombe arrived exactly on time, as is his habit (and a most unusual one for an African). He wore a button-down white shirt, red tie, blue tweed suit, and carried in his hand his black homburg, with which he waved genially to passing acquaintances. He was accompanied by three shirt-sleeved toughs wearing red and white baseball caps with the words "Votez CONAKAT" inscribed on their visors. Tshombe ordered a scotch and soda (he does not smoke) and settled down to talk about his trip to America. He had, he said, "a very good impression." At first, he'd been suspicious that American financial interest in Africa was merely another form of colonialism but now he saw that this was not so. "I would welcome both American private investment and technical assistance from your government," he said. "If America does not come in, it is certain that the Communists will. That fellow Lumumba is already a Communist."

Tshombe said he had been most interested in the American system of government with its division of power between the federal government and the states. "We would like something rather on the American model," he said. "We are willing to have a federal president and to give the central government control of the army, the customs, and that sort of thing. What we do not want to do is to abrogate our control over the entire economy. We are willing to share our mining revenues with the rest of the Congo but we want at least 50 per cent of the wealth derived from the province kept in Katanga." Tshombe went on to say that he felt the Congo was so large and its people so diverse that it could only be held together under a unitary system of government by a dictator. "If a unitary form of government is imposed," he said, "the Congo will die."

How did he intend to prevent this? "We will win the provincial elections, consolidating our power here. Our delegates to Leopoldville then will work for a revision of the *loi fondamentale*."

What about secession? He denied emphatically a statement made by Sir Roy Welensky, Prime Minister of the Federation of Rhodesia and Nyasaland, to the effect that Katanga might want to secede from the Congo and join the Federation after independence. "Why should we want to become a colony again?" Tshombe asked. "We are not anti-white here but the time has come for us to rule ourselves." This was ten weeks before Tshombe declared Katanga's independence. He gave no indication at the time that he was considering such a step.

As for the local elections, Tshombe said that he was not worried. "We have the support of the majority of the tribes. Even 60 per cent of the Balubas support us [this is certainly an exaggeration—25 per cent would have been closer to the mark]. But we would welcome an effective opposition within the provincial assembly."

The provincial elections in May, 1960, did not come off as smoothly as Tshombe had expected, nor were the results as favorable as he had predicted. The voting took place in an atmosphere of rising tension. In recent weeks, at least thirteen had been killed in clashes between the Lundas (CONAKAT) and warriors from the Baluba and Chokwe (BALUBAKAT CARTEL) tribes. A three-day strike affecting twenty-four local firms had shaken the whites, many of whom were purchasing firearms. SA-BENA reported its international flights out of Katanga fully booked through August. Partisans of the two parties kept strictly to their own home areas, visited only their own bars, even drinking their own beer exclusively ("Simba" for CONAKAT members, "Kasai" for BALU-BAKAT CARTEL supporters). Sendwe, chugging around the country in his battered blue Opel, was campaigning hard. Tshombe, still debonair and confident, secure in the knowledge that he could count on winning a majority of the rural votes, confined his campaign largely to the cities, where BALUBAKAT was strong. When votes were counted for the sixty-member Provincial Assembly, the result was almost a draw: CONAKAT had won twenty-five seats, BALUBAKAT twenty-two, while thirteen seats went to splinter parties or independents. At this crucial moment in Katanga's history, Tshombe showed his skill as a politician by quickly bringing all thirteen independents into line, thus gaining control of the government. In elections held two weeks later, during which the Provincial Assembly selected the delegates to the Senate in Leopoldville, CONAKAT won eight seats and BALUBAKAT settled for six. Among the latter's six delegates was Sendwe. Tshombe, however, decided to remain in the Provincial Assembly. BALUBAKAT did not take its defeat with good grace. It turned down Tshombe's offer of a coalition government, and the Baluba delegates walked out of the assembly three times, paralyzing its proceedings, because a two-thirds attendance was required by law if business was to be transacted. In desperation, the province's Belgian governor declared a state of emergency when Tshombe threatened to secede unless the quorum law were amended to allow him to govern effectively. Faced with a breakdown in the administration of all the Congolese provinces, in only one of which a party had won an absolute majority, the Belgian Parliament quickly amended the quorum law to permit the provincial assemblies to operate with a 50 per cent attendance.

How much influence had whites wielded in the Katanga elections? In 1944, the white settlers in Katanga formed an association essentially professional in character called UCOL (*Union pour la Colonisation*). UCOL devoted itself to such matters as trying to get a reduction in the bond ($1,000 for a man, $500 for his wife and children) demanded of intending settlers in Katanga. As the wind of change began to blow through the Congo, UCOL sprouted a political arm, called the *Union Katangaise* (UKAT), under the leadership of handsome, greying Elisabethville attorney Jean Humble, a veteran of thirty years in Katanga. From the beginning, UKAT was opposed to the excessive centralization of the colonial government, favoring a federal organization for the six Congolese provinces with Belgium as the seventh member of the federation. In the last resort, UKAT favored the secession of Katanga and *Anschluss* with the Federation of Rhodesia and Nyasaland. Despite its protestations the organization was designed to perpetuate white privilege, if not white supremacy. Tshombe and CONAKAT immediately attacked UKAT and it soon backed away from this position. But UKAT had more success in convincing Tshombe of the desirability of federalism. Although UKAT itself was never openly associated with CONAKAT (UKAT was officially dissolved in 1960), many of its prominent members either joined CONAKAT or openly acted as advisors to Tshombe's party. CONAKAT also unquestionably received funds from local whites. This is true, too, although to a lesser extent, of BALUBAKAT.

There were three reasons why the majority of Katanga's

whites supported (and support) CONAKAT rather than BALUBAKAT: Tshombe was better known and more trusted than Sendwe, his party favored the federal form of government that appealed to most whites, and both Tshombe and CONAKAT had a record of cooperation with and friendship for the whites. BALUBAKAT made no new white friends when, a few weeks before the elections, one of its newspapers published a list of fifty prominent Belgians who would be required to leave the country "within twenty-four hours" after the Congo's independence or be "liquidated."

It is more difficult to say how much assistance, if any, *Union Miniere* gave as a corporation to CONAKAT. It is certain, again, that individual mining-company employees gave both money and advice to CONAKAT. It is also interesting to note that UMHK, in its annual report for 1960, lists $2.5 million under the heading of "exceptional expenses." The company goes on to explain that "these expenses were incurred through the political events in the Congo in July, 1960, and are comprised mainly of expenses of evacuating members of our personnel and their families, expenses for their return to Katanga, and various allowances." However, even if every white man, woman, and child of the *Union Miniere* families had been evacuated—which was not the case—that would have put the cost at $416 per person. Since mining-company personnel were evacuated almost exclusively by road (a distance of less than 200 miles) and most of them were back at work within three or four days, it is obvious that the entire $2.5 million could not possibly have been spent for this purpose.

It was widely reported in Elisabethville just before the elections that *Union Miniere* was financing CONAKAT. It was also said that it was covering its bet by slipping a bit under the table to BALUBAKAT. This would make sense. *Union Miniere* could hardly afford to antagonize either party and it is not a crime to make a donation to a political party. There can be little doubt, however, that the majority of *Union Miniere's* staff, had the choice been theirs, would have backed CONAKAT. As it was, they, like the rest of the Congo's whites, had no vote. They could only influence the outcome of the elections by providing funds or advice to the rival parties. In short, the influence of the whites over the election results was probably far less than is widely believed. CONAKAT won primarily because in Tshombe it had a strong candidate with appeal for the majority of Katanga's tribes. It was as simple as that.

The results in the other five Congolese provinces went more or less according to form. In neighboring Kivu Province, Anicet Kashamura's *Centre du Regroupement Africain* (CEREA) won twenty-two of seventy seats in the Provincial Assembly and ten of twenty-three of Kivu's seats in the Congolese National Assembly. In Kasai, Kalonji's wing of the MNC won twenty-one of seventy seats in the Provincial Assembly and eight of Kasai's twenty-two National Assembly seats. In Orientale, Lumumba's MNC won fifty-eight out of the seventy provincial seats and twenty-one of the province's twenty-five national seats. In Equateur, Paul Bolya's PNP emerged as the most powerful of many parties, none of which had a majority. In Leopoldville Province, the *Parti Solidaire Africain* of Cleophas Kamitatu and Antoine Gizenga barely edged out Kasavubu's ABAKO, winning thirty-five of the ninety seats in the Provincial Assembly to ABAKO's thirty-three, and thirteen of Leopoldville's thirty-three National Assembly seats.

A study of the election results reveals several things. In the first place, Lumumba emerged as the only leader with a really solid territorial base. His MNC was the only party to win an absolute majority in the provincial elections. In addition, Lumumba's MNC managed to win a total of forty-two of the 140 seats in the Kasai and Kivu Provincial Assemblies. This indication of at least a pretense to national appeal was fortified by the results of the elections to the National Assembly, where the MNC won thirty-three of 137 seats, obviously far from a majority but still the largest single total. Although twenty-one of these seats came from Orientale, Lumumba was able to boast that his party held at least a few seats from four of the other five provinces, Katanga being the only province where he failed to score (the MNC won five national seats in Kivu, four in Kasai, two in Equateur and one in Leopoldville). This is the way the National Assembly looked:

MNC (Lumumba)	33
PNP (Bolya)	22
PSA (Kamitatu)	13
ABAKO (Kasavubu)	12
CEREA (Kashamura)	10
CONAKAT (Tshombe)	8
MNC (Kalonji)	8
BALUBAKAT (Sendwe)	6
Others	25

The federalists (Kasavubu, Tshombe, and Kalonji) could muster only thirty-eight out of 137 seats, the remainder going either to avowed "unitarians" or to delegates without strong feelings one way or another. It was obvious that Lumumba was the outstanding candidate for Prime Minister, that no stable Congolese government could be formed, and that the chances for revising the constitution in favor of a federal system, under which the provinces would have real power, were dim.

In the second week of June, 1960, Walter Ganshof van der Meersh, the Belgian Minister for General Affairs in Africa, asked Lumumba to form a government. The Batetela leader's first retort was to claim the right to form a government from his own MNC, as the largest party in the assembly, although it held less than 30 per cent of the total seats. When told that this was impossible, he set about forming a coalition government.

Relations were already bad between Lumumba and the local Belgians (in contrast to the politicians at the Round Table Conference), who—he claimed (with some justice) —had supported his opponents during the elections. Lumumba now set about worsening relations between the various Congolese leaders in his drive for power. His principal weapons in his attempt to form a government were bribery, bullying, and exacerbation of tribal rivalries. A political Donnybrook resulted. When Lumumba failed to form a government (granted he was given little time to do so), the Belgians sent for Kasavubu and asked him to take over the task. At this point, Lumumba threatened to withdraw his delegates and form his own private government. Tshombe, meanwhile, had shown no desire to take advantage of the confused situation. He had, in fact, offered to join Lumumba's coalition in exchange for the ministries of Economic Affairs, Defense, and State. The Leopoldville impasse was finally settled by a compromise, whereby Kasavubu became President and Lumumba Prime Minister. Tshombe agreed to participate in the coalition government then formed (the average age of the cabinet ministers was thirty-five and none had administrative experience beyond the town-council level), receiving only the Ministry of Economic Affairs, the powers of which were further watered down by the creation of ministries of Economic Coordination and Planning, of External Commerce, and of Finance. Tshombe insisted that he rejected the idea of a unitary form of government for the Congo but stated that CONAKAT was always willing to negotiate on the constitutional question with other Congolese parties. The Katanga leader returned to Elisabethville in a somber mood.

Tshombe's disappointment was understandable. He and his federalist allies had failed at Brussels to win any support for their views. Although CONAKAT had won the provincial elections, the BALUBAKAT CARTEL had walked out of the assembly and formed a rival government in the northern part of Katanga. Lumumba, Tshombe's arch foe, had won the battle for the prime ministership. CONA-KAT's demands for ministries in the central government had been whittled down by Lumumba until the party, despite Katanga's huge contribution to the economy of the Congo, had only a negligible influence in national affairs. There was trouble in the air and Tshombe was not the only one who could smell it. Nervous whites, not only in Katanga but in all the Congo, dismayed by the turn events were taking, were shipping their families out of the country on "holidays."

It was a dark hour—for Katanga and for the whole of the Congo.

VI

CHAOS AND SECESSION

"The Congolese people will always stretch out a brotherly hand to the Belgian people."

—PATRICE LUMUMBA,
January 28, 1960

"Katanga is an independent, sovereign, and constitutional state."

—Article One of the Katangan Constitution

THE EVENTS which led to the Congo's disintegration into chaos and to Katanga's secession were triggered off before the new African nation was a day old, when Lumumba issued a calculated insult to King Baudouin in a speech in which the Congolese Prime Minister reminded the Belgian monarch of the "contempt, insults, hangings, and shootings" under Belgian colonial rule. Somewhat shaken by Lumumba's performance, 200 V.I.P.-visitors to the independence celebrations departed. Fortunately, U.N. representative Ralph Bunche remained behind. Local whites uneasily waited for the next outbreak. They did not have to wait long.

On July 4, troops of the *Force Publique* mutinied at Thysville's Camp Hardy, a military post on the main road between Leopoldville and Matadi. The rebellious soldiers threatened their officers with bayonets and helped themselves to ammunition from the camp's armory. A flying visit from Kasavubu and Lumumba retrieved the situation to some extent, although the Congolese soldiers still refused to report for duty, beat up their officers, and kept the majority of them and their wives confined to a small area of the camp. The following day, a group of Congolese troops stationed at Camp Leopold II outside the capital met to air their grievances. Officers who attempted to break up the meeting were placed under arrest. On July 6, a delegation of soldiers obtained an interview with Lumumba. They demanded the departure of their white officers, as well as pay raises and promotions. Lumumba refused to accede to their demands. Meanwhile, isolated incidents of mutiny, rape, and assault by Congolese soldiers were taking place all across the Congo. On July 7, soldiers from Camp Leopold II stoned a government car. Aware now of the seriousness of the situation, Lumumba fired the Belgian Commander, Lieutenant-General Emile Janssens, and announced one-rank promotions for the entire army, whereupon the *Force Publique* became the only army in the world without a single private.

But these moves were too little and too late. Soldiers carrying bayonets and bicycle chains were already in the streets of Leopoldville. The capital's 700 African police placed their five Belgian commissioners under arrest. Lumumba himself was saved from a mob of riotous Congolese soldiers only when his house was surrounded by red-bereted Belgian commandos. In Elisabethville, *Force Publique* mutineers shot two Belgian officers and four white civilians. Violence broke out at Kongolo, Matadi, Luluabourg, Sanda, and Stanleyville. The mutineers, told by their officers that "independence is for civilians," were determined that it should not be for them alone. To them, independence meant not freedom but license. The Congo's whites began to stream for the borders, by car, plane, riverboat, and on foot. Their flight added to the confusion and angered the mutineers, who smelled their fear and hostility.

That the *Force Publique* should act savagely ought not to have surprised anyone: The *Force Publique* was a color-bar army, composed of poorly paid ($6 a month for a private as opposed to $10,000 a year for Congolese national assemblymen), illiterate savages, kept in line in the past only through the application of harsh discipline. The *Force Publique* had mutinied before—in 1895, 1897, 1901, and as recently as 1944. Its 23,000 men, officered by 1,006 whites, were selected from the most backward and savage tribes. In the years immediately after its formation in 1891, soldiers of the *Force Publique* were not only allowed but expected to live off the land. A little rape and stock-theft in off-duty hours was not considered serious, as long as discipline was maintained in the ranks. And the Congolese, who served a seven-year hitch, stayed in the ranks. When independence came to the Congo, only seven Africans had reached the rank of sergeant-major, although the first twenty Congolese officer cadets were attending the Belgian military academy in Brussels. Units of the *Force Publique* were often segregated by tribe and never allowed to serve in their home province. The logic behind this is obvious: A soldier doesn't mind what he has to do to the civilian population as long as they aren't his own people. When there were insufficient volunteers to fill the ranks, chiefs were given power to "designate" recruits. These men, inevitably, were trouble-makers.

Once the *Force Publique* had run amok, there was little that could be done. Kasavubu and Lumumba agreed on the appointment of Sergeant-Major Victor Lundula as commander of the military forces (the name of which was changed to the *Armée National Congolais*, or ANC) and of Joseph Mobutu, a former sergeant turned journalist, as his chief-of-staff. But at the time neither Lundula nor Mobutu had any influence with the mutinous ANC. It was (or should have been) clear that the only hope of stopping the Congo's descent into chaos was the intervention of outside armed forces to restore order. The Belgian Army, units of which were at the ready in the three Congolese bases assigned to them by the Brussels Conference, were the obvious if not the most politically desirable force to undertake this task. Unfortunately, neither Lumumba nor Kasavubu had the political courage to make such a request—the only legal means under which the Belgian troops could have gone into action. Two men had the courage to take such a step: Tshombe and the thirty-four-year-old Congolese Foreign Minister, Justin Bomboko. Their action, however, was quickly disavowed by Lumumba, who stated that intervention was a violation of the Congo's sovereignty. There can be little doubt, however, whatever the validity of Bomboko's move, that the Belgians had a right to intervene in the Congo. Only a convinced Marxist would assume that such a step had as its goal the reassertion of Belgian rule. Belgian citizens had been raped, murdered, and maltreated, and Belgian property was threatened. Under the circumstances, Belgium had a clear right, recognized by international law, to intervene to restore order. Instead of drawing back in horror at such a move, other nations with citizens and property in the Congo, such as the U.S. and Great Britain, which would have been justified in intervening, perhaps should not have shrunk from their responsibilities to their nationals and to the world.

There is just a chance, and an extremely slim one at that, that order might have been restored without Belgian intervention. The Congolese politicians were doing their best to calm the troops, as was a very brave group of Belgian officers, led by Colonel Heniquiaux, that went unarmed to negotiate with the mutineers. It is possible that the rebellion might have burned itself out or at least been contained until new Congolese troops could have been trained and put into the field against the mutineers. It is difficult, however, to reproach the Belgian Government, which was under heavy pressure from its own people, for intervening to protect Belgian lives. The result of this intervention, however, while it temporarily returned a semblance of order to parts of the Congo, was to rupture relations between Belgium and the Congo, smash the fragile coalition built by Lumumba and Kasavubu, throw the Congo as a pawn into the Cold War, and bring about a total collapse of order elsewhere in the country. In two weeks time, according to the Belgians, 251 white women were raped, 230 men and women were "severely mal-treated" and fifteen were killed (ten by shooting, two by burning, and three by stoning). Not all the fighting, of course, was between blacks and whites. The disappearance of law and order resulted in a series of inter-tribal wars, particularly in Kasai and northern Katanga.

On July 6, Tshombe flew to Leopoldville where he had secret discussions with Kasavubu and Lumumba. The nature of these talks is not known. It may have been that Tshombe once more pressed his demand for a federal form of government and threatened secession if he did not get it. Or it may have been that he just wanted to form a first-hand impression of developments in the capital. In any event, he flew back to Elisabethville the following day, called for intervention on the part of Belgian troops in Katanga, and issued a request for help to the Federation of Rhodesia and Nyasaland, a request that was refused by Britain, which is responsible for the Federation's foreign affairs. When the security situation deteriorated on July 9, *Union Miniere* closed down and evacuated its employees' dependents. The Belgian troops, sallying from their base at Kamina in northern Katanga on July 10, quickly restored order, disarmed the rebellious *Force Publique* in Elisa-bethville (who had machine-gunned Italian Vice Consul Tito Spoglia and five other whites that same day), and dropped paratroopers into Kongolo, from which most of the white inhabitants had fled by riverboat. There was very little fighting (about 100 were killed) between the *Force Publique* and the Belgian forces, and peace quickly returned to Katanga's urban areas. Tshombe followed this up by appointing a Belgian, Major Guy Weber, to reorganize the army forces in Katanga. The *Force Publique* troops, who were not Katangans, were disarmed and sent to their homes, the only effective step taken against the mutineers by any Congolese leader or government. Then, on July 11, 1960, less than two weeks after the Congo had become a nation, Tshombe took his fateful step: He declared Katanga to be a free and independent nation.

When Kasavubu and Lumumba flew to Elisabethville to parley with Tshombe on July 12, their plane was not allowed to land. Tshombe's action was unanimously approved by the Katangan Assembly (minus its twenty-two Baluba delegates) on July 17. The CONAKAT Minister in the Central Government was recalled the same day, and Central Government officials were deported on July 18. Interior Minister Munongo made a one-minute speech and the first two Katangan flags were hoisted over Elisabethville (local drapers were not able to supply additional flags for some time). The 8,000 whites who had fled from Katanga to Rhodesia cautiously began to return.

It is ridiculous to assert that Tshombe seceded only because the rest of the Congo was plunging into chaos or that he feared a Communist takeover. The Katangan people, with the exception of the Balubas, had never felt themselves to be a part of the Congolese nation. Language, ethnic bonds, communications, and history all contributed to create among them a feeling of separate exclusiveness. Even those Katangan tribes who, like the Balubas, opposed Katanga's secession, did not do so because they felt any love for Lumumba or had any strong nationalist sentiments but because they feared Tshombe's Lundas and wanted allies against them. The unity of the Congo was never more than a political fiction based on the façade of a common

Belgian colonial administration which effectively concealed the fact that the Congo was not one but several contiguous territories. The Congo, in fact, is more comparable to the four territories of British East Africa—Kenya, Uganda, Tanganyika (now independent) and Zanzibar—separate territories with individual identities, than it is to, say, Ghana. Tshombe had never made any secret of the fact that he would accept a federal Congo, prefer a confederal one, or be overjoyed at the prospect of an independent Katanga. He had made it equally clear that he would not accept a unitary Congo. But the Belgian Government would not listen to Tshombe and the "unitarians" were not prepared to negotiate on the constitutional question. The descent of the Congo into chaos thus was not the cause but the pretext of Katanga's secession. Tshombe assumed the posture of an anti-Communist not because he wholly swallowed the story that Lumumba was a Red (which had only the smallest grain of truth in it), although he certainly was influenced by his white advisors in this respect, but because he felt that it would win him important allies in America, Britain, France, and Belgium.

Having hoisted his proud new green, white, and red flag ("red for the blood shed for Katanga's freedom, white for purity, green for hope"), formed his government, printed currency and stamps, posted patriotic posters around Elisabethville ("*Katanga anakinga Afrika kwa Ukomonisti*"—"Katanga defends Africa against Communism"), and gained the support of local *Union Miniere* officials and other whites (the mining company reopened its plants on July 11, and production was back to normal within a week; *Union Miniere's* July production was off only 15 per cent), Tshombe had four tasks before him if Katanga was to survive. The first was to build up his armed forces from scratch, the second was to secure diplomatic recognition, the third was to crush his enemies within Katanga, the fourth was to maintain in the south and re-establish in the north an effective administration.

Within a week Major Weber had received ample assistance in his task of creating a Katangan gendarmerie in the arrival of Majors Champion and Crevecoeur. In addition, most of the Belgian officers who had served with the *Force Publique* units disbanded in Katanga agreed to stay on to train new units and were given permission to do so by the Belgian Government. In the rest of the Congo, all those Belgian officers unpopular with their troops had been expelled and those allowed to remain had little authority. If Katanga had to start from scratch in creating an army, it at least had professional officers to undertake the task. Also, these officers had fresh material untainted by the mutiny and drawn from the Katangan tribes with which to work. As witness to the thoroughness of the screening of the *Force Publique*, only 300 of the 2,800 Congolese soldiers serving in Katanga at the time of Tshombe's declaration of independence were allowed to remain in the armed forces.

The necessity for a very rapid build-up of the Katangan forces became pressing for two reasons: the intervention of the United Nations in the Congo and the collapse of Katangan authority in the northern (Baluba) areas of the province. Of these causes, the first was by far the most important.

As white civilians fled the Congo (30,000 left the country within the disastrous first week of the mutiny) and the Belgian paratroopers sallied from their bases, the Congolese politicians, frightened, confused, and angry, sent frequent and often conflicting appeals for military assistance "against the Belgian aggression" to nations as disparate as the Soviet Union, the United States, and Ghana. Finally, on July 14, three days after Katanga's declaration of independence, the U.N. Security Council, on the request of Kasavubu and Lumumba, authorized international intervention in the Congo. In its resolution, the Security Coun-

cil called "upon the Government of Belgium to withdraw
their troops" from the Congo and stated that it was the
intention of the U.N. to reorganize the Congolese security
forces "to meet fully their tasks." U.N. Secretary-General
Dag Hammarskjold, in a statement that same day to the
Security Council defining his interpretation of his mandate,
made it clear that he did not feel the U.N. should intervene
in the Congo's internal affairs or act to end Katanga's
secession. By July 18, 4,000 U.N. troops of five African
nations, most of them ferried to the Congo by U.S. planes,
had reached Leopoldville (132 USAF Hercules and Globe-
master transports carried 75 per cent of the U.N.'s troops
and 95 per cent of its supplies to the Congo). Two days
later, the Belgian troops began to withdraw to their bases.
On July 22, the Security Council passed another resolution,
calling on all nations to "refrain from any action which
might tend to impede the restoration of law and order (or)
undermine the territorial integrity and the political independence of the Republic of the Congo." This resolution,
innocent as it may appear, was a clear case of intervention
in the internal affairs of the Congo and therefore, under
the U.N.'s own charter, illegal. By the phrase "territorial
integrity" of the Congo, the international organization obviously condemned the Katangan secession and threw its
weight behind the Leopoldville Government. It undertook
not to restore order in the Congo but to fight the battles
of the Leopoldville politicians against those of Elisabethville. The U.S., as a veto-holding member of the Security
Council, thus must bear a heavy responsibility for the events
that later took place in Katanga.

On July 23, the Belgian forces had completed their
withdrawal from the Congo, in accordance with the Security Council resolution. However, they remained in
Katanga on the invitation of Tshombe's Government,
which certainly had *de facto* if not *de jure* authority.

When the U.N. first announced its intention of sending

troops to the Congo, Tshombe publicly stated that he did not need them, did not want them, and would not have them in Katanga. He certainly had a good deal of justice on his side. At the time, all of Katanga was quiet. The vast majority of the 8,000 whites who had fled to Rhodesia during the events of the second week of July had returned. The mines were working, the shops were open, Katanga was at peace. It was patently obvious that there were plenty of other places in the Congo, namely Kasai and Kivu provinces, where there was trouble enough to occupy the U.N. for years. If it was coming to Katanga, it was clear that the U.N. was coming for a political purpose and that this purpose was to end Katanga's secession. That this was the case was obvious not only from statements made in the U.N. but from the complexion of the international organization's military force in the Congo. At the time, this consisted of 2,100 Ghanaians, 1,400 Moroccans, 2,000 Guineans, 2,100 Tunisians, 1,800 Ethiopians, 700 Irish, 1,000 Swedes, and a handful of Liberians. Troops from Mali, Indonesia, and Egypt were on the way. The Ghanaians, Moroccans, Guineans, Malians, Indonesians, and Egyptians had all declared their unalterable opposition to Tshombe and to Katanga's secession. Only a fool (and Tshombe was never that) could believe that the admission of U.N. troops to Katanga could end in anything but bloodshed and disaster.

Tshombe opposed the U.N. entry into Katanga with all the forces at his disposal. He was not, however, in a position to contest the issue by force of arms; and he did not have sufficient diplomatic backing (no nation had recognized Katanga's secession) to keep the U.N. out by this means. In this respect, he depended on Belgium. Brussels, however, let him down and agreed to the replacement of the Belgian troops by those of the U.N. Hammarskjold, assuming that Tshombe was a Belgian stooge, thought that was all there was to the matter. But Tshombe soon made it clear that he didn't care what Brussels had said, U.N. troops were not coming in. His fear, he stated, was that "in their luggage" would come the Lumumbists, bringing with them "anarchy, disorder, pillage, murder, and misery." He had a point.

Before he would agree to the admission of U.N. troops, Tshombe demanded a guarantee that they would not come from countries "with Communist tendencies" (i.e., Ghana or Guinea), that his government should retain the right to refuse entry to anyone, that his troops should remain in control of the airports and other points of entry into Katanga, and a reaffirmation that the U.N. would not intervene in Katanga's internal affairs. In principle, Hammarskjold was unable to agree to a conditional entry. He went a good way unofficially to meet Tshombe's demands by giving the initial troop assignments in Katanga to Irish and Swedish units. The Secretary-General told the Central Government that the U.N. could not guarantee the safety of any of its officials who might try to come to Katanga, thus leaving entry control (except for U.N. personnel) in Tshombe's hands. Katangan troops were given joint control with the U.N. of Elisabethville airport, and Hammarskjold reiterated his earlier statement that he had no intention of forcing a political solution on Katanga. In the end, Tshombe made the best of a bad bargain by accepting at first only a token force of 237 Swedes who flew into Elisabethville's sandbagged airport on August 12 as Hammarskjold's "personal bodyguard." Tshombe, carrying a tourist brochure called "Elisabethville Welcomes You," met the Swedish diplomat at the airport where the pair reviewed a Katangan gendarmerie honor guard led by Belgian officers. Tshombe scored a nice point by having "Vers l'Avenir," Katanga's unofficial anthem played (Education Minister Joseph Kiwele, who died in November, had not yet had time to compose "La Katangaise," the official anthem), at which time Hammarskjold had no choice but to stand at attention in front of the fluttering Katangan flag, symbol of a sovereignty unrecognized by the U.N. The Swedish soldiers were more jeered than cheered by Africans and whites alike. There was a quick build-up, however, and within a week there were more than 2,000 United Nations troops in Katanga. As the U.N. moved in, 1,700 Belgian troops in battle dress paraded in Elisabethville on August 15 before their commander, General Roger Gheysens, and flew off to Germany to reinforce the NATO forces there. Belgian women wept and there were shouts of "*Vive la Belgique*" from the men as the troops left. Approximately 600 Belgian officers and NCO's, however, remained with the Katanga gendarmerie.

Had the U.N. chosen to do so, it could have performed a real service for Katanga and the Congo by quickly moving into the northern part of the province, which was becoming restive. In the event, the U.N. moved slowly; once established in the north, it stuck pretty much to its main bases and refused to intervene against Baluba terrorists on the pretext that this would constitute interference in the internal affairs of the Congo. As it was, the U.N. forces not only were not a positive force for peace in northern Katanga but they were a detriment to the security situation. The African is quick enough when it comes to sizing up a general situation. The anti-Tshombe Balubas in the north soon understood that the U.N. was not on Tshombe's side. Tshombe himself had very few security forces available in the north. The dissident Balubas took advantage of the situation to stage a reign of terror while the U.N. stood by.

The story of what happened in the north during the last three months of 1960 is not a pretty one. It is not a well-known story because its telling does not suit the purposes of Tshombe's enemies (or of the U.N.'s uncritical friends). It is a story, however, that must be told.

The great Baluba chief Kabongo Boniface early in the game had declared his support for BALUBAKAT. Clan and personal rivalries certainly played a major role in this decision. When the Belgians reached Katanga in 1890, the Baluba emperor, Dai Mande, lay dying on his couch of leopard skins. His two younger brothers, Kasongo Nyembo and Kabongo, were engaged in a bitter fratricidal war that eventually resulted in the collapse of the Baluba empire. The Belgians considered reconstituting the Baluba empire under the chieftaincy of Kasongo Nyembo, who had the better claim. Instead, they divided authority among the Balubas between the two brothers. The two Baluba chiefs who rule today are not, of course, the same men. The real name of the present Kasongo Nyembo is Ndaie Emmanuel; that of Kabongo Boniface is Dibwe Kaloa. But the two brothers of Dai Mande had so much prestige that their successors have always used their names. The two cousins who now rule the partitioned empire are great rivals, each claiming precedence over the other as the true ruler of a united Balubaland. Since Kasongo Nyembo supported CONAKAT, it was inevitable that Kabongo Boniface should throw his support behind BALUBAKAT. It can be seen, then, that it is fallacious to say that all Balubas oppose Tshombe and support BALUBAKAT, although a substantial number do so. Of the estimated 600,000 Balubas and Balubacized Africans of Katanga, about 400,000 are anti-Tshombe. But, as can be seen, the minority that favors him is a substantial one.

When Katanga declared its independence, there were virtually no military forces available to maintain order in Balubaland except for the Belgians stationed at Kamina. When the United Nations moved into Katanga, these 1,700 Belgian troops moved out. The U.N. had neither the forces nor the stomach to maintain effective control in the bush. Kasongo Nyembo's 90,000 Balubas remained loyal to Katanga, as did the 79,000 Balubas of northern Kolwezi territory, northwestern Kabongo, and Kaniama. Feeling was mixed among the 60,000 urban Balubas in the big cities, but here Tshombe's forces were strong enough to keep order.

Upon the Katangan declaration of independence, Tshombe sought to win the support of BALUBAKAT by offering it five of fifteen ministries in a coalition government. BALUBAKAT rejected this offer, although the representatives of the Chokwe tribe came over to CONAKAT. Tshombe then formed his own government. Of the fifteen ministries, four went to pro-Tshombe Balubas, three to Batabwas, two to Bahembas, two to Lundas, and one each to the Bayekes, Basonges, Chokwes, and Ndembos. It is interesting to note that the Balubas were allocated the largest number of seats of any ethnic group—including Tshombe's own Lundas—in the cabinet.

Chief Kabongo Boniface, although he had backed Sendwe before Katanga's declaration of independence, quickly switched his allegiance to CONAKAT. It is not known whether or not pressure was applied to Kabongo Boniface to bring about this switch. The Katangan Government claims that the Baluba chief, who had been elected to the Congolese Senate, was so appalled by what he saw of events in Leopoldville during the mutiny and so pleased by Tshombe's appointment of Balubas to his cabinet, that he voluntarily took his support away from Sendwe and gave it to Tshombe. The "unitarians" claim, however, that Kabongo Boniface, on his return from Leopoldville, was held in Elisabethville and told that he would not be allowed to go back to his own country unless he renounced BALUBAKAT. One is inclined to accept the CONAKAT version, if only because Kabongo Boniface was brutally murdered and mutilated by the BALUBAKAT *Jeunesse* (Youth Wing) a few weeks after his return to his village.

This was the signal for a general uprising among Sendwe's followers in northern Katanga, who quickly established the so-called "Baluba Republic of North Katanga" at Manono. On the murder of Kabongo Boniface, however, many of his supporters switched their allegiance to his cousin, the pro-Tshombe Chief Kasongo Nyembo. In effect, civil war broke out among the Balubas of northern Katanga. Anti-Tshombe guerrillas cut both the north-south and the east-west railway, setting up pockets in which there was no administration whatsoever. The U.N. forces established rather ineffective "neutral zones" around these pockets but made no effort to penetrate them.

Within these pockets, the BALUBAKAT *Jeunesse* ruled supreme. Many Baluba chiefs accepted the *dawa* (literally, "medicine"—it means taking an oath of loyalty, usually accompanied by magical ceremonies such as those employed by Kenya's Mau Mau terrorists) of the *Jeunesse* and then set about eliminating their traditional rivals. At least eighteen other chiefs, in addition to Kabongo Boniface, were murdered for remaining loyal to Tshombe. The *Jeunesse* also killed at least two Protestant missionaries, a doctor, two settlers, and thirty-eight white miners and businessmen, most of them in Manono. Hundreds of Africans also died at their hands.

Those who suffered most were members of the Katangan "establishment," the educated, the prosperous, those politically associated with CONAKAT and with the church.

The first troubles began at Manono in early August, when Tshombe issued a call for all chiefs to come to Elisabethville for a conference (chiefs from twenty-one tribes responded to the call, heard Tshombe explain himself, and approved his actions). The *Jeunesse* warned the twenty-three chiefs of Manono district not to leave their villages. Of these, only three tried to do so. Two made it to Manono but decided against going on. The third, Chief Hubert Mwamba, was ambushed by the *Jeunesse*, flayed with bicycle chains, and scalped. He died of his wounds.

On September 13, the *Jeunesse* took over Manono and plundered the town for five days, during which time most of the white and senior African employees of GEOMINES, the tin-mining firm which dominates the town, were beaten and several killed. Katanga requested permission to reinforce its gendarmes in Manono and was turned down by the U.N., which did nothing itself, although there was a company of Irish troops in Manono at the time. In November, at least ten other prominent Africans, including Chief Vincent Yangala, were killed by the *Jeunesse* after condemnation in kangaroo courts. Chief Yangala's genitals were cut off, gasoline was poured on him, and he was burned alive. His penis was carried triumphantly through the streets of Manono on a spearhead before being turned over to his rival, Chief Kiluba, for use in making *dawa*. So much for the brave new world of Jason Sendwe.

A ten-man Katangan patrol led by the local administrative officer Gregoire Kulu, was ambushed by about 100 *Jeunesse* near Kialo in Kabalo district on October 6. The patrol was overrun (Kulu had ordered his men not to fire). The *Jeunesse* cut off Kulu's legs, jammed sticks into the stumps, and forced him to run on them, before burning him alive. A Belgian NCO named Leclerc who had accompanied the patrol had his legs cut off below the knees, his anus cut out, and his arms and thighs skinned before his head was torn off. Two other members of the patrol suffered similar fates. Similar atrocities took place throughout Kabalo district during October. At that time, U.N. soldiers from Mali were in Kabalo and responsible for law and order there. They did little to justify their presence.

Katangan and U.N. Irish troops were able to hold Albertville against the *Jeunesse* bandits, although various outlying wards of the city were plundered in late August. In the countryside, the terrorists ran wild, holding up trains from Kabalo (on one of these operations, they murdered three white civilians) and massacring (at Nyemba, on November 9) a ten-man Irish patrol. The one survivor of the massacre was later found in the bush and beaten to death by the *Jeunesse*.

The reign of terror began in Bukama district on September 13 with the murder of the chief of the Lualaba sector and all his staff. In September, twenty-two men, women, and children were massacred at Mukulakulu, their hands were cut off, dried, and attached to the hats of the *Jeunesse* leaders as trophies. Trains coming from Kamina were halted and their passengers slaughtered at Bukama. The local witchdoctor, a gentleman by the name of Arthur Kabengele, is said to have demanded a finger and the genital organs from each victim for use in making *dawa*.

The list of atrocious killings that took place in northern Katanga makes sickening reading. The most common weapon used was the bicycle chain, fastened to a stick, its links honed to razor sharpness. A few blows from such a weapon can tear all the flesh from a man's leg in a matter of seconds. Those unequipped with bicycle chains relied on clubs, spears, and sharpened sticks. Many victims were burned alive or impaled. The more distinguished prisoners were castrated. While this was going on, there were U.N. soldiers in northern Katanga who were theoretically responsible for public order. Some of them appear to have done their best to carry out this function while others seem to have done little. Granted that they were terribly short-handed; but at this time there were more than 1,000 U.N. troops in southern Katanga where they were not needed to maintain order, where everything was quiet. They were there to force Tshombe back into the Congo. They were drawing generous pay, exchanging American dollars at black-market rates, and having a pretty good time for themselves. Meanwhile, innocent African men, women, and children were dying horribly in the north.

Tshombe had no forces at his disposal to send to the north. Although nine tons of ammunition reached Katanga in September, he still had inadequate reserves. His new army, only a few weeks old, was still untrained and unfit for action. It was then that Tshombe began to recruit white mercenaries to give himself a ready-made striking force.

The first appeal went out on August 9, 1960. Katangan agents fanned out into South Africa, the Rhodesias, and British East Africa in search of volunteers. The pay was good (about $300 a month for a private) and the only condition (and one not always observed) was that the men were expected to be combat veterans, since there was no time available for training. The mercenaries were to serve under their own officers in all-white units. All things considered, the response was negligible. At the outside, it produced no more than 500 men, including local volunteers from the white civilian population. This does not include, of course, a perhaps equal number of Belgian officers and NCOs training the Katangan gendarmerie.

But the White Legion, as it was called, led by Captains Richard Browne and Alistair Wick (both Britons), did its job: It filled the vacuum left by the dissolution of the *Force Publique*, the U.N.'s unwillingness or inability to act, and the unprepared state of the new Katangan gendarmerie.

Beginning in February, 1961, the White Legion, accompanied by a few gendarmes, cleaned up Luena and Bukama, and reopened the Elisabethville-Kamina railway (the Katangan gendarmerie demonstrated that it was not yet sufficiently disciplined by shooting sixty-eight Baluba prisoners at Luena). In March, the Legion recaptured Nyemba, took Nyunzu, stormed Kabalo, and occupied Manono. In all of these districts an effective administration was re-established, lives and property were safeguarded. This is not to say that the Legion was wholly successful in its sweep; it was not. The anti-Tshombe Baluba warriors and *Jeunesse* simply melted away in front of it into the bush where the Legion lacked the men and the bush knowledge to follow them. But they did restore order in the principal towns, a task that the U.N. could and should have done. Perhaps this is why so many U.N. soldiers feel so bitterly about the mercenaries.

The term mercenary should be used with caution. Most of the men of the White Legion were mercenaries in the true sense of the word: They fought primarily for money, although some of them said rather vaguely that they felt they were "fighting Communism." In the course of time, however, three other categories of whites were serving with Tshombe's forces. The first, on hand from the beginning, were the cadres of Belgian officers and NCOs who stayed on to train the gendarmerie at the invitation of Katanga and with Belgium's blessing. These men were not mercenaries. They were professional soldiers of the Belgian Army temporarily assigned to Tshombe's forces, much as American officers are attached to the South Vietnamese Army. Being professional military men, most of them were conservative in their politics and glad to help Tshombe against what they considered to be a Leftist if not a Communist regime.

Early in 1961, a second element was introduced: the presence of foreign officers, most of them French. Although these officers came as private individuals and were paid for their services—and could technically be called mercenaries—that is really clouding the issue. Most came because they believed in what they were doing, much as did the Americans who served in the RAF during World War II before America awoke from its sleep. In contrast were the Indian Gurkha troops of the U.N., who for hundreds of years have been mercenaries, fighting first for the British and now for the Indians, with equal skill and ferocity.

Lastly, and these were not to become a factor until December, 1961, there were volunteer whites from the local Katangan community. Few of them were paid and hence they cannot be called mercenaries. They volunteered to fight against the U.N. for the very simple reason that U.N.

troops were destroying their homes and killing their friends —a pretty good reason for any man to take up arms.

Meanwhile, events outside Katanga had become even more confusing. A few days after Katanga's secession, Albert Kalonji, the Baluba leader of Kasai, had announced the formation of his own "Mining State" of South Kasai, a kidney-shaped area covering one-third of the province, containing half its population and all of the industrial diamond mines operated by the Industrial, Forestry, and Mineral Company of the Congo (FORMINIERE). Lumumba had countered by sending Congolese troops to Kasai. These seized Bakwanga, capital of the "Mining State" and so distinguished themselves by their actions among civilians that Hammarskjold termed it "genocide." Kalonji fled to Elisabethville where he signed a defense pact with Tshombe.

Lumumba grew more and more erratic. If Tshombe was unhappy with the U.N.'s actions, Lumumba was equally disappointed. In his opinion, the function of the U.N. in the Congo was to support him with its bayonets against Tshombe. When the U.N. only harassed Tshombe and undermined his administration, Lumumba considered that he had been betrayed. He called for the withdrawal of all white U.N. troops, expelled the Belgian Ambassador to the Congo, Baron Jean van den Bosch, declared a state of emergency, announced a series of measures designed to abrogate freedom of speech, assembly, and association, and accused Hammarskjold of being a "colonialist stooge." There began a series of Congolese attacks on U.N. troops.

The Security Council met for the fourth time on August 21, to consider the situation in the Congo. At this meeting no new resolution was passed, but the Swedish diplomat survived a vicious Russian attack aimed at his interpretation of the mandate. A similar assault was defeated at the fifth Security Council meeting in September. During the same month, Lumumba illegally accepted a Russian offer of aid in the form of the loan of twenty-nine Ilyushin transport planes, 100 trucks, and more than 200 technicians. These provided him with the transport with which he attacked Kalonji in Kasai.

By September 5, everybody in the Congo was pretty well fed up with Lumumba. On that date, Kasavubu fired him and appointed Joseph Ileo, the President of the Senate, former editor of *Conscience Africain,* the man who had led the 1959 revolt within the MNC against Lumumba, as Prime Minister. Lumumba promptly countered by dismissing Kasavubu. The Senate got into the act by refusing to endorse either action. Since the U.N. had more or less endorsed Kasavubu's move, it was finally and completely compromised in Lumumba's eyes. And neither the President nor the Prime Minister, of course, could trust the other. Joseph Mobutu, the thirty-one-year-old Chief-of-Staff of the Congolese Army and former Lumumbist, seized power (after Kasavubu had dismissed General Lundula, Commander of the Congolese Army, on September 13), dismissed both Ileo and Lumumba (the former accepted his decision, the latter did not), forced the withdrawal of the Communist-bloc embassies, and established a government of university graduates (this was inevitably and irreverently referred to in Leopoldville as the Student Council). There were now, in effect, two governments in Leopoldville, no government in Kivu and secessionist governments in Katanga and Kasai. A rump Lumumbist government was established in Stanleyville, the capital of Orientale Province, by Antoine Gizenga, Lumumba's Deputy Prime Minister.

There followed weeks of shadowboxing by Lumumba, Kasavubu, and Mobutu, and it would have been ludicrous had it not been so tragic. No side was prepared to move against either of the others. Kasavubu sulked in the presidential palace. Lumumba hid in the Prime Minister's residence under guard of Ghanaian U.N. troops. Mobutu's Student Council toiled manfully and largely ineffectually to keep the government moving. Periodically, Kasavubu or Lumumba sallied into the center of Leopoldville to deliver harangues.

Finally, late in November, Lumumba slipped out of his villa and made a break for Stanleyville. He was caught at Port Franqui in Kasai by Mobutu's troops, beaten up, brought back in chains to Leopoldville, and imprisoned at Thysville, where the Congo's tragedy had had its beginning with the mutiny of the *Force Publique* six months before. But even with the stormy petrel of Congolese politics temporarily in safe-keeping, his shadow still loomed large. A rumor that Lumumba had escaped was enough to send Leopoldville's whites scurrying for the ferries.

This was the time for reconciliation in the Congo. Kasavubu, Ileo, Mobutu, and Tshombe are all men who understood the need for considerable local autonomy within the Congo. Had they been able to reach agreement, the problem of Katanga might have been solved.

But once again the enigmatic, mercurial Lumumba was to cause dissension in the Congo, this time not through his life but through his death.

VII

MURDER, DIPLOMACY, AND IMPRISONMENT

"Prove it!"

> —Katangan Interior Minister
> GODEFROID MUNONGO, replying to
> allegations that his government had
> murdered Lumumba.

"It was Hell."

> —MOISE TSHOMBE, describing his
> detention by the Leopoldville
> Government to the Katangan
> Assembly.

THE SITUATION could not have been more confused and frightening than it was in the Congo during the first month of 1961. Mobutu's troops had launched an invasion of Lumumbist Kivu and Orientale provinces. Gizengist columns were threatening Kasai and northern Katanga, where they were attacked by Tshombe's infant air force. Kasavubu, fed up with the maneuvers of the unpopular Rajeshwar Dayal, head of the U.N.'s Congo operations, was demanding the Indian's recall. Meanwhile, the five so-called Casablanca powers (Ghana, Guinea, Mali, Morocco, and the United Arab Republic) were demanding Lumumba's release and restoration to the premiership and the disarming of Mobutu's "lawless bands." Lumumba, imprisoned at Thysville, had come within an ace of provoking a mutiny among his guards with the object of effecting his release, a move that was forestalled only by the arrival of Kasavubu and Mobutu at the camp.

Meanwhile, the U.S. position on Katanga had begun to shift. Kasavubu had always been regarded as more stable than Lumumba. Mobutu's gentle *coup* had been generally welcomed as a move designed to return stability to the Congo. But the U.S. had become disillusioned with Kasavubu because of the Bakongo leader's inability or unwillingness to act decisively. Mobutu, while he had made an earnest effort to restore order to the Congo, had proved himself to be one of the weakest strongmen in political history, a black Hamlet plagued by indecision, unwilling to assume power himself, and with no candidate to put forward. Under the circumstances, the U.S. and the U.N. began to think in terms of a new deal in the Congo involving the release and presumably the return to power of Lumumba.

Against this darkening background, Kasavubu and Mobutu decided it was essential to place Lumumba in safekeeping. It will never be known whether at that time the decision was reached that Lumumba should die. It is certainly not beyond the realm of possibility, because they were well aware that official U.N. opinion favored his return to power. Kasavubu and Mobutu understood Lumumba very well. They realized, if the U.N. and the U.S. did not, that Lumumba's return to power would in all probability mean their own deaths and further civil war in the Congo. Obviously, the only way to make sure this would not happen was to kill Lumumba or have him killed by someone else. If such a decision was taken, it was largely because of the justified fear on the part of the Congolese that the U.N. and the U.S. intended to force Lumumba's release, despite advice to the contrary from Clare Timberlake, America's able Ambassador to Leopoldville. This is speculation, of course. It may have been that Kasavubu and Mobutu were sufficiently confident of their position to risk letting Lumumba live providing he was transferred to a place of detention from which it would be difficult for him to escape or for the U.N. to free him.

This is the story of what happened to Lumumba as told to me by a high and unimpeachable source in the Belgian Government, a man with many years experience in the Congo who enjoyed the confidence of both Tshombe and Kasavubu:

Kasavubu and Mobutu had first thought of imprisoning Lumumba on a small island in the Congo's estuary, deep in Bakongo country. But it was decided that the *Force Publique* garrison at Matadi was too unreliable and the position too vulnerable to outside intervention. The Leopoldville Government then entered into negotiations with Tshombe to persuade him to imprison Lumumba. Tshombe, however, was no fool. Much as he would have liked to see Lumumba safely out of the way, he was unwilling to take the responsibility for the Batetela leader's safety. Tshombe knew that Lumumba, who had been subjected to sporadic ill-treatment, was not in good health. He, above all men, was aware of the hatred with which Lumumba was regarded both by the Katangan tribes and by their white allies. Tshombe— so the story goes—refused to have anything to do with the problem. As a bargaining counter, the Central Government reportedly offered to arrest anti-Tshombe Balubas in Leopoldville, including BALUBAKAT leader Jason Sendwe, now Vice Premier in the Leopoldville Government, if Tshombe would guard Lumumba. The Katangan leader again refused. Kasavubu is then said to have appealed to "King" Albert Kalonji, Baluba leader of the "Mining State" of South Kasai, to take Lumumba off his hands. Kalonji, of course, was an even more bitter enemy of Lumumba than Tshombe. The Baluba had been Lumumba's top lieutenant until 1959, when he broke away to form his own wing of the MNC. When Lumumba formed his government in June, 1960, the MNC (KALONJI) was the only party to go into opposition. Later that year, Lumumba sent his troops into Kasai, shedding much Baluba blood and chasing Kalonji from his Bakwanga capital. Kalonji was more than agreeable to Leopoldville's suggestion that Lumumba and nine of his aides, also held by Mobutu, should be tried for the "genocide" (Hammarskjold's term) of the Baluba people. He agreed to imprison Lumumba in return for favorable consideration on Kasavubu's part for recognition of his autonomous "Mining State" when constitutional talks, already under consideration, should take place.

On January 17, Lumumba, former Senate Deputy Speaker Joseph Okito, and former Minister for Youth and Sports Maurice Mpolo were taken from Thysville prison and loaded aboard a plane bound for Bakwanga, Kalonji's capital. All three showed signs of having been maltreated during their imprisonment. During the flight, Lumumba and his two aides were severely and brutally beaten by their captors.

When they reached Bakwanga, the pilot found the air strip blocked by fuel drums and parked trucks. The Bakwanga control tower—so the story goes—refused to remove the obstructions (stranger things than this have happened in the Congo during the last two years). The pilot, either on his own initiative or on instructions from Leopoldville, then flew on to Elisabethville.

Lumumba's arrival in a near-dead condition came as a complete surprise to Tshombe. The Belgian Government, as soon as it heard of Lumumba's arrival, instructed its Consulate General in Elisabethville to have nothing to do with Lumumba's detention and to see to it that no Belgian officers were involved. Unwilling as Tshombe was to have Lumumba on his hands, he was even more unwilling to release him or to return him to Kasavubu and run the chance of his again assuming power. Munongo was especially opposed to letting Lumumba go. The three badly beaten prisoners were taken to a villa outside of Elisabethville.

The Katangan Government's story is that the trio was then transferred to a small farmhouse-shack near Mungulunga in the Dilolo Department of Lulua Province (Chokwe country in the angle between Northern Rhodesia and Angola). The shack measured fifteen feet by nine feet and had sandstone walls. The three prisoners were guarded there by a fifteen-man detachment of gendarmes and police commanded by Captain Julien Gat.

The Katangan Government, which had refused repeated U.N. requests to see the prisoners, announced that Lumumba and his comrades had dug their way out of the house, overpowered two guards, stolen their guns and a car, and had escaped on February 10. Three days later, Interior Minister Munongo announced that their car had been found near Kasaji (a few miles from Mungulunga) and that Lumumba, Okito, and Mpolo had been killed by villagers, presumably Chokwes, although he refused to identify their tribe or the name of the village "because we do not want them to suffer any possible reprisals in the future." Lumumba, he said, was buried in a secret grave near where he fell. The villagers, he said, would receive the $8,000 reward placed on the heads of the three men by the Katangan Government.

Munongo's story was immediately challenged as a cover-up. His only reply was: "Prove it!"

According to my informant, three Katangan cabinet ministers (of whom Tshombe was not one) visited Lumumba at the Elisabethville villa where he was held a day or two after his arrival. A drunken orgy ensued, and Lumumba was again beaten by his guards for the amusement of the visiting dignitaries. But Lumumba had been too

thoroughly roughed up during his imprisonment at Thysville and the plane trip to Katanga: He died under the blows
of his tormentors. His two companions, who had witnessed
the murder, were then shot and their bodies disposed of.
Later, the escape plot was hatched.

The U.N.'s version of what happened, published on
November 14, 1961, tallies roughly with this. The U.N.
discounted the Katangan Government's story and said that
"on the evidence so far available" (the Central Congolese
Government refused to let the commission of inquiry visit
the Congo or Katanga), it appears that Lumumba and his
companions were killed in a villa outside Elisabethville on
the day of their arrival. "In all probability," it said, the
murder took place in the presence of Tshombe, Munongo,
and Kibwe. The U.N. named a Colonel Huyghe and Captain Gat, both Belgian mercenaries, as being involved in the
actual killing of Lumumba. One witness (whose testimony the commission treated "with caution") said that
Munongo himself had plunged a bayonet into Lumumba's
chest. Tshombe described the U.N. report as "completely
false."

No one aside from those actually present at the time
knows how Lumumba died. There would seem to be three
possibilities: that he was executed in cold blood on agreement between the Leopoldville and Elisabethville governments; that he was mistakenly beaten to death at the villa;
or that he was, in fact, killed while escaping. The circumstances surrounding Lumumba's death are, in themselves,
irrelevant. The inescapable fact was that he had died while
in Katanga. Tshombe's enemies would have believed the
worst of him no matter what the evidence, such as it was,
had shown. In this instance, they were probably close to
the truth.

Lumumba's death was a pivotal event in the stories both
of Katanga and of the Congo. The Katangan announcement of his death came on the eve of a Security Council

meeting on Katanga. Demonstrations took place at the U.N. and outside Belgian embassies in half a dozen countries. Anti-Tshombe opinion, which the Communist bloc was quick to exploit, hardened among the more radical wing of the Afro-Asian nations. In the heat of the moment, the Security Council passed a foolish resolution calling for the withdrawal of "all Belgian and other foreign military and paramilitary personnel, political advisers, and mercenaries" and authorized the use of "force, if necessary, in the last resort" to prevent civil war. The resolution was foolish because, had it been implemented, the removal of all white personnel from the Katangan Government, personnel which the United Nations could not replace, could only have resulted in the same chaos in Katanga that existed in areas such as Kasai and Kivu. There was nothing intrinsically wrong with the resolution to use "force, if necessary, in the last resort" to prevent civil war. But in its application it was used against Katanga rather than against anyone else.

As far as the rest of the Congo was concerned, Lumumba's death probably had a beneficial result. It failed to produce the violent reaction among his followers that outsiders had said it would. And it permanently removed from the scene the *eminence grise* of Congolese politics. It served as a warning to the other Congolese politicians of the wages of extremism and made negotiation between them possible. It erased the one important Congolese politician subject to the influence of Communism. His political heir, Antoine Gizenga, at no time was to pose the threat that Lumumba had.

The murder of Lumumba was a savage act. It was followed by an equally savage one (that failed to produce the liberal outcry provoked by Lumumba's death): the execution in Stanleyville of nine anti-Lumumbist politicians, held and mistreated for months in Stanleyville, while the U.N. confined its efforts to release them to timid negotiations. In reprisal, Kalonji executed six Gizengists (including

Jean-Pierre Finant, former President of Orientale Province, Major Jacques Fataki, former commander of the Stanleyville gendarmerie, and Gilbert Nzuzi, twenty-two-year-old leader of the Lumumbist youth movement) handed over to him on February 9, by Mobutu. On January 21, Congolese Foreign Minister Justin Bomboko had stated that Lumumba was to be placed on trial, presumably for genocide. Had he been in Kalonji's hands rather than Tshombe's, there probably would have been no difference in his fate.

Lumumba's death was, on the face of it, a crime. This should not be allowed to conceal the fact, however, that Lumumba was an erratic, incompetent, corrupt racist whose demagogic actions brought death and suffering to literally thousands of Congolese. He used his intelligence and diligence in the cause of evil, and in the end he was his own victim. If it was necessary for one man to die for the good of the Congo, the most logical candidate for this honor was Lumumba.

His murder, as well as that of the anti-Lumumbists in Stanleyville and the Gizengists in Bakwanga, illustrated only one point, and one that everybody but the radical African states and the more fuzzy-minded U.N. delegates should have known: The average Congolese (and some considerably above average) are only slightly removed from savagery. Yet even after these bloody events, the U.N. and the U.S. continued to act as if this were not the case. The murder of the thirteen Italian airmen at Kindu late in 1961 and of the twenty-one Belgian priests at Kongolo this year, were the direct result of this ostrich-like attitude.

With Lumumba out of the way, Kasavubu moved quickly to consolidate his position and forestall any attempt by the U.N. to disarm the Congolese troops (7,500 under his banner, 7,000 Gizengists, 5,000 Katangan gendarmes, and 3,000 Kalonji Balubas) or install a "unitarian" government. Mobutu stepped aside, and on February 8, a new government was formed with Ileo as Prime Minister. Five cabinet portfolios were set aside for Katangan, Orientale (where Gizenga had established a regime recognized by the Communist and Casablanca blocs), and "Mining State" ministers. Tshombe was offered a Vice Premiership, and Kasavubu announced that he would favor a wide measure of provincial autonomy when the Congolese leaders got together for constitutional talks.

This was a crucial moment in the Congo's history. Had the U.N. chosen to give Kasavubu and Ileo their full and genuine support, a political settlement might have been obtained in the Congo. As it was, the U.N. concentrated on a negative tactic: passage of resolutions for the eviction of Belgian personnel and authorizing the use of force. Tshombe's reaction was immediate and forceful. He warned that a blood bath would ensue if the U.N. tried to remove white employees of the Katangan Government. Ghana and Guinea, which had been making the most noise in the U.N., he pointed out, were—because of the authoritarian nature of their regimes—least qualified to propose any solution to the Congo's crisis, particularly since it was they who had "incited" Lumumba. To demonstrate that his white personnel were fully at his disposal and not he at theirs, Tshombe announced that his government would no longer accept the one-third subsidy of their salaries from Belgium (there were, at the time, about 800 white military men and 1,300 advisors and administrative personnel in the Katangan service). He warned that the chiefs and people of Katanga would take up arms to resist any United Nations "colonial regime."

That February, 1961, was the time for the U.N. to make a concerted effort to cooperate with the Congolese leaders in re-establishing security and stability can be seen from a study of the encouraging white population figures. Six months before independence, Leopoldville Province had a white population of 34,000. This had fallen to 3,000 during the August, 1960, troubles but was now up again to

9,000. The Katangan population, down from 34,000 to 10,000 during the first troubles, now had doubled. Even in bloody Kasai, where the population had fallen from 9,000 to 1,500 in August, 1960, 500 whites had returned. The only areas where the white populations were still declining were those theoretically under control of Gizengists: Orientale, Kivu, and Equateur (in reality, Gizenga controlled nothing; where his flag flew, authority of any kind simply did not exist). The combined pre-independence white population of these provinces, 38,000, had fallen to 8,500 during August, 1960. By February, 1961, it had dropped again to 4,500. Not only was the U.N. singularly ineffective in re-establishing order in these regions but it did little to assist in the evacuation of terrified white women and children from these provinces. The U.N. had planes available to evacuate to Stanleyville Gizengists who felt themselves in danger in areas under the control of the Leopoldville Government (including Lumumba's widow, Pauline, and forty-one of the dead Premier's thugs). But it showed little interest in evacuating whites from Stanleyville. One is eventually led to the conclusion that the U.N. was not terribly concerned with what happened to the Congo's whites. If a Lumumbist was maltreated, a general outcry could be expected from the Communist bloc, the Afro-Asian nations, and from liberal circles in Britain and America. If a white woman was killed or molested, there might be a complaint from Belgium, but she was already discredited in the minds of the majority of the U.N.'s members, so it made little difference.

Meanwhile, without the help of the U.N.—or almost in spite of it—the Congolese were taking definite, measurable steps toward recreating that territorial integrity of the Congo to which U.N. delegates were so fond of giving lip service. On February 28, Ileo, Tshombe, and Kalonji met in Elisabethville and signed a mutual defense pact to prevent the establishment of a U.N. "regime of tyranny."

The same day, in Brussels, Belgian Foreign Minister Pierre Wigny "invited" all Belgian mercenaries serving with the Katangan forces to return home (it was at that time—March 3, to be exact—that French officers began to play a part in Katanga with the arrival of the paratrooper Colonel Roger Trinquier and two other officers; later in the game, French officers were to play an important role in Katanga).

In early March, relations between the U.N. and the Congolese had deteriorated to the breaking point after *Force Publique* soldiers at Matadi attacked and captured the 135-man Sudanese garrison, which suffered two dead and thirteen wounded in the action. Later, the Congolese stormed ashore from boats and seized the Atlantic port of Banana, thus completely cutting the U.N.'s line of ocean communications.

Against this crisis background, fourteen top Congolese leaders met at the lovely mountain city of Tananarive, capital of the Malagasy Republic (ex-French Madagascar) to seek a solution to the Congo's political problems. The prime mover of the conference was Tshombe, but it was attended by Kasavubu, Ileo, Kalonji, Adoula, Kamitatu, Jean Bolikango (of Equateur), Barthelemy Mukenge (the north Kasai leader), and virtually every other Congolese leader of importance except Gizenga. Gizenga had been invited and had indicated his intention to come (he had asked for and received a promise of U.N. transport). Orientale provincial president Jean Manzikala and Victor Lundula, commander of the Gizengist troops in Stanleyville, both were enthusiastic about the prospects of such a conference. Tshombe and Kasavubu delayed the conference for three days while they waited for Gizenga. He did not show up. Why? One can only conclude that he was warned not to by his Communist and radical African supporters (such as Ghana), forces that were willing to wreck the Congo if they could not dominate it.

The Tananarive Conference got down to business without Gizenga on March 8, 1961. Tshombe opened the initial six-hour session by suggesting that all Congolese leaders should proclaim "a common front against the most recent Security Council resolutions on the Congo, which violate our sovereignty" (the resolution to use "force, if necessary, in the last resort" and that demanding the withdrawal of all Belgian military, paramilitary, and advisory personnel from the Congo). Tshombe maintained that the recent military pact signed by himself, Ileo, and Kalonji made unnecessary the presence of U.N. troops in the Congo. He said that the "military system imposed by Belgium" had failed and described the "regroupment" of the Congo's six provinces as "inevitable." The Katangan President proposed the creation of a commission to coordinate the hiring of foreign technicians. At the end of the first session, the conferees issued a communiqué calling on the U.N. to "abstain from all further action on the Congo pending results of this conference" and warned that any use of force on the part of the U.N. would only bring bloodshed and chaos to the Congo and "aggravate the situation very seriously."

The following day the Congolese leaders announced their intention of recognizing the existence of new states within the Congo and creating new ones based on ethnic, geographic, and economic considerations. Only viable states were to be recognized. At the close of the nine-hour session, the conferees dispatched a telegram to Nkrumah denouncing his attempts "abusively to allocate to himself the right to speak in the name of the Congo."

The three-day conference wound up on March 10. In a final communiqué, the conferees expressed their political design for a new Congo in more detail. The present centralized structure was to be replaced by a "Community of Congolese States," a loose confederation of nearly sovereign states. There was to be a central government at Leopoldville in a "neutral zone" somewhat similar to the District of Columbia. Kasavubu was to remain President, serving on a "Council of States" made up of the presidents of the member states, whose original number would probably be ten (it was later thought that this figure might be doubled). Foreign policy, general internal policy, currency, and military affairs were to be the province of this "Council of States," the decisions of which would have to be unanimous. There was to be an executive "coordinating body" to implement the decisions of the Council and, perhaps, a central assembly of some sort. There were to be no customs or immigration barriers between the various states.

It was further agreed that the military pact between Ileo, Tshombe, and Kalonji was confirmed, that the conferees would "respect" neighboring states and "abstain from military intervention."

In a final telegram to Hammarskjold, the Congolese leaders warned that the planned dispatch of 4,700 Indian troops to the Congo would "aggravate tension" between the U.N. and the Congolese population and demanded that the Security Council resolution on disarming Congolese troops and removing foreign advisers be revoked.

The Tananarive Conference had not constructed a comfortable political mansion in which all of the Congo's disparate peoples and rival leaders could live in harmony and govern themselves effectively. But it had laid the groundwork for the construction of such an edifice. Much remained to be done and final agreement was by no means certain. There remained the troublesome questions of delimiting frontiers, agreeing on the division of revenue, and ratifying a new constitution. These questions were to be dealt with at further conferences tentatively set for Bakwanga and Elisabethville.

But very real gains had been registered at Tananarive. The leaders of the Congo (excluding Gizenga) had gathered together in amity and hammered out over the conference table a plan to which they were able to give unanimous assent. Gizenga had been isolated and shown up in his true colors as a wrecker with little support even in his own province, a man representing only himself and the foreign interests whose puppet he was. Most important of all, for the first time the Congolese themselves had done what the U.N. was too timid or ill-informed to do: They had recognized the indisputable fact that the Congo's political center of gravity lay not in Leopoldville but with the local leaders in the provinces. Having recognized this, anything was possible; having rejected it, as the U.N. had done, captivated by the chimera of the Congo's territorial "integrity," nothing was possible. What emerged from Tananarive was a compromise between partition and federation. It might not suit Kwame Nkrumah's vision of the Congo. It might not even suit John F. Kennedy's. But it was a realistic solution that took into account the facts of the Congo as they were, rather than as some people might have wanted them to be. Most important of all, it was a Congolese solution, freely arrived at by the leaders of the people in open negotiation.

Much of the credit for Tananarive must go to Tshombe. He was a moving power in calling the conference and he played the dominant role once it was convened. With Kalonji riding high in Kasai, chaos in Kivu, Mobutu's troops moving against Stanleyville, and Kasavubu quarrelling with the U.N., he was in a position to hold out for Katanga's independence. He did not. He forged a confederation that, if it reduced the authority of the central government, at least provided for the Congo to be one nation, under one flag, with a single policy. The links that bound the Congo together would at least have been stronger than those existing among the four states of ex-French Equatorial Africa or Houphouët-Boigny's *Conseil de l'Entente.*

Said Tshombe at the conclusion of the conference: "We have resolved our problems ourselves and now we want both West and East to leave us alone."

Despite the holes in the Tananarive agreement, it had much to recommend it, if only because it was a Congolese solution. Tass, the Soviet news agency, recognized this by denouncing Tananarive as "a conference of puppets and traitors." One would have thought that the U.N. and the U.S., if they were really interested in seeing a peaceful reconstruction of the Congo (even if its design was not of their making), would have adopted a conciliatory posture, made concessions wherever possible, and done nothing to disturb the good-will and community of interest established at Tananarive. This, however, was not the case.

The U.N. contemptuously brushed aside Tananarive as if it had never taken place. Radical African and Asian diplomats in New York seized on Gizenga's absence to claim that a third of the Congo had not been represented at Tananarive, hence the resolutions of the conference were of no importance. This, of course, was why Gizenga had not gone in the first place. His Communist and Afro-Asian advisers were determined to go to any lengths to prevent the re-establishment of Congolese unity unless such unity was to be achieved on their terms, not on those of the Congolese. The claim that Gizenga represented a third of the Congo was ridiculous. Gizenga is a Bashiko tribesman from Leopoldville Province with no tribal support whatsoever in the areas which were allegedly under his control. Nor could he claim even the MNC leadership: He had never been a member of the party, much less an officer; his party was the *Parti Solidaire Africain*, the leadership of which he had lost to Kamitatu, who was at Tananarive and approved the conference's decisions. Even Gizenga's colleagues in Orientale were disenchanted with him, as witnessed by the stand taken by Lundula (who soon opened secret negotiations with Leopoldville) and Manzikala, who favored his attendance at the conference. In short, Gizenga represented only himself. He was supported, as was demonstrated by his easy arrest in January, 1962, by only a company of hired thugs. What passed for his "control" over a third of the Congo was only a total lack of any form of authority in those regions. The position adopted by many Afro-Asian delegates on this question was either woefully uninformed or callously and criminally biased.

In any event, the U.N. passed off Tananarive as unimportant. In a report of the U.N.'s eleven-nation Congo Conciliation Commission, a new conference based on the unworkable *loi fondamentale* was suggested. There was no retraction of the Security Council resolution of February 21. The 4,700 Indian troops, flown in on U.S. planes, arrived in the Congo despite the protests of the Congolese leaders. Meanwhile, the temporary head of the U.N.'s Congo operation, the Sudanese Mekki Abbas, began negotiations with both Kasavubu and Gizenga.

Kasavubu wanted more control over U.N. air and sea traffic into the Congo. He also wanted Dayal, then temporarily in New York, removed. The U.N. (and the U.S.) wanted the Tananarive Conference downgraded and the Congolese National Assembly reconvened, any changes in the state's constitutional structure to spring from this rather than from negotiations among the Congolese leaders. This suited Gizenga. He would have preferred, of course, to have had his claim as the Congo's legitimate Premier (based on the fact that he had been Lumumba's Deputy Premier) recognized. But Tananarive had dangerously isolated him; he was quick to realize that. By agreeing to the recall of the National Assembly, Gizenga thought that he could wipe out Tananarive, shift his odd-man-out status to Tshombe, and still have a chance of emerging on top when the deputies reconvened. He was not hard to convince when Kamitatu came to Stanleyville for secret negotiations with him on April 3.

Meanwhile, the second conference of Congolese leaders, designed to build upon the foundation of Tananarive, was set for April 21, 1961, and its venue changed from Bakwanga to Coquilhatville, a port on the Congo River in Equateur Province, an area under Central Government control.

Relations between Tshombe and the U.N. had deteriorated markedly since Tananarive. Tshombe, like Kasavubu and the rest of the Congolese leaders, had decided that he had made a mistake in handing over control of the Elisabethville airport to the U.N. On the night of April 3, a force of thirty-two Katangan gendarmes and policemen, led by a Belgian officer, parked a dozen vehicles across the airport runways and attempted to enter the control tower. They were arrested by Swedish troops who immediately sealed off the airport to Katangan military personnel and placed a ban on all Katangan flights, military and civilian. Tshombe termed the arrest of his soldiers and the closure of the airport a cause for war and called for the mobilization of the entire province. Radio Katanga broadcast repeated calls on the morning of April 4, for the people to assemble in the center of the city, where Tshombe would speak to them. The Katangan leader, meanwhile, was negotiating with Georges Dumontet of France, the principal U.N. representative in Katanga. They quickly reached an agreement whereby Katangan and U.N. forces would share control of the airport. But Tshombe was not happy. The U.N. had announced, after his troops had recaptured Manono from the Baluba rebels a few days earlier, that Indian troops were being sent to Katanga and that they would use force if necessary to prevent armed clashes. In other words, the U.N. was going to use its bayonets to prevent Tshombe from re-establishing his control over northern Katanga.

Tshombe told the crowd of about 6,000 that all contacts with the U.N. military and civilian personnel in the future were banned. He announced that water and electricity to the Swedish camp outside the city had been cut. He asserted that if the U.N. had not agreed to joint control of the airport he would have asked the crowd to retake it for him. The crowd, armed with *pangas* (machetes), iron bars, and muzzle-loading rifles, streamed toward the airport. There they tore down the U.N. flag, broke telephone wires, smashed windows, and overran the main entrance. They were finally brought under control by Katangan police. This was the first serious incident between Katanga and the U.N. It was not to be the last.

The U.N. quickly flew Irish and Indian reinforcements into Katanga and warned that the feared Indian troops would be used if Tshombe again "interfered" with the U.N.'s operations. Tshombe backed down and rescinded his sanctions against the U.N. Meanwhile, Tshombe's White Legion and gendarmerie completed the conquest of the north with the capture of the vital railway junction of Kabalo, and of Nyunzu. In Kabalo, Tshombe's forces clashed with U.N. Ethiopian troops after the latter had disarmed some gendarmes, theoretically to prevent clashes between them and Baluba warriors. Two Belgian, twelve British, and fourteen South African mercenaries and 200 Katangan gendarmes were captured in the clash and both sides suffered casualties.

Tshombe retaliated by freezing U.N. bank accounts in Katanga, cutting rail and telephone links from the U.N.-held Kamina base, mining the road north of Kamina to the Iluba power station held by seventy Irish troops, blocking the Manono and Albertville airstrips, and forbidding the sale of aviation gas to the U.N.

So occupied was Tshombe with his troubles that he did not reach the Coquilhatville Conference until April 23, two days after it had begun. Obviously, he was not in a happy frame of mind. Despite Tananarive, the U.N. had flown Indian troops into Katanga and implemented against

Katanga the resolution to use "force, if necessary, in the last resort." Katangan blood had been shed, Tshombe's authority placed in serious doubt, and his pride hurt. All this had taken place on the eve of vital negotiations affecting the political stability of the Congo.

At the Conference, Kasavubu confirmed that he had reached an accord with the United Nations and that it was his intention to convene the National Assembly. This, of course, was a direct contravention of the Tananarive resolutions. Tshombe smelled a rat, as well he might have: The U.N. had built up its force in Katanga to 7,000 men with another 1,500 expected daily, more than half the total strength of the U.N. in the Congo. Recent events had proved that the U.N. was quite ready and willing to employ this strength against him. Worst of all, the Baluba leader Jason Sendwe, Tshombe's arch foe, had arrived uninvited at the conference, demanded, and received a seat. Tshombe immediately set three conditions for his participation in the Coquilhatville Conference: denunciation of Kasavubu's agreement with the U.N., a protest to the U.N. against its actions in Katanga, and the expulsion from the conference of delegates who had not participated in the Tananarive talks. Turned down, Tshombe stalked from the conference and ordered his plane readied to return to Elisabethville the following day. On April 26, Congolese soldiers began rounding up Tshombe's retinue in Coquilhatville. The Katangan President and his Foreign Minister, Evariste Kimba, were arrested and confined to the airport.

Ileo, trying to convince Tshombe to return to the conference, told him that "your arrest was not authorized by our government but you shocked the conference by walking out." Tshombe, who may be many things but certainly is not a coward, replied to Ileo: "If that is how you run the Congo, you can have it."

Tshombe may have acted precipitately in walking out

of the conference. But the fact remains that Kasavubu had gone back completely on the Tananarive Conference by agreeing to the expulsion of all Belgian military and political advisers from the Congo and by okaying the "force, if necessary, in the last resort" resolution. Kasavubu had shown that he meant this by handing over to the U.N. his own top five Belgian advisers.

With Tshombe out of the way, the chances for the establishment of a Congolese confederation were finished. The fragile fabric of Congolese trust and cooperation established at Tananarive was rent and was not to be re-established for many months, during which much blood was to flow. It should be remembered that this was so because the U.N. willed it and the U.S. permitted it. Had the U.N. and the U.S. given their full support to the Tananarive resolutions, it is likely that peace, unity, and stability could have been produced in the Congo.

Most U.N. officials, almost all foreign diplomats, and not a few Congolese had assumed that Tshombe's regime would collapse with his arrest. Indeed, it is possible that this was the purpose of his detention. Such, however, was not the case. On hearing of their President's arrest, the Katangan cabinet declared a state of emergency. Interim powers were delegated to a quadrumvirate consisting of Munongo, Kibwe, Kiwele, and Assembly President Charles Mutaka. Munongo, easily the most powerful of the four, assumed the captive Kimba's Foreign Affairs portfolio, which meant that it was he with whom the U.N. would have to deal. Munongo could easily have sold Tshombe out in return for U.N. support for himself as Katangan President; he certainly would have done so if Tshombe, as the U.N. was so fond of implying, was nothing but a Belgian stooge (unless one assumes that every Katangan politician by definition is in the Belgians' pocket). That such a move never entered Munongo's mind is evidence of the genuine nature of Tshombe's leadership in Katanga.

Munongo immediately set about securing Tshombe's release through traditional (and some highly untraditional) diplomatic means. He kept the Lunda leader's image before the people by plastering Katanga's towns with pictures of Tshombe inscribed "He suffers for us—let us be worthy of him." To take the pressure off in Elisabethville and increase the chances of Tshombe's release, Munongo offered to negotiate with the U.N. on the question of foreign advisers serving with the Katangan Government and gendarmerie. In Brazzaville, President Fulbert Youlou of the (ex-French) Congo Republic, impounded five U.N. planes, closed his airport to U.N. traffic, and cut the ferry service to Leopoldville in protest against Tshombe's arrest.

But having once broken with Tshombe, the Leopoldville Government was determined to crush him. On May 7, an old personal enemy of Tshombe's, Foreign Minister Justin Bomboko, announced that the Central Government would try Tshombe and Kimba on four counts, two of them punishable by death. These were: assassination of political prisoners (Lumumba and his colleagues) and massacre of the northern Katanga Balubas, rebellion under the specific direction of foreign elements, theft (of the Central Government's property when Tshombe declared Katanga's independence), and counterfeiting (for issuing a Katangan currency). Then Bomboko, speaking in Coquilhatville, mouthed some fateful words:

"We are going to do everything in our power to liberate Katanga, by force if necessary." It was clear that part of the U.N.'s deal with Kasavubu had included the total subjugation of Katanga, in violation of the United Nations Charter. The U.N. proved this to be the case by its own actions.

But if Kasavubu and the U.N. had found life with Tshombe difficult, they found a political solution to the Congo's woes impossible without him. Although the U.N. was able to arrest and deport a few mercenaries (others left

voluntarily when Munongo released them from their con-
tracts), Munongo refused to budge on the basic questions.
He still maintained Katanga's sovereignty, promised that
he would destroy the mines and dams if Leopoldville attempted to impose its will by force, and demanded
Tshombe's release.

Finally, on June 22, 1961, Tshombe—largely through the
intervention of Mobutu—was set free. He said in Leopoldville (where he had been imprisoned) that he intended to
work "with my Congolese brothers to make a very great
country." He added, however, that "we have no need of
the gentlemen of the U.N." To obtain his release, Tshombe
had agreed that Katangan delegates should attend the reconvening of the Congolese National Assembly (scheduled
to take place within a few days), that its copper should be
exported through the Congo rather than through Angola,
and that the Katangan gendarmerie should be reorganized
under the leadership of twenty Congolese officers, who
were to accompany him to Elisabethville.

No sooner was he back in Elisabethville than Tshombe
reasserted Katanga's independence and adherence to the
principles of Tananarive. The Congolese officers were sent
back to Leopoldville. Katanga did not send a delegation to
the National Assembly. Tshombe's action was a betrayal
of trust. On the other hand, his arrest while attending a
political conference was obviously illegal. By the fact of
his detention, any agreements he made in Leopoldville certainly were made under coercion. Consequently, he had
no moral duty to abide by them. (In any event, the Katangan Assembly invalidated all such agreements.)

Tshombe's arrest, whoever advised it, was a mistake. It
solved nothing and created many problems. It was regret-
table, of course, that Tshombe walked out of the Coquilhatville Conference. On the other hand, he was certainly
justified in so doing since Kasavubu clearly had gone back
on the Tananarive accord. It is, however, difficult to fault

Kasavubu for coming to terms with the U.N. He lacked the military strength to do anything else. The one villain in the whole unfortunate mess obviously was the U.N. which placed pressure on Kasavubu at a time when delicate negotiations were under way and progress had been made toward reconciliation in the Congo. To intervene at a time like that merely to force the Congo to conform to a particular constitutional pattern would seem to be both stupid and criminal.

The Congolese House of Assembly met at heavily guarded Lovanium University outside Leopoldville for the first time in ten months on July 25, and elected a Gizengist, Joseph Kasongo, as its President. Katanga, which had demanded another summit conference outside the Congo before the reconvening of the Assembly, was not represented except by Sendwe's BALUBAKAT delegates. On July 29, Tshombe flew to Brazzaville in a last-ditch attempt to explain to Kasavubu why he felt a new conference was needed before a Congolese government could be formed. He made it plain, as he had on a score of other occasions, that he was willing to share Katanga's wealth with the rest of the Congo. Kasavubu, however, refused to see him and Tshombe flew back to Elisabethville on August 1. The same day, Kasavubu called on Interior Minister Cyrille Adoula, a man of the Left but not a Lumumbist, to form a new government. Named as Vice Premiers were Tshombe's two most bitter enemies, Antoine Gizenga and Jason Sendwe.

On August 1, 1961, the die was cast. Despite pious protestations to the contrary, the one aim of the United Nations and of the Congolese Government became the overthrow of Tshombe's regime and the reintegration of Katanga in the Congo. It was war.

VIII

THE PHONY WAR

"Katanga's secession is ended."

> —U.N. Representative CONOR CRUISE
> O'BRIEN, September 13, 1961.

"The unpalatable truth is that the United Nations
has used force to try to subjugate a small area
of the Congo whose people and leaders have the
courage to stand up for their convictions."

> —SIR ROY WELENSKY, Prime
> Minister of the Federation
> of Rhodesia and Nyasaland,
> September 15, 1961.

ON AUGUST 4, 1961, less than three days after his in-
stallation as Prime Minister, Adoula made his position quite clear when he said that his government intended
to end Katanga's secession "within the next few days." In
his inaugural address he accused Tshombe of "provoca-
tions" and stated that "nothing would keep the Congolese
people from recovering their heritage."

Chief U.N. Representative in the Congo Sture Linner
gave the first firm indication that "the fix was on." Despite
the fact that the Security Council's resolution instructed
the U.N. forces to prevent civil war "by force, if necessary, in the last resort," the Swede indicated that a double
standard was to be applied in Katanga's case. Military action

by the Central Government against Katanga, Linner said, executing some rather puzzling mental gymnastics, would not be considered civil war and the "U.N. would therefore not intervene." It was made clear, however, that if Katanga moved to secure its frontiers through a preventative offensive, this would be considered civil war and the U.N. would take action against Tshombe. In other words, it was a heads-you-lose-tails-I-win situation.

In an eleventh-hour effort to achieve reconciliation, Tshombe on August 6, agreed to send CONAKAT's National Assembly delegates to Leopoldville, although he stated that this move did not mean Katanga "had in any way abandoned its actual position or its acquired rights."

Leopoldville and the U.N. were in no mood for reconciliation. On August 6, those countries that had for the past eight months recognized Gizenga's rump regime as the Congo's legitimate government—Russia, Red China, Yugoslavia, Czechoslovakia, Poland, the U.A.R., Mali, and Ghana —were informed by a Gizengist spokesman that Adoula's Government was now the only Congolese government. Plainly one of the conditions of Gizenga's renunciation had been a U.N. promise to smash Tshombe. Two days later, Mobutu, who was known to be a friend of Tshombe's, pointedly and publicly pledged his personal loyalty and that of his army to Adoula. Something was obviously in the air.

That something became clear on August 25, when U.N. Special Representative in Katanga Conor Cruise O'Brien announced the arrival of a battalion of Indian troops as the first step in the disarming of Katanga's 13,000 police and gendarmes (according to the Belgian Government, there were 201 Belgian officers and noncommissioned officers in Katanga at the time). The following day, O'Brien delivered a virtual ultimatum to Tshombe: Go to Leopoldville and negotiate with Adoula or face the consequences. As Tshombe and Munongo (who was also present) told

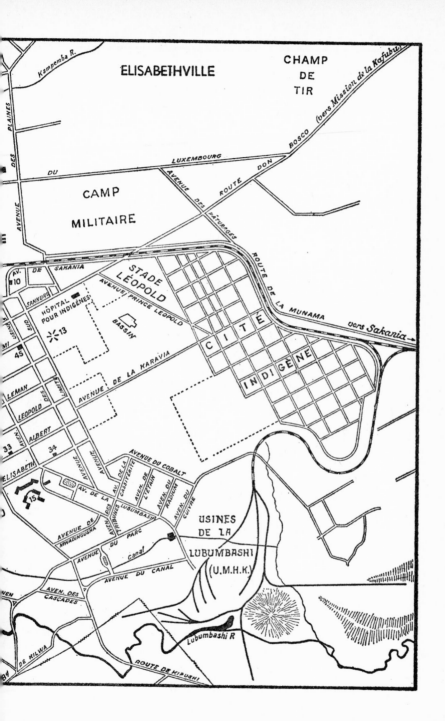

the story, O'Brien informed them that Tshombe must go to Leopoldville or "have the U.N. forces put at the disposal of the Adoula Government to liquidate Katanga." O'Brien said that he had merely conveyed Adoula's "invitation," not issued an ultimatum, although he agreed that U.N. intervention was "possible." O'Brien admitted that the U.N. had promised Adoula its full support, even to the extent of military aid. This in itself, as Munongo pointed out to him at the time, would be "interference without precedence" in purely internal matters, a clear violation of the U.N.'s own charter. Tshombe immediately called together his cabinet, which rejected the Adoula–O'Brien ultimatum and refused to negotiate "under United Nations threats."

Two days later, on August 28, 1961, O'Brien took the first open step designed to bring down Tshombe's regime. A task force of Indian and Swedish troops commanded by Indian Brigadier K.A.S. Raja moved into Elisabethville before dawn, seizing the airport, Radio Katanga, the post office, the telephone exchange, Katangan army headquarters, and several hospitals. Their objective: to arrest and deport all Europeans serving in the Katangan administration and armed forces.

Within a few hours, more than 100 of an estimated 512 of such officers (201 of whom were Belgians) had been rounded up. As Irish-manned armored cars prowled through Elisabethville's shady streets, U.N. units in the capital, Albertville, Manono, Nyemba, and Nyunzu flushed white officers from their hiding places. Tshombe, realizing that his forces were caught off guard, went on the air to appeal for calm and formally released some 200 white officers and advisers from their posts. He reasserted his claim to independence, however, and said that the U.N. had given him written assurance that the Katangan gendarmerie would not be disarmed and that the Congolese army would not be admitted to Katanga. By noon, O'Brien was sure enough that he had the situation well in hand to withdraw his troops from the post office and other installations. Tshombe was again "invited" to go to Leopoldville for negotiations with Adoula.

The dragnet for the mercenaries continued for the next two days quietly but with insignificant results: Most of the white officers not apprehended during the first sweep had had time either to go into hiding or to join their units in the bush. Having failed to provoke an incident during the arrests, O'Brien next (August 31) demanded that Tshombe suspend Munongo, charging that the Interior Minister had plotted a "murderous conspiracy against United Nations personnel and organized atrocities on large sections of the population." O'Brien said that the atrocities charge referred to police treatment of Elisabethville's Kasai Balubas, 700 of whom had "sought refuge with the U.N.," many of them badly beaten up. Munongo must not, Brigadier Raja said, "be left in control of the Katangan armed forces."

These were serious charges, yet O'Brien presented no specific proof indicting Munongo personally in any atrocities. It is certainly true that atrocities against Balubas were committed in Elisabethville, both by the civilian population and by the police. The Balubas were, after all, regarded by the mass of Katangans, who are not very sophisticated people, as a seditious group. Theirs was the misfortune to be trapped in Elisabethville while their northern kinsmen were at war with Tshombe's troops. It is also true, however, that the U.N. deepened the schism between the Balubas and the other Katangan tribes by sending patrols into Elisabethville's five African communes, offering Balubas free food and refuge with the U.N. Once it had the Balubas in its camps (they soon numbered 35,000), the U.N. stamped their identity cards to entitle them to rations. This permanently branded them as allied with the U.N., regarded by the rest of the Katangans as an enemy "tribe," and made it impossible for the Balubas to return to the city. This in turn made those Balubas who remained in the communes increasingly suspect in the eyes of the other tribes, thereby increasing the likelihood of incidents. There was certainly a Baluba problem: there had been one for centuries. But the crisis proportions of the present situation were at least to some degree of the U.N.'s own making.

This does not excuse, of course, the atrocities perpetrated against the Balubas: they were horrible and unforgiveable. But they were the product of history, tribal rivalries, and present-day politics. They were not solely of Munongo's making. He could not have stopped them had he wanted to. By the same token, the U.N. had never thought to demand Lumumba's removal when his troops were engaged in an infinitely more horrible "genocide" against the Balubas of Kasai. Even more recently, less than a month before, the troops of the Central Government had gone on a rampage in Kasai killing 700 Luntu tribesmen. One did not hear Linner's righteous voice demanding the resignation of Congolese Interior Minister Christophe Gbenye. One came to the conclusion that there was one standard for a Gizengist like Gbenye and another for a pro-Western Katangan such as Munongo. O'Brien's charges that Munongo was organizing a "murderous conspiracy" against U.N. personnel were based on evidence that could hardly be termed conclusive. The charge stemmed solely from the evidence of Andre Cremer, a thirty-six-year-old Belgian who claimed that Munongo had hired him to assassinate U.N. officials. The Belgian Government the following day identified Cremer, who had taken refuge with the U.N., as a convicted car thief eluding a three-year jail sentence. He had recently been dismissed from the Katangan Army. Cremer was killed the following month by Ethiopian troops when he attempted to break out of a U.N. prison camp in Leopoldville.

In any case, as O'Brien well knew, there was no question of Tshombe removing Munongo. The Bayeke leader

was Tshombe's strong right arm, the man who had ruled
Katanga while Tshombe was in detention. Both the army
and the police were personally loyal to the Minister of the
Interior. To have removed him would have broken the
morale of the army and driven the Bayekes out of their
alliance with Tshombe. It would seem that there were two
purposes in the charge: to establish a pretext for U.N. intervention in Katanga and to spread dissension within
Tshombe's Government. As O'Brien obviously knew he
would, Tshombe refused to suspend Munongo.

The next day, September 1, O'Brien announced that the
U.N. was breaking off relations with Tshombe's Government "except for the minimum contacts necessary for public order and the security of our forces." The gauntlet was
thrown down. The U.N. no longer recognized Tshombe's
regime as the Government of Katanga.

After four days of "war by press conference," during
which each side sought to blacken the other, Tshombe
called an emergency meeting of the Katangan Assembly
to consider "the danger threatening our country." Foreign
Minister Kimba told the deputies, two of whom called for
"war against the United Nations" that "no further concessions" would be made to the international organization.
Meanwhile, the CONAKAT *Jeunesse*, which is no better
than its parallel Baluba organization, was getting out of
hand: Katangan police had to fire into the air to disperse
a crowd of youths who stoned a U.N. hospital and set
a U.N. vehicle afire. On September 9, the Third Battalion
of the Third Gurkha Rifles flew into Elisabethville to reinforce Raja. By that date, the U.N. deadline for the deportation of all mercenaries, 273 had been repatriated and another sixty-five were awaiting evacuation. Only 104 were
unaccounted for. The hour was at hand.

O'Brien moved swiftly and ruthlessly. At four o'clock
in the morning of September 13, Gurkha troops supported
by Irish armored cars attacked Katangan gendarmes who

had reoccupied the post office in the center of Elisabethville. Other Indian troops seized Radio Katanga and Swedish
units engaged gendarmes guarding Munongo's home. After
two hours of heavy fighting, the knife-wielding Gurkhas
stormed the post office. Tshombe and Munongo were
reported fleeing toward Rhodesia. Kibwe was in U.N.
custody.

O'Brien proclaimed: "Katanga's secession is ended. It is
now a Congolese province run by the Central Government
in Leopoldville." The Irishman added that the U.N. had
moved on the instructions of the Leopoldville Government.
The action, he added, had been taken to prevent civil war
between Katanga and Central Government troops, who
planned an invasion. In Leopoldville, where Hammarskjold
had flown the same day for "consultations," Adoula announced the dispatch of a special High Commissioner to
assume authority in Katanga. His name: Egide Bochely-
Davidson, a man regarded by many Western diplomats as
being strongly pro-Communist. His background: High
Commissioner of State in Gizenga's Stanleyville regime.

It was obvious, then, from O'Brien's statement and from
the rapid dispatch of the Gizengist gauleiter to Elisabethville that the move was prearranged and had only one aim:
to topple Tshombe's regime. The mercenary gambit had
been nothing but a cover.

But Katanga's fourteen months of independence were
not to be ended so easily. Heavy fighting continued into
the afternoon as the gendarmerie regrouped and snipers
took up their positions throughout the city. Three Katangan
counterattacks were launched against the post office but
all failed. Tshombe's transmitter came on the air within
hours as "Radio Free Katanga" and called for a fight to the
death. Several hundred Bayeke warriors responded by join-
ing 500 Katangan gendarmes besieging 158 Irish troops at
Jadotville. A U.N. column dispatched to relieve Jadotville
was halted when a Katangan Fouga Magister jet trainer,

one of Tshombe's midget air force, attacked it in support of the gendarmes and Bayeke warriors. Another Fouga strafed Elisabethville airport, destroying a U.N. transport plane on the ground, hit O'Brien's Elisabethville headquarters, and attacked the U.N.-held Kamina base in the north. Katangan gendarmes, reinforced by 5,000 of Kasongo Nyembo's Baluba warriors, harried Kamina's outer defenses, cutting the 300-man garrison's water supply and forcing its withdrawal to a tight perimeter around the airfield. Tshombe and Munongo turned up in Elisabethville where they directed the resistance. The city's light and water was cut. Bochely-Davidson, sent to preside over the subjugation of Katanga, found himself able to take control only over Elisabethville's shell-pocked airport, finally gave up, and flew back to Leopoldville. O'Brien called for reinforcements but found them difficult to procure because Katanga's two jets, flown by South African and Belgian mercenaries, controlled the daylight skies.

On September 15, the third day of the fighting, O'Brien announced that the U.N. had lost seven dead and twenty-six wounded. Katangan losses he set at 200 dead, 500 wounded, and 100 prisoners. Eyewitnesses reported that Indian troops had fired on ambulances and killed wounded gendarmes. The U.N. countered with atrocity claims against the Katangans.

The following day, Tshombe issued a proclamation demanding "total war" against the U.N. and expressing the determination of his government and his people "to fight to the last man and the last round of ammunition for Katanga's independence and freedom."

On September 17, the Irish garrison at Jadotville surrendered. Heavy Katangan assaults were launched against O'Brien's headquarters. It became patently clear that the U.N. had bitten off more than it could chew. Its total military strength in the Congo was 20,000—slightly more than half of them in Katanga. But these had no air support or artillery and only a few armored cars. Tshombe's 11,600 troops, supported by tribal warriors and the Fouga jets, were more than a match for the U.N. troops. It was obvious that the U.N. had made the fatal mistake of believing its own propaganda. It had maintained for so long that Tshombe was a Belgian puppet supported only by a handful of mercenaries against the will of his people that it had expected his government to topple at the first blow. It failed to understand, or could not admit, that he was a popular, courageous leader at the head of a people fighting on their own ground against foreign troops. Important segments of world opinion were marshalling in condemnation of what appeared to be a clear violation of both the letter and the spirit not only of the Security Council's resolution but of the U.N.'s own charter. The U.N. had placed itself in a position from which it could not extricate itself. The only solution seemed to be a cease-fire. Hammarskjold, the one man with the prestige, intelligence, and understanding to bring some sort of solution out of the Katangan chaos, left Leopoldville by air at 3:51 P.M. GMT on September 17 for Ndola, Northern Rhodesia, in an attempt to arrange a truce with Tshombe.

The tragedy that was to occur at Ndola, like the death of Lumumba, was to result in the shift of at least a portion of world opinion against Tshombe, as if he personally were responsible for what happened. It is interesting to consider whether events might not have taken a different course, had Hammarskjold survived. Certainly part of the reason for the U.N.'s failure in the Congo has been the mediocrity of its personnel. This could not be said of Hammarskjold. If there was a solution to the impasse between Katanga and the Congo, he was probably the man to find it. As things worked out, he was not to have the chance.

At 11:35 P.M. Ndola time (six hours after leaving Leopoldville), Hammarskjold's plane, which had flown nearly due east from Leopoldville and down Lake Tanganyika to avoid Tshombe's jets, made radio contact with Ndola tower as it descended from 16,000 to 6,000 feet.

At ten minutes past midnight on September 18, Hammarskjold's aircraft, the DC-6B *Albertina,* chartered from the Swedish firm of TRANSAIR, circled in clear weather over Ndola airport, the site at which he had chosen to meet Tshombe. The plane reported that it had the airport's lights in view. Then the radio went dead and the plane disappeared. Tshombe, who had made the 120-mile journey from his capital to the Northern Rhodesian town earlier in the day, waited in the control tower. Nothing happened and Tshombe eventually returned to the residence supplied for him by the Rhodesian Government at nearby Kitwe. Through a monumental press snafu, most wire services and newspapers (not the *Chicago Daily News,* I hasten to add) reported that Hammarskjold had arrived in Ndola and was conferring with Tshombe in the airport control tower.

The fifty-six-year-old Swede was, in fact, lying dead amid the smouldering wreckage of his plane in a forest glade seven miles northwest of Ndola. Hammarskjold's body, except for burns on his hands, a wound on his neck, and an abrasion of the forehead was curiously composed and unmarked. The dead bodies of nine members of his entourage (including one woman) and the plane's crew of five were horribly maimed and charred. The only survivor the search party found when it reached the wreckage in the early afternoon of the 18th was Harry Julian, a thirty-five-year-old American security guard. Julian, who had sustained third degree burns over 30 per cent of his body, had other injuries and was suffering from shock and sunstroke (he had lain by the plane's flickering wreckage for fourteen hours). He died six days later.

The full story of Hammarskjold's death may never be known. Apparently there were no reliable witnesses to the crash. Julian died while still incoherent and under sedation.

There are a number of theories, of course. One is that the plane was sabotaged in Leopoldville, another that it was shot down by one of Tshombe's Fougas.

Sabotage was possible, although U.N. spokesmen say the plane was closely guarded at Leopoldville airport before its take-off. Should investigation ever prove that it was a case of sabotage, this should by no means be taken as proof that Tshombe was the perpetrator. Tshombe liked Hammarskjold personally and is intelligent enough to realize that Katanga had nothing to gain through the Secretary-General's death. The only people who did stand to gain by it were the Russians, who had just lost a bitter battle to unseat Hammarskjold and were determined that he should not continue as Secretary-General.

It is possible that the plane was shot down. If so, it was shot down by a Katangan jet. Tshombe's mercenary pilots were a wild bunch with no love for the U.N. They and their planes were capable of such an action. The evidence of their log books (which can, of course, be falsified) and the personal testimony of Major Joseph Delin, the senior Fouga pilot, is that no Katangan planes took off on the night of Hammarskjold's crash. The rumor that the plane was shot down is based largely on an unconfirmed report that an unidentified plane circled Ndola shortly before the arrival of the DC-6B. This may in fact have been the Secretary-General's aircraft. There have also been reports that there were a series of explosions and flashes before the plane crashed. These reports, until further substantiation is obtained, must be treated with extreme caution. Some bullets, fragments of exploded cartridge cases, and percussion caps were found in the bodies of two of the victims—both security guards. The guards were armed and their shells probably would have exploded in the crash or during the fire that swept the wreckage.

A third theory is that the plane crashed as the result of engine failure caused by previous damage from ground-fire. The *Albertina*, the personal aircraft of Irish General Sean McKeown, U.N. military commander in the Congo, had taken off from Elisabethville airport on the morning of September 17 to pick up Hammarskjold in Leopoldville. On take-off, Katangan machine guns had damaged one of its engines. The pilot, however, made Leopoldville safely. There the engine had been repaired. Hammarskjold had been due to leave Sunday morning in a DC-4. He delayed his departure, however, until repairs to the larger plane were completed. It may have been that the patched-up engine developed a malfunction, although investigations reveal that all four engines had some power at the time of the crash. It would seem to be stretching coincidence that any malfunction should take place just as the plane was about to land.

The most logical explanation of the tragedy is the most obvious one: pilot error. The plane's pilot, Per Hallonquist, had done a great deal of flying during the previous weeks, although not during the previous twenty-four hours. The plane had no navigator aboard and its radio operator, as revealed in hearings held in Ndola in January, 1962, had had no air-radio experience. Thus a heavy burden of duties fell on Hallonquist. Fellow Swedish pilots at Elisabethville told me a few days after the crash that Hallonquist was a cautious, meticulous, almost old-maidish flier who kept a large notebook full of information about airfields and load limits. Curiously enough, there was no "Ndola" page in his notebook, which was found near the wreck. The direction of the plane when it crashed— almost in line with Ndola's landing strip—would seem to indicate that Hallonquist was turning to make his approach run (the plane's undercarriage and flaps were down) when he badly misjudged his altitude.

The report published in February of the official Rhodesian inquiry into the crash dismissed the possibilities that the plane had either been shot down or sabotaged. It found that the bullets lodged in two of the bodies had not passed through gun barrels and asserted that the plane was serviceable and in good condition at the time of the disaster. In conclusion, the commission of inquiry named pilot error, probably as the result of inattention to or misreading of altimeters, to be the cause of the crash. A U.N. commission, also inquiring into the cause of the crash, will probably come to the same conclusion.

Whatever the cause of Hammarskjold's plane crash, his death came at a time when the highest degree of skill and understanding was required to retrieve the U.N.'s position in Katanga. Those who wielded responsibility after his death demonstrated those qualities in only negligible quantities.

Tshombe stayed on in Ndola for talks with Mahmoud Khiari, the Tunisian chief of U.N. civil operations in the Congo. Most of us covering the phony war headed back to Elisabethville. Conditions were chaotic. Elisabethville airport was closed to all traffic. The main road through Kasumbalesa to Elisabethville was studded with roadblocks manned by villagers, CONAKAT *Jeunesse*, and gendarmes. They were always suspicious, frequently drunk, and quite prepared to cut the throat of any white man who could not convince them that he wasn't a *Onusien* (U.N.) spy. Consequently, most of us used the much longer, infinitely rougher but considerably safer track that wandered through the bush of Northern Rhodesia for nearly 200 miles before wiggling across the Katangan border at Kipushi, only twenty miles from Elisabethville. Transport, of course, was difficult to obtain because the Rhodesian car dealers were well aware that their vehicles stood a good chance of being shot up in Elisabethville. However, I was able to hire a venerable Ndola taxi driven by an African who fortunately was unaware that there was a war on in Elisabethville. Edson (for that was his name) was delighted at the prospect of a visit to Elisabethville and assured me that he was from "near Elisabethville" and knew the local languages. As we approached Kipushi, Rhodesian Canberra jets, attracted by the column of dust we raised, began buzzing the car. Edson turned slightly grey. Then we began to run into roadblocks set up by Rhodesian troops guarding the border zone. It was hot and most of the troops (a white unit) were stripped down to their shorts but carrying rifles with fixed bayonets or Bren guns.

"Whooo-eeee," whistled Edson, clucking in disapproval, "what all these white bosses doing out here for bush like animals?"

The Katangan police at Kipushi at first were unsure whether we should be allowed to enter, and then, having admitted us, seemed to think that it might be a good idea to put us in jail.

"Edson," I said, "explain to these gentlemen that you and I are on intimate terms with Mr. Tshombe and that we are going to Elisabethville to document the valor of the victorious Katangan gendarmerie."

Edson, who was twisting in his hands the battered brown hat which a Katangan gendarme, with a nudge from his rifle butt, had suggested he remove when in the presence of officials of the Katangan state, moaned unhappily.

"Boss," he said, "I'm from Nyasaland and I just can't speak these people's language. And tell them to stop pointing these guns at me, please."

Edson's confession left the issue even more in doubt since the Katangan border guard spoke little French. Finally, after a delay of several hours, we were allowed to proceed. There were two more roadblocks manned by gendarmes nervously fingering the triggers of submachine guns in the twenty miles between Kipushi and Elisabethville, but we managed to pass.

It was well after dark when we reached the outskirts of Elisabethville. Tracer bullets were streaking across the ink-black sky like swift and angry fireflies. From the center of the city came the dull crump of exploding mortar shells. The suburbs—and the rest of the city, for that matter— were blacked out. We cut our lights and groped our way tentatively down the tree-lined streets, momentarily expecting a blast from Katangan or U.N. snipers. Edson seemed decidedly ill at ease. I know I was.

Out of the shadows stepped a Katangan paracommando in battle dress and red beret, his French burp gun trained on our windshield. He explained in a miraculous combination of broken French and Swahili that the road ahead was swept by U.N. fire. After suitable protestations of mutual regard and undying loyalty to President Tshombe, he waved us on by a route that would take us through the *Union Miniere* slag heaps from which there was a reasonable chance of reaching the Grand Hotel Leopold II without ending up in the meat wagon. There were bridges knocked out around the slag heaps and the woods surrounding them and, in trying to find a way through, we got hopelessly lost. Finally, we stumbled upon the *Union Miniere* Club and the manager very graciously provided us with beer, sandwiches, and mattresses on which to sleep.

The situation in Elisabethville was odd. The U.N. held the post office, the railway underpass just north of the Leopold II, the railway station, the hospital between the station and the post office, its headquarters in the north-western part of the city, and the airport. Twice daily, trucks convoyed by armored cars roared through the city to supply and reinforce these strong points. Around each of these points there was sporadic but often heavy firing. Streets that could be covered from these bastions were dangerous. But a block away from heavy fighting it would be perfectly safe because one would be shielded by a line of buildings. There was, of course, always the danger of being hit by a U.N. or Katangan sniper anywhere in the city, but large portions of the residential areas, white and black, were perfectly quiet, with mothers pushing baby carriages down the shady streets. The whole atmosphere was unreal. It was not war, yet men were dying. It was almost like a stage set with people going through the act of war mechanically. And then you saw that the blood on the men brought into the casualty stations was real. It almost surprised you. On the whole, one was reminded of the so-called *sitzkrieg* on the Western Front in Europe before the Nazis jumped off.

From the point of view of news, there was really not a great deal to be had in Elisabethville. The one story that had not been covered to any degree was that of the 35,000 Baluba refugees guarded by Swedes in camps east of the city. I knew that the Balubas had been without food for two days and without water for twenty-four hours. Their camps had no sanitary arrangements and there was considerable danger of epidemic. The few U.N. doctors in the camp were kept busy delivering twenty babies a day and treating the wounded. It was rumored that the Balubas, who used to be cannibals (Tshombe claimed they had eaten forty people within the past week), had already tried to break out of their camps and reach the city but that they had been turned back by heavy fire from Katangan gendarmes and white civilians.

O'Brien denied that the Balubas had broken out but said that the camps had been fired on by Katangans, presumably in an attempt to provoke the refugees into turning against their U.N. guards. O'Brien said that a dozen Balubas had been killed and sixty-five injured by this harassing fire.

Two other journalists agreed to accompany me. Edson, who had not moved out of the hotel and apparently was living exclusively on ice cream cones, said he was happy where he was. And when was I going back to Rhodesia, please?

As we drove east along jacaranda-lined Avenue Droogmans, a greasy smudge of smoke hung over the railway station's burning fuel dump to the south. The nervous stutter of machine guns, the high-pitched roar of a 106-millimeter recoilless rifle, and the dull thud of mortar shells exploding drifted up on a warm, flower-perfumed wind from the U.N.-held underpass.

Near the industrial section, we were met by a stream of cars heading toward the center of the city at high speed. The cars were driven by tightlipped whites and loaded with the impedimenta of hasty flight: mattresses, bird cages, pots, bundles of clothes. At the Victory Stadium, we were waved down by a gigantic blond Belgian civilian.

"If you go down that road, man" he warned, "you'll not come back alive. The gendarmerie have pulled out and the Balubas are on the rampage. They've already chopped one white man to bits and wounded several others. We've got plenty of guns and ammunition and we're going to try to hold them here."

We went on but we weren't very happy. Across the shell-pocked road sprawled two derelict Katangan 40-millimeter dual purpose guns, their tires flat. In the railway yard to the south, snipers banged away at each other. Feeling immensely naked and exposed, we rattled across the level crossing. It had been shelled and one of its steel gates was twisted into a metal finger that pointed accusingly at the smoke-smudged sky.

Bel Aire, a modest white residential sector of small cottages set among flowering hibiscus and bougainvillaea, was rapidly emptying. Whites were fleeing in their cars toward town. Their African servants, a few belongings balanced on the tops of their heads, were slipping away into the bush. Most of the houses were tightly locked and shuttered, although a few families had fled in such haste that the doors of their homes hung open.

A thousand yards ahead, after passing a U.N. roadblock, we began to pass lone Balubas walking towards Bel Aire. Swerving around a tree felled across the road, we came face to face with a small knot of Balubas. Farther down the road, there was a larger group of Balubas walking slowly towards us, their chins sunk low on their bare chests. Some of them carried spears, clubs, or *pangas*. Others had bicycle chains fastened to sticks.

We braked to a stop. Before we could turn around, a Baluba loped up, grabbed the handle of the door and began to shake a knife in the face of Bob Targett of the (London) *Sunday Times*, who was driving. Other Balubas started running toward the car. Targett quickly reversed. The Baluba at his window began to scream and make short jabs at him with the knife. Mercifully, the Baluba seemed unable to work the door handle. Out of the corner of my eye I saw a squat Baluba dressed in ragged shorts and a dirty undershirt swing his *panga* in a gigantic arc. As the blow descended toward my closed window, I could clearly see the tendons knotting in his forearm.

Instinctively I threw up my forearm and turned my head away to protect my eyes. There was a crash and the car was filled with a milky cloud of flying glass as the *panga* smashed the window and bit deep into its frame. I was conscious of the fact that I was covered with blood from a score of superficial wounds.

Targett had managed to keep the car moving in reverse and we bumped over the felled tree and off the road. Other Balubas were beating against the sides of the car with clubs. Targett accelerated and the Balubas, howling with rage, went flying as we pulled onto the road again and sped away. The Irish soldiers at the U.N. roadblock said nothing as we passed them.

That was the way it was in Elisabethville in September, 1961. There was really no war. Just organized, large-scale murder. The situation was largely of the U.N.'s making. Its nose had been bloodied and now it wanted peace. Tshombe, although told by some of his advisers to press for a complete victory, was willing. "It is useless to continue this bloodshed," he had said to reporters at Ham-marskjold's funeral service in Ndola.

On September 20, exactly a week after the fighting had begun, Tshombe and Khiari signed a provisional cease-fire agreement that came into effect at one minute past midnight on the 21st. The agreement banned the movement of rein-forcements, munitions, and arms, provided for an exchange of prisoners, and set up a mixed four-man Katangan-U.N. commission to supervise the truce. The U.N. officially set its own casualties at thirteen dead, sixty-eight wounded, 158 captured, and twenty-five missing. Katangan casualties were provisionally listed as five whites and fifty-three Africans killed, twenty-seven whites and ninety-one Afri-cans wounded, and about 300 captured (these are hospital figures; many other Katangans believed to have been hit either treated themselves or went to private physicians).

What had the U.N. accomplished? In a positive sense, exactly nothing. It had not ended Katanga's secession; it had not cleared out the mercenaries. In a negative sense, it had accomplished a great deal. What little trust Tshombe had had in the international organization was destroyed. The chance of fruitful negotiations between Leopoldville and Elisabethville was greatly reduced. The prestige of the international organization certainly declined as the result of this obvious violation of its own charter.

Who was to blame for the blunder? Conor Cruise O'Brien, the forty-four-year-old Irish diplomat, was the U.N.'s special representative in Katanga from June, 1961, through the September troubles. O'Brien, who resigned from both the United Nations and the Irish Foreign Service in December, 1961, is an intelligent, cultured, arrogant, restless, and ambitious man. He accepts without question the highminded integrity and intelligence of himself and of those who happen to agree with him. Those who do not agree with him inevitably are men of small intelligence and low motives.

O'Brien, the only son of an Irish journalist, was educated at Trinity College where he won first-class honors in history. His doctoral thesis about the Irish nationalist Charles Parnell was later published as a book (O'Brien frequently writes under the pseudonym of Donat O'Donnell). In 1942, he entered the Irish treasury, transferring two years later to the foreign service. He served in Paris (he speaks excellent French, as well as Russian and Spanish) before returning to Dublin in 1957, where he set up the Irish Foreign Office's United Nations section. He served with the Irish delegation in New York, and, in 1960, became Ireland's Assistant Secretary for External Affairs. In May, 1961, he received two years leave of absence to head the U.N.'s operation in Katanga.

O'Brien, a tousled, large-headed, dark man is not many of the things his detractors say he is. He is not, for instance, particularly anti-British, although he has stated that he "despises" British elements who support Katanga's secession, including Prime Minister Macmillan (others named by O'Brien: Captain Charles Waterhouse, Sir Roy Welensky, Lord Salisbury, and Lord Lansdowne). He also alleges that his resignation from the U.N. and his own country's foreign service was the result of British pressure. Nor is O'Brien a violent man, although he does not shrink from the use of violence to accomplish ends he believes to be just.

Nor was O'Brien, as his supporters try to maintain, a close confidant of Hammarskjold. The Secretary-General picked him primarily for reasons of international politics, as O'Brien himself admits. An Irishman, O'Brien is a citizen of a small neutralist country with an anti-colonial tradition. As such he was acceptable to the Afro-Asian bloc. As a Catholic (although only a nominal one: his twenty-two-year first marriage, which was dissolved late last year, was a civil ceremony) and a white man, he was acceptable to the more conservative Western countries.

It is clear now that O'Brien was temperamentally unsuited

for service in Katanga. An incisive, erudite, witty man, he lacked the patience for endless discussions—which is the only way anything is ever accomplished in Africa. His personal relations with Tshombe were never good (Tshombe said after Hammarskjold's death that he would never negotiate with O'Brien and that he wanted him recalled). The Irishman was forever seeing sinister and occult forces working against him: first it was the Belgian Government, later the British and the French Governments, and finally the "British gutter press." It never occurred to him that he might not be up to the job of peacefully reintegrating Katanga with the Congo. Frustrated and embittered by his failure, he struck out at Tshombe with U.N. troops in an action that caused grave doubts as to the future of the international organization, not only in the Congo but in the world.

The February 21st resolution of the Security Council, a resolution which O'Brien himself terms "completely revolutionary in character," authorized the use of force only "if necessary, in the last resort" to prevent civil war. By no stretch of the imagination could it be said that U.N. troops were acting to prevent civil war. O'Brien has sought to justify his actions by pretending that he was authorized to use force to implement the Security Council resolution calling for the removal of foreign mercenaries. But this clearly was not the intention of the Security Council. In addition, O'Brien has written that, in his opinion, once force had been used, "we should not desist until the secession of Katanga had been ended." Such an attitude, which had never been authorized by any Security Council resolution, clearly disqualifies O'Brien as both biased and insubordinate.

On whose instructions did O'Brien act when he launched his attack against the Congolese? This is one of the strangest parts of the entire drama. O'Brien claims that he received verbal instructions in Elisabethville from Mahmoud Khiari to take over various public buildings, to arrest any white officials found there, and to seize Tshombe, Munongo, Kibwe, and Kimba. Upon whose authority was Khiari acting?

O'Brien relates he later discovered that neither Sture Linner, chief of the U.N.'s Congo operations (and Khiari's direct superior), nor General McKeown, the U.N.'s commanding general, had any knowledge of any such instructions. Nor did Dr. Bunche or General Indar Jit Rikhye, the U.N.'s military adviser in New York. In Bunche's opinion, Hammarskjold had never given any such instructions and knew nothing about them.

Khiari claims to have been in personal, direct contact with Hammarskjold, through a channel unknown to anyone else, using secret, unnumbered telegrams. O'Brien does not believe it.

Hammarskjold's attitude toward O'Brien (according to the Irishman), between the time the Swede arrived in Leopoldville and his death at Ndola, would indicate that Hammarskjold had not authorized the Khiari–O'Brien offensive and did not approve of it. O'Brien relates that on September 14, the second day of the fighting in Elisabethville, he began to receive "grim" telegrams from Hammarskjold in Leopoldville that left him "numb." O'Brien adds that statements he made to the press in explanation of his actions and of U.N. policy "were met with harsh reprimands" from Leopoldville. Two incidents related by O'Brien indicate what little confidence Hammarskjold had in O'Brien and how much he disapproved of his actions.

The Irishman recalls that Denzil Dunnett, the British Consul in Elisabethville, conveyed to him on September 17 or 18* an invitation from Tshombe to negotiate a cease-fire. O'Brien, who would seem to have lost all sense of proportion by then, forwarded Tshombe's suggestion to

---

* O'Brien does not remember which but it must have been the 17th, since Hammarskjold died early on the 18th.

Leopoldville with the recommendation *that it be rejected.* In other words, O'Brien, the representative of an organization dedicated to peace, was quite prepared to continue shedding blood until the world's objectives, as he saw them, had been met and his actions vindicated (he later stated that he was willing to meet Tshombe any place in Katanga but not in Rhodesia). Hammarskjold cabled back that he was prepared to meet Tshombe in Ndola. Having failed by telegram to stop Hammarskjold from negotiating a cease-fire with Tshombe, O'Brien next tried to intervene personally. He cabled Leopoldville proposing that Hammarskjold's plane should land at Kamina and that he (O'Brien) should join him there and accompany Hammarskjold to Ndola. O'Brien admits that he "wanted very badly to clear away the thunderous cloud of disapproval I knew was over me in Mr. Hammarskjold's mind" and to keep the Swede from negotiating with Tshombe. O'Brien knew "from the tone" of Hammarskjold's telegrams that the Secretary-General "thought I had let him down." O'Brien describes his feelings at the time as "rebellious, uneasy, and sick at heart."

Hammarskjold again overrode O'Brien's advice. According to the Irishman, the Secretary-General's reply was "polite and cool": He had no need of O'Brien's services in the matter.

If O'Brien is to be believed, Hammarskjold had no prior knowledge of the Irishman's intention to resort to force and did not approve of it. One is inclined to believe O'Brien in this matter: Hammarskjold was both too fair and too intelligent to have initiated or agreed to such a thing.

If one accepts O'Brien's account of Khiari's verbal instructions (and there were four witnesses to the meeting in addition to O'Brien and Khiari), O'Brien is cleared of everything except diplomatic failure and a certain incompetence in the execution of his instructions. But if one accepts the belief of O'Brien and Bunche (as related to O'Brien), did Khiari in fact have Hammarskjold's approval for the operation or did he order the offensive against Katanga on his own initiative? If the Tunisian did act on his own initiative, what was his intention? The answers to these two questions are known only to Hammarskjold, who is dead, and to Khiari.

Surely, if Khiari, as he claims, was in personal contact with Hammarskjold through unnumbered, coded telegrams, copies of these telegrams must exist somewhere in the files of the United Nations. The reputations of three men— Hammarskjold, Khiari, and O'Brien—demand that there should be a full and impartial investigation of the question. When the U.N. acts in violation of its own charter and becomes a threat itself to world peace in the process, the common good requires that the truth should be known.

But the phony war of September and the mystery that surrounds it were to be only the prelude to an even greater disaster.

IX

THE DECEMBER WAR

"Let Katangan fighters arise at the given moment
in every street, every lane, every road, and
every village."
—MOISE TSHOMBE, speaking to the
people of Katanga on November
26, 1961.

T HE INK of the cease-fire agreement was not yet dry
when the Central Government made it clear that it
was intent on war in Katanga. On September 22, 1961,
Adoula stated in Leopoldville that the Central Government
would resort "to its own means to put an end to the secession of Katanga." The Congolese Prime Minister wrote
to Linner expressing "extreme reserve" about the agreement concluded between Tshombe and the U.N. Earlier,
Adoula had stated that the Congolese troops were "ready to
answer force with force in Katanga." Also on September
22, Mobutu broadcast an appeal to the Katangan gendarmerie to refuse to obey its white officers.

On the face of it, any invasion of Katanga by Central
Government troops would constitute civil war, an event the
U.N. officials in the Congo were bound to prevent under
the terms of the Security Council's resolution of February
21 "by use of force, if necessary, in the last resort." Yet
both Linner and Khiari, again indulging in curious mental
and semantic gymnastics, declared that, in their opinion,

such a move would be only a "police action" and hence could not be stopped.

On September 23, the Congolese cabinet unanimously approved the House of Assembly's motion, carried the previous day in secret session, that Katanga should be attacked. Gizenga, now Vice Premier in Adoula's government, was the prime mover in these maneuvers. Central Government troops on the Katangan border were alerted to be ready to attack and reinforcements were flown into Luluabourg, the capital of Kasai. On September 27, Tshombe appealed to Adoula for negotiations "with the shortest delay and on neutral territory," a suggestion Adoula quickly rejected. If Tshombe wanted to talk, said Adoula, he must come to Leopoldville. Since he had spent two months in detention after his last visit to territory under Central Government control, Tshombe's unwillingness to come to Leopoldville certainly was understandable.

Meanwhile, relations between Tshombe and the U.N. had not improved. Katanga and the U.N. repeatedly charged each other with violating the cease-fire agreement. O'Brien denied Tshombe's charge that he was flying in reinforcements, but said that the U.N. had flown in additional armored cars four hours before the signing of the cease-fire agreement. Bars, cafés, laundries, and breweries in Elisabethville refused to do business with U.N. personnel, either voluntarily or out of fear of reprisals from the CONAKAT *Jeunesse*. No one had much confidence in the permanence of the cease-fire, and 431 white civilians, mostly women and children, took advantage of the truce to flee from Katanga. Four Ethiopian F-86s, the first of fourteen Ethiopian, Swedish, and Indian jets, flew into Leopoldville. Meanwhile, O'Brien kept up constant pressure on Tshombe to expel his remaining 104 white mercenaries. On October 1, Tshombe formally released these men, although few apparently left the Katangan forces. On October 5, Khiari complained that Katanga had refused to let the four-man cease-fire commission visit the Katangan strongholds of Kipushi, Kolwezi, and Jadotville. Mercenaries and war materials, the Tunisian said, were entering Katanga through Kipushi.

Tshombe would have been a great fool had he not, under the circumstances, been bringing in reinforcements. As Khiari pointed out, neither the Central Government nor the U.N. in Central Government territory were bound by the cease-fire agreement. As the Tunisian put it, the Central Government was free to "arm itself to the teeth" for action against Katanga but Tshombe, under the terms of the cease-fire, had no right to reinforce his troops to defend Katanga against such attacks. By the same token, while it could not bring jets into Katanga, the U.N. could bring them to Luluabourg, thirty minutes' flying time away. Yet it was clear that the jets were for future use against Katanga.

On October 20, 5,000 Central Government troops (including 4,000 former *Force Publique* mutineers who had served in Katanga) crossed from Kasai into Katanga and were engaged by Katangan gendarmes. Adoula stated that the troops were carrying out a "police action" against outlaws and added that the operation was part of a plan to end Katanga's secession. Norman Ho, a U.N. spokesman in Leopoldville, stated the same day that Katangan planes had made air strikes in the area of the Kasai–Katanga border. The raids, he said, were "a serious breach of the cease-fire in Katanga" and six U.N.-Swedish jets in the future would give aircover to Mobutu's troops. Ho had nothing to say about the civil war nature of the Congolese offensive.

The Congolese troops, however, did not act much like liberators. They put villages to the torch, slaughtered women and children, and sent an estimated 10,000 families fleeing to the south. On November 1, another 1,500 Gizengist troops under the command of General Lundula were flown into Kivu, presumably in U.N. aircraft, to attack Katanga from that direction.

Mobutu announced on November 2, that he had ordered the offensive and that his troops had captured seventy-two villages within a 30-mile belt inside Katanga. But Kimba (Tshombe at the time was in Geneva for medical treatment) denied Mobutu's claim of victory and said Katangan troops had thrown back the Congolese at both Kaniama on the Kasai front and at Kongolo on the Kivu front.

The following day, Linner, in a report to the Security Council, made the remarkable statement that the activities of the Katangan Air Force "represent offensive civil war action" prohibited under the resolution of February 21. He thus conveniently ignored the stipulation in the cease-fire agreement between the U.N. and Katanga which allowed the gendarmerie to reply to an attack from beyond Katanga's frontiers. Khiari with a straight face then stated that the Congo was not considered as "beyond Katanga's frontiers." Perhaps he thought Katanga feared an invasion from Angola or Rhodesia.

It soon became clear that Kimba was closer to the truth as regards the military situation than Mobutu. On November 5, Leopoldville admitted that Katangan gendarmes had defeated and inflicted heavy losses on the Congolese troops north of Kaniama, taking many prisoners and much equipment. Tshombe, speaking in Geneva, once more stated his willingness to negotiate a settlement with Adoula. Said he: "We want to come to an agreement with our brothers in the Congo but there must be no coercion or repression. We will defend ourselves when attacked."

But if Mobutu's troops could not fight very well, they had other talents that were revealed only on November 6, when ten white refugees reached Brussels from Luluabourg. It was revealed then that, enraged at their defeat, Congolese soldiers had arrested 400 whites, raped fifteen women including some nuns, and beaten up eighteen missionaries.

Linner and Ho, so quick off the mark with information about the Katangan air attacks on Congolese troops, were surprisingly slow in hearing about this sort of thing or about announcing it to the world. About the only creditable aspect of the whole nasty incident was the fact that Mobutu had the courage to arrest 123 of the soldiers involved and to send them back to Leopoldville. The fact remains that the U.N. was directly responsible for what happened at Luluabourg because it encouraged the Leopoldville Government to move against Katanga. This was to be far from the last time that innocent men and women were to pay a bitter price for the U.N.'s actions.

Things were not going so well on the Kivu front either for Tshombe or for anyone genuinely interested in the maintenance of law and order. The Katangan gendarmes pulled out of Albertville on the approach of a large body of Baluba warriors backed up by Gizengist troops who quickly captured the lightly-held towns of Kabalo, Nyunzu, Manono, and Nyemba. Only in Kongolo did 1,600 gendarmes stand firm.

The Congolese troops immediately distinguished themselves in their usual fashion. At Kindu (in Kivu Province) they seized and brutally beat thirteen Italian U.N. airmen. The Italians had flown some Malayan Ferret armored cars into Kindu. Drunken Congolese soldiers accused them of being Belgian mercenaries, beat them, shot them all, and then dismembered their bodies. According to witnesses, parts of the bodies were thrown into the Congo River. Others were sold in the market place and a human hand was presented to a World Health Organization doctor by a giggling Congolese soldier. Colonel Alphonse Pakassa, the commanding officer of the Gizengist unit, who refused either to withdraw his troops from the airport or to punish the murderers, when questioned by General Lundula on the subject of the massacre, came up with the quote of the week: "You know how soldiers are." Linner, however, managed to top this one by stating later that it was "inopportune" to disarm the Congolese troops at Kindu. These same troops were later to slay twenty-two Belgian priests at Kongolo. One began to wonder just how many men and women were going to have to die because of the criminal stupidity of U.N. officials and the political bias of some member states of the United Nations. It was, or should have been, clear from the beginning that the Congolese invasion of Katanga amounted to civil war. It was, or should have been, clear from the beginning that the U.N., by allowing half-savage Congolese troops to enter Katanga, was signing the death warrants of hundreds of innocent civilians, black and white. Yet the U.N. preferred to carp about Tshombe's violations of the cease-fire agreement. Certainly he violated the cease-fire by reinforcing his troops and bringing in military supplies. And more civilians, white and African alike, would be dead today if he had not done so.

In Albertville, the activities of the Congolese troops were slightly less dramatic. Demonstrating admirable restraint, they restricted themselves to looting white homes, stealing cars, and arresting whites and Africans identified by BALUBAKAT *Jeunesse* as pro-Tshombe. All but about thirty of Albertville's 1,200 whites fled across the lake to Tanganyika, as drug-crazed Balubas emptied the prison. In Leopoldville, U.N. spokesman George Ivan Smith primly described "the behavior" of the Congolese troops as "impossible."

Meanwhile, Tshombe reiterated his recognition of Kasavubu as the head of a confederal Congo and repeated that he was "always ready" to negotiate with Adoula. He asked only that the U.N. should end its "subversive" acts in Albertville and that the Central Government should halt hostilities in northern Katanga. But neither Leopoldville nor the U.N., despite the tragedies of Luluabourg, Kindu, and Albertville, were in a mood for negotiations. Adoula declined the offer and demanded Katanga's unconditional reintegration into the Congo.

The Security Council met on November 13, in an air of mixed anger, frustration, and quiet desperation. Tshombe's white soldiers, military successes, wealth, and defiance had raised the antagonism of the Afro-Asian bloc to an almost hysterical pitch. The U.S. and the Western powers were anxious that the U.N. should not fail in Katanga. On the other hand, it was clear that they had nothing really positive to suggest.

Bomboko, speaking for the Leopoldville Government, made three main points: Leopoldville expected the U.N. to give it "direct assistance" in maintaining law and order; it wanted all of Tshombe's white mercenaries turned over to it for punishment for their "dastardly crimes against the Congo" (in November, the Belgian Government withdrew the passports of its nationals still serving in the Katangan forces); and it wanted a new and clear U.N. mandate on the Congo.

What Bomboko was asking for, obviously, was a new U.N. military offensive against Katanga to replace that of the Central Government which had ended in defeat. In view of the happenings at Kindu, turning over the mercenaries to Leopoldville would have been the equivalent of murdering them in cold blood.

The one draft resolution before the Security Council contained no more wisdom and balance. Sponsored by Ceylon, Liberia, and the U.A.R. (the Security Council's three Afro-Asian members), it authorized U Thant, the new Acting Secretary-General, "to take vigorous action, including the use of the requisite measure of force, if necessary, for the immediate apprehension, detention pending legal action and/or deportation of all foreign mercenaries and hostile elements."

The resolution strongly deprecated "the secessionist activities illegally carried out by the provincial administration of Katanga." The three powers also attacked the Katangan regime for resisting the U.N.'s attempt to topple it by force!

That such a resolution, a clear violation of the U.N.'s charter forbidding interference in the internal affairs of a member nation, should even be debated seriously must some day be recalled with astonishment, regret, and perhaps amusement. The "hostile elements" phrase could in fact quite easily be interpreted to mean that the U.N. had the right to deport any Katangan not in agreement with it, including Tshombe, his entire government, his 11,600 gendarmes, and every member of CONAKAT.

But not only was the resolution debated, it was accepted virtually as written. The U.S. State Department, perhaps becoming vaguely aware of the nature of the monster it had helped to create, made a feeble attempt to expand the resolution to cover Gizengist activity as well as that of Katanga. U.S. delegate Adlai Stevenson also proposed that negotiations should be urged upon the Katangan and Congolese governments and that the Congolese Army should be reorganized, retrained, and equipped with a small air force. These amendments Soviet delegate Valerian Zorin promptly vetoed. He let pass a Stevenson amendment "rejecting" Katanga's independence. Unlike Britain and France, the U.S. lacked the moral courage even to abstain from the resolution, much less to veto it. It passed by a vote of 9-to-0 and the U.N. found itself in a virtual military alliance with the Congolese Government, with U Thant holding *carte blanche* to end Katanga's secession in any way he saw fit.

The Security Council resolution of November 24th amounted to an obvious declaration of war against Katanga. Tshombe was quick to realize this.

Addressing 8,000 cheering Africans in Elisabethville on November 26, Tshombe told them that the U.N. would soon "undertake war on our territory." Said the Katangan President:

"Tomorrow or the day after, there will be a trial of strength. Let us prepare for it. Let Katangan fighters arise at the given moment in every street, every lane, every road, and every village. I will give you the signal at the opportune time. You will not be able to have guns and automatic weapons but we still have our poisoned arrows, our spears, our axes."

Meanwhile, U Thant had conferred with his eighteen-nation Congo Advisory Commission composed of delegates from Malaya, India, Pakistan, Senegal, Canada, Ethiopia, Ireland, Liberia, Sweden, Nigeria, Ghana, Guinea, Indonesia, Morocco, Sudan, Mali, Tunisia, and the U.A.R., all nations that had, or had had, military units in the Congo (the last eight had withdrawn their troops). The Acting Secretary-General appealed to them for more troops and transport. The U.N.'s military strength in the Congo at the time amounted to 15,418 men, a force clearly inadequate to both crush Tshombe and maintain order in the remainder of the country. About two-thirds of the U.N.'s troops were deployed in Katanga. I cabled to my paper in late November that the "military subjugation of Katanga which is, after all, larger than Portugal, cannot be undertaken with any prospect of success unless a minimum of 25,000 troops are placed at the disposal of the United Nations." To undertake Tshombe's overthrow with fewer troops would be doubly criminal since it clearly could not succeed and hence the lives lost on both sides would be wasted. But the U.N. was intent on war. U Thant's only concession to Tshombe and the West was to replace O'Brien (already recalled to New York "for consultations") with Brian Urquhart, a Briton, as special representative in Elisabeth-ville.

Katanga's fortunes unquestionably had suffered at the U.N. through the publication on the eve of the Security

Council meeting—the timing can hardly be considered
coincidental—of the commission of inquiry's findings con-
cerning Lumumba's death. At this critical moment, a second event occurred that was to blacken Tshombe in the
eyes of many of those otherwise not ill-disposed toward
him.

U.S. Senator Thomas J. Dodd of Connecticut, a man
sharply critical of the State Department's position regarding
Katanga, was visiting Elisabethville. On November 28, a
private dinner party to which U.N. officials and members
of the consular corps were invited was given for Senator
Dodd at a private home in Elisabethville. Katangan paracommandos guarding the nearby home of Gendarmerie
Commander General Norbert Moke became suspicious
at the number of cars arriving at the villa. A car bearing
U.N. plates arrived. In the car was Urquhart with his assistant, forty-six-year-old Australian-born George Ivan
Smith. When the paracommandos recognized the pair, they
chased them into the house, dragged them out into the
street, beat them up, and threw them into a truck. A Belgian employee of the *Banque du Congo* tried to intervene
on their behalf and was himself beaten and thrown into the
truck. At this moment, Senator and Mrs. Dodd, accompanied by the U.S. Consul in Elisabethville Lewis Hoffacker
and preceded by a motorcycle escort of Katangan gendarmes, arrived on the scene. Hoffacker, sizing up the situation at a glance, jumped from the car and, with the
assistance of the escort, dragged Smith and the Belgian
from the truck and drove immediately to Tshombe's residence. Urquhart, meanwhile, was driven away to the Katangan army camp by the half-crazed paracommandos.
Three hours later, Urquhart was released on the personal
intervention of Tshombe, Munongo, and Kimba. He had
suffered cracked ribs and a broken nose from his beating.
A Gurkha driver and a Sikh major were killed while

searching for Urquhart. Tshombe later "abjectly apologized" for the incident.

It is necessary to pause for a minute to give credit to Lew Hoffacker. Hoffacker is everything that a State Department official should be and seldom is: intelligent, courteous, resourceful, courageous, unpretentious, and well-informed. In the days to come (he was a newcomer to Katanga) we were to see a great deal of each other. During the fighting that followed, he always made it his business to get about (at some danger to himself), to find out what was going on, and to do everything he could to ease tension. Had we more men like him in Africa (and in the higher echelons of the State Department), it is unlikely that the U.S. would have made the major errors it did make in Katanga.

It is difficult to evaluate the effect that the brutal and stupid beating of Urquhart and Smith had on the U.N.'s actions. It would be silly to imply that the U.N. later waged war against Tshombe because of the incident. U Thant already had his mandate and his plans were laid. But the incident did go a long way toward exacerbating relations in Elisabethville between the Katangan Government and the U.N., and it did provide Tshombe's foes with a potent propaganda weapon. Urquhart's broken nose seemed to wipe out the memory of the thirteen Italians slaughtered at Kindu by the Congolese troops.

The situation in the north had not improved. A force of about 3,000 Congolese troops, including the Kindu murderers, was pressing south against Kongolo while Baluba warriors edged in from the east and west. COTANGA, the textile company that operates in Kongolo, ordered the evacuation by air of its employees. Sendwe arrived in Albertville to set up a Baluba government. Kongolo's 1,500-man gendarme garrison, running short of ammunition, dispatched a request for arms and munitions to Elisabethville. But the U.N. refused to let a Katangan plane fly the war materials into the beleaguered town. Under the circumstances, Tshombe had no alternative but to order Kongolo's evacuation. One month later, twenty-two Belgian priests were murdered by the same troops whom Linner had found it "inopportune" to disarm after the Kindu massacre. And so there were twenty-two more murders on the head of the U.N.

Meanwhile, Tshombe had not given up hope of a negotiated settlement with Leopoldville. On November 29, he dispatched a message through Welensky, suggesting the appointment of a distinguished statesman from an uncommitted independent African country to act as mediator between Katanga and the Central Congolese Government. The following day, Tshombe flew to Brazzaville, across the river from Leopoldville, in the hope that he might personally be able to arrange a meeting with Adoula on neutral territory. His overture was rejected. The Katangan President then flew on to Paris.

But the die was already cast and the U.N.'s own propaganda drums were beating. On December 1, a report from Linner was published in New York which alleged that Tshombe's regime was "approaching the point where it cannot control the forces it has unleashed, and where it cannot change the direction of its policy away from violence and toward peaceful collaboration with the U.N."

"Unless the regime alters its course immediately," Linner continued, "neither Mr. Tshombe nor his associates may be able to control its direction, and elements of their military forces and of the civil population may initiate further hostilities against the United Nations."

The report, capitalizing on the Urquhart-Smith incident, was a clear attempt to develop the thesis that no peaceful solution was possible in Katanga. Tshombe, as he was to show within a fortnight, was in full control of both his army and his people. He was quite capable of changing his policy to one of "peaceful collaboration" with the U.N., had there been any point in so doing. But to expect Tshombe to quietly lie down and lick the U.N.'s boots while it was openly preparing for war against him was expecting rather much. Over the last ten months, the U.N. had done everything possible, including resorting to arms and unleashing the Central Congolese troops, to overthrow Tshombe's regime and subjugate Katanga to Leopoldville. Under the circumstances, collaboration with the U.N. was out of the question. Tshombe's reply to Linner was more realistic than the Swede's charge:

"When I put my people on guard against the danger the U.N. represents for Katanga, I am said to be conducting a campaign of incitement. If I understand things correctly, Katanga is not only being forced to let itself be strangled but must also permit this to happen in silence."

On December 2, while Tshombe was in Brazzaville, the situation in Elisabethville deteriorated sharply. It is difficult to apportion the blame but each side seems to have been at fault. The initial incident took place at Elisabethville airport when Indian troops arrested and disarmed thirty-two Katangan gendarmes who allegedly had drunkenly molested an African woman. Within hours, other gendarmes had set up roadblocks, arrested eleven United Nations personnel, fired on a U.N. aircraft, killed one Swedish soldier and wounded two others when they tried to force their way through a roadblock. The U.N. moved all its civilian personnel within its Elisabethville defense perimeter as U Thant directed Linner and Smith "to act vigorously to reestablish law and order and protect life and property in Katanga." Smith tersely ordered Kimba to have the roadblocks removed or face the consequences.

On December 4, Smith announced that Kimba had threatened to shoot down U.N. aircraft flying over Katanga and added that he regarded this as "a very grave statement." Kimba denied this, asserting that his statement applied only to unannounced and unscheduled aircraft. Kimba added that he had agreed that U.N. personnel should have freedom of movement in Elisabethville when engaged in their "normal" duties. But the Katangan roadblock across the highway leading from the city to the airport ten miles away remained in position, although Kimba agreed (Smith said) to remove it.

Speaking in Paris, where he allegedly had gone to see his seventeen-year-old son before continuing to a Moral Rearmament Conference in Brazil, Tshombe sounded a grave note:

"If the United Nations forces undertake fresh armed intervention in violation of the cease-fire," he said, "the Secretary-General will bear heavy responsibility for the hostilities. This time I give a solemn warning to the United Nations and its executives: Any new conflict would today be a major one, because since September 13, and since the attack of the Congolese National Army, the people of Katanga have realized that they are a free nation, determined to preserve their liberty."

Those of us stationed in other parts of Africa packed our bags and bought our airplane tickets to Ndola (Northern Rhodesia), the jump-off point for Elisabethville.

We had not long to wait. On December 5, Urquhart (who was U.N. Special Adviser in Katanga; Smith's title was U.N. Chief Representative) charged that "in a final act of bad faith," Katangan gendarmes were infiltrating through the bush toward the airport. Within a matter of minutes, Gurkha troops had assaulted the main roadblock on the airport road, held by a company of paracommandos led by three white officers and supported by three armored cars and some 60-millimeter mortars. When the smoke cleared, thirty-eight gendarmes lay dead. The Indians had suffered one dead and four wounded. It was war. And this time there was nothing phony about it.

With Tshombe away in Paris (was it coincidence that the fighting began then or did the U.N. command believe that its chances of success would be improved by Tshombe's absence?), Munongo took charge. Said he, replying to false press reports that the Katangan Government had fled:

"We are all here, resolved to fight and die if necessary. The United Nations may take our cities. There will remain our villages and the bush. All the tribal chiefs are alerted. We are savages; we are Negroes. So be it. We shall fight like savages with our arrows."

The first fighting centered in the air and along the road connecting U.N. headquarters with Elisabethville airport. The U.N. air force of fifteen jets (six Swedish Saabs, five Indian Canberras, and four Ethiopian Sabres) took off from Luluabourg and swept south over Katanga. The jets attacked bridges, cannoned the railway between Jadotville and Elisabethville, strafed trucks, and, by destroying four Katangan planes on the ground at Kolwezi, quickly established U.N. air superiority in the skies over Katanga. If this did not ensure the U.N. of victory, it at least made its defeat impossible, since control of the skies meant that it could move and reinforce its troops at will, while Tshombe could not.

At the northwestern end of the highway linking U.N. headquarters and the airport, twenty-nine Seventh Day Adventist missionaries (including nineteen women and children), most of them Americans, found themselves pinned down by gun fire in their mission buildings, which lay between the opposing lines. They managed to flee to safety only after Seventh Day Adventist World Secretary-General Chester Torrey, an American, had been wounded. There was heavy fighting at the old airport (proposed site of Elisabethville University), near the traffic circle where the initial clash had taken place. Elsewhere, firing was sporadic but indiscriminate enough for Georges Olivet, Swiss International Red Cross representative in Elisabethville, to cable an appeal to his Geneva office to call on the U.N. to stop firing on Red Cross vehicles. Meanwhile, in New York, U

Thant authorized George Ivan Smith to take "counteraction" on the ground and in the air against the Katangan gendarmes.

Having smashed the threat of the Katangan Air Force, Brigadier K.A.S. Raja began to build up his forces to sufficient strength to enable him to take the offensive. Washington put U.S. Air Force Globemasters at the U.N.'s disposal (one was damaged by Katangan ground fire as it came in for a landing at Elisabethville) and these giant planes (a total of twenty-seven U.S. aircraft was employed) began bringing in troops, artillery, and armored cars. This resulted in the Katangan authorities placing Lewis Hoffacker under house arrest. Anti-American feeling spread throughout the city. Meanwhile, heavy fighting broke out around the railway underpass connecting the industrial section with the center of the city. Swedish troops, who initially had occupied the underpass, were forced out again after an attack by an all-white Katangan unit.

Tshombe quickly returned by air from Paris to Ndola, stopping at Brazzaville for a hasty conference with his ally, President Fulbert Youlou. From Ndola, escorted by a small body of gendarmes and accompanied by Joseph Lambroschini, the French Consul in Elisabethville, he drove by car to his embattled capital. In the north, heavy fighting between gendarmes and U.N. troops broke out at the tin-mining center of Manono.

As the U.N. jets stepped up their air attacks on December 7, and U.N. armored cars hammered gendarmes dug in on the fringes of Elisabethville's northern residential sector, the Rhodesian Railways dispatched a ten-car mercy train to Elisabethville to evacuate white women and children.

The situation was becoming increasingly unpleasant. Fifty U.N. mortar shells rained down on the Prince Leopold Hospital one night as African patients crawled screaming into the corridors. A terrified African woman about to give birth jumped from the operating table and disappeared into the night. The U.N. at first denied mortaring the hospital but later admitted it, stating that the hospital adjoined Camp Massart, the gendarme headquarters. It was, in fact, more than 800 yards from Camp Massart. This was the first of many incidents that led one to believe that the U.N. had both unskilled gunners and less than candid spokesmen.

On the same day, *Union Miniere* described as "unfounded and entirely untrue" accusations by U Thant that the company had built armored cars and bombs for the Katangan gendarmerie and shielded mercenaries with cover jobs. *Union Miniere* suggested that the U.N. was making these accusations to justify attacking *Union Miniere*'s installations, an eventuality that came to pass a few days later.

The U.N. jets next turned their attention to the center of the city. Screaming in at treetop level while excited gendarmes and white civilians popped away at them with anything from .22 pistols to submachine guns, they blasted the post office and the radio station, severing Katanga's communications with the outside world. It is difficult to see how this had any connection with ensuring the safety of the U.N.'s lines of communications and the security of its personnel, the avowed purposes of the U.N. attack. One came to the conclusion that the U.N.'s action was intended to make it more difficult for correspondents to let the world know what was going on in Katanga, since the only way press dispatches could be filed was to drive them 150 miles to Northern Rhodesia over a road studded with tribal roadblocks and subject to U.N. air attack. This did not always work to the U.N.'s advantage, however: Since the U.N. command in Elisabethville had direct communications with Leopoldville and New York, there was at least one occasion when it denied atrocity charges before these had appeared in the press. Meanwhile, the U.S. airlift of troops and war materials into Elisabethville continued.

On December 10, General McKeown, speaking in Leopoldville, asserted that if the U.N. had fired on cars with Red Cross markings, it was because these vehicles were carrying mercenaries (nobody thought to ask McKeown if a white civilian doctor serving with the Katangan forces was considered a mercenary by the U.N.). The General stated that the Red Cross had only ten vehicles in Elisabethville but fifty had been spotted with Red Cross markings. There is a possibility that mercenaries did use cars marked with red crosses for reconnaissance. It is also true, however, that many civilians placed their cars at the disposal of the Katangan Government for use as ambulances, which explains the presence of more Red Cross vehicles than those officially registered.

U.N. air attacks continued with strikes against *Union Miniere*'s Kolwezi fuel dump which set 750,000 gallons of diesel oil afire. Two hundred youths of the CONAKAT *Jeunesse* stoned and partially looted the American Consulate in protest against the U.S. airlift. The Association of Enterprises of Katanga (Chamber of Commerce), a grouping of eighty companies giving work to 60,000 Katangans and supporting 240,000 others, filed a protest to "the civilized countries of the world" against "the systematic and willful destruction of the economic potential of Katanga." Late on the 10th, the first refugee train bringing 360 white women and children to safety reached Northern Rhodesia.

On December 11, Youlou cabled Kennedy beseeching him "in the name of peace and humanity, to intervene in Katanga to arrange a cease-fire." On the following day, U Thant denied that the purpose of the U.N.'s Elisabethville operation was "to force a political solution of the Katanga problem by smashing the military strength of the present political leadership, and also the political leadership itself." He said that the goal was to "regain and assure our freedom of movement, to restore law and order, and to ensure that for the future U.N. forces and officials in Katanga are not subjected to attacks."

One of the worst atrocities of the war occurred on December 12. Indian-piloted Canberra jets, safe in the knowledge that the daylight skies were theirs (the Katangan Air Force's few remaining propeller-driven light planes were able to make night attacks only), roared in over Shinkolobwe and shot up the former uranium mine's hospital, leaving two children and two men dead. Four pregnant women were wounded, as were forty-four other Africans. The hospital was clearly marked with a huge Red Cross on its roof and was more than 1,500 yards from the nearest building. The previous day, while U Thant was still talking, U.N. jets had attacked the Le Marinel hospital, without, however, causing any casualties. Shinkolobwe was known to be an important Katangan military base. Putting the best possible interpretation on this tragic incident, one can only surmise that the Indian pilots did not see the Red Cross on the roof and thought they were attacking a military camp. However, far too many hospitals, churches, and other civilian installations were hit by U.N. air and ground fire to accept this as plausible. Even granting that, as the U.N. charged, Katangan gendarmes often fired from the shadows of churches or hospitals, the U.N. record in this respect left much to be desired. By December 12, the end of the first eight days of fighting, Katangan losses amounted to about 100 killed and 179 wounded (seventy-five gendarmes and the rest civilians of both races). An estimated 1,500 whites were homeless. The U.N. set its own losses at ten dead, thirty-four wounded, and thirteen missing.

Later in the day, U.N. jets attacked the Jadotville railway, strafed the Mulungwishi post office, cannoned an ore train in Kolwezi railway station, damaged a processing factory at Luilu, knocked out an electric generator at Luena, and destroyed a locomotive north of Elisabethville. It is not clear what bearing these attacks had on the re-establishment of the U.N.'s communications or the safe-guarding of its personnel. The whole operation was beginning to look very much like an old-fashioned imperialistic punitive expedition. All that was missing was the gun-boat.

By December 12, Raja had nearly 6,000 troops at his disposal to attack 3,000 Katangan gendarmes reinforced by 250 (at the very most—some estimates ran as low as fifty) white mercenaries and perhaps 100 local white volunteers. Mortar shells hailed down on the center of the city as the softening-up process began. Again, the gunnery was either disgracefully amateur or totally indiscriminate. Among the "military objectives" hit: a beauty shop, the apartment of the French Consul, SABENA Airways office, the Roman Catholic cathedral, Elisabethville's museum. A car pulled up in front of the Grand Hotel Leopold II, where all of us were staying. "Look at the work of the American criminals," sobbed the Belgian driver. "Take a picture and send it to Kennedy!" In the backseat, his eyes glazed with shock, sat a wounded African man cradling in his arms the body of his ten-year-old son. The child's face and belly had been smashed to jelly by mortar fragments. The war—and life —were over for him. His mother, also wounded, sat wordlessly beside her husband.

On the same day that this child died, Britain, France, Greece, the Malagasy Republic, and the former French Congo were all pressing for a cease-fire. But U Thant did not want one, the eighteen-nation Congo Advisory Committee did not want one, the U.S. did not want one. Or rather they did not want one until Tshombe had been taught a lesson and was prepared to accept conqueror's terms from Adoula.

There was never much doubt about the U.N.'s ability to storm Elisabethville. It had absolute control of the air, numerical superiority in men, and better equipment (the U.N. had Ferret armored cars, heavy mortars and 108-milli-meter guns; the biggest gun the Katangans had was 75-millimeter and they were equipped only with light mortars). The only real questions were how much human misery the U.N. was going to inflict before capturing the city and whether, once its troops jumped off, they would complete their offensive quickly enough to prevent large-scale looting by the city's African civilian population.

The attack on the city continued as U.N. jets blasted the Lido Hotel near the zoo in the northwestern part of the city, traversed the city with mortar barrages, set aflame a large fuel dump, and captured the tallest building in the city, the so-called "new hospital," which contained no medical equipment, patients, or medical personnel and was being used by the Katangans as an observation post. The U.N. was far from being alone in being less than candid about the conduct of the war.

The propaganda battle continued as *Union Miniere* asserted that "it is evident that the objective pursued by the U.N. troops is the complete destruction of the economic potential of Katanga, a policy aggravated by total disregard for human life." U Thant countered this by publishing the names of 200 mercenaries serving in Katanga, although this would seem to have little to do with the moral right of the international organization to kill innocent Africans (Belgian Foreign Minister Paul-Henri Spaak later revealed that of these 200, one was dead, five were not Belgians and forty-eight had not been in the Katangan service for "several months"). In Elisabethville, George Ivan Smith flatly denied that the U.N. had hit any industrial installations. This was obviously untrue. He could have read his statement by the flickering light of the burning railway fuel dump.

On December 13, the U.S. Globemasters flew a battalion of 700 Ethiopian troops and large quantities of war material into Elisabethville. U.N. jets destroyed a small Katangan transport plane on the ground at Ngule, 125 miles from Elisabethville, and knocked out two armored cars. In Elisabethville, U.N. ground forces lobbed more than 200 mortar shells into the center of the city, blowing up two fuel dumps, jets blasted gendarmes dug in at the Lido Hotel near the American Consulate and hit targets of opportunity in the center of the city. The Katangan Government announced late in the day that Olivet, the Red Cross representative, had disappeared while on a mercy mission to U.N. headquarters to arrange for the evacuation of civilians from the part of the city subjected to the heaviest fire. Ten days later, Olivet's wrecked ambulance was found in the combat area. The vehicle apparently had been hit by a U.N. bazooka. A shallow grave nearby contained Olivet's body, that of a Dutch Red Cross representative, and that of a Belgian woman ambulance driver.

Tshombe, meanwhile, had appealed to Pope John and to President Kennedy ("as a free man and a Christian") to arrange a cease-fire. To his people he said: "Whatever happens, all Katangans, black and white, will fight to defend their country. Resistance will be total and not one inch of ground will be yielded without a fierce fight to the last man, to the last drop of blood." While Tshombe was awaiting a reply from the American President, the U.N.'s long-awaited offensive got underway. On the 14th, the air and mortar attacks were intensified. Gendarmes with quart bottles of beer strapped into the baggy pockets of their combat fatigues fired back at the planes from the streets and hurried forward to reinforce the Katangan positions. Later the same day, Tshombe repeated his willingness to negotiate with Adoula anywhere on "neutral" ground. He suggested the Malagasy Republic as a suitable site for such a meeting, or some other point in former French Africa and called on his "African brothers" to assist in arranging such a meeting. Tshombe also directed a public appeal to "the free and civilized world to end this barbarous and useless carnage." In an obvious reference to the U.S., Tshombe charged that "a great power that itself prizes liberty" was encouraging and financing the United Nations' intervention in Katanga. On December 15, there was heavy fighting around the railway underpass and the mortar barrage continued to rain down on the center of the city. At 10:30 that night, fresh Ethiopian troops waded across Kiboko ("Whip") Creek and attacked in strength Katangan troops entrenched on the golf course to the northwest of the city, in an attempt to slash Elisabethville's communications with Kipushi on the Rhodesian border. To the east, Swedish and Irish troops moved up to the railway line and began their assault on Camp Massart, which guarded the other route to Rhodesia. In the north, Gurkha troops supported by armored cars blasted their way to within five blocks of the heart of the city. G. C. Senn, the International Red Cross' replacement for Olivet, accused Swedish troops of firing on two of his ambulances.

Everybody had been expecting a frontal assault from the north, if only because the U.N.'s fire had been concentrated there and it obviously had the strength to storm the center of the city. Raja's pincer attack would have been a brilliant move, had he made it in sufficient strength to seal off the city quickly. Had he done this, he would have seized Tshombe and Munongo, captured most of the mercenaries, and destroyed or captured half the gendarmerie in the city. This would have ended Katanga's secession forever.

As it was, the Swedes and the Irish moved so cautiously and so unskillfully that their intention soon became obvious. The Ethiopians, although they attacked with great courage, found themselves opposed by gendarmes and white volunteers possessed of an equal bravery and tenacity. Three times the white-led gendarmes counterattacked and threw the Ethiopians off the golf course. Eventually, the U.N. seized the course. But it had taken them eight hours to do so. By then, Tshombe and his Government had withdrawn to Kipushi on the Rhodesian border behind a shield of mercenaries and gendarmes. Most of the gendarmes had been withdrawn from the center of the city and were busy digging in to protect the road junction to the south of the city. There was still a gap several thousand yards wide through which General Moke (or Major René Faulques, if you prefer—this thin, ascetic Frenchman, winner of the Legion of Honor and veteran of Indochina and Algeria, was the mercenary who commanded and was responsible for most of the gendarmerie's staff work) could evacuate his somewhat battered and depressed but largely intact army.

During those last days of the fighting, the atmosphere in Elisabethville had a dream-like quality of unreality. The streets were filled with rubble and lined with blasted palm trees and shattered cars, their tires flat and their windows broken. Four trainloads of white women and children— about 1,100 people all together—had been evacuated to Northern Rhodesia. Perhaps another 100 had made the risky road trip to safety. This left Elisabethville, which before independence had had a white population of 14,000, with about 3,000 white males and perhaps 1,000 women. Many of these—nearly a quarter—had been driven from their homes by the fighting. Perhaps 200 were huddled in the Grand Hotel Leopold II, sleeping eight to a room and on mattresses in the lobby and in the corridors. During the fighting, the *Leo Deux* had been fairly gay. There was whisky but no beer or soda. The restaurant always managed to produce something in the way of food. This and *Michel's* were the only places in town where you could get anything to eat. At the latter it was still possible to munch a *chateaubriand bernaise* and enjoy a modest bottle of beaujolais by candlelight, while machine guns chattered in the darkened streets and mortar shells whistled overhead. Both places were hangouts for gendarmes and *Les Affreux* ("the Terrible Ones"), the mercenaries, who ate in their camouflaged battledress with their floppy jungle hats on their heads and their rifles slung over their shoulders. We got to know some of the mercenaries pretty well.

All of us will remember Luigi, who in many ways was a typical mercenary. Luigi, despite his nickname (many mercenaries, for obvious reasons, preferred to use a *nom de guerre*), was a Pole. Like most Poles, he was a Catholic. Like almost every Pole outside Warsaw's orbit, he nurtured an abiding hatred of Communism which, as is natural, he associated with Russia, his country's ancient foe and present conqueror. The Poles, because of their geographical position on the eastern marches of Western European civilization, have had to develop certain martial qualities. They've had to fight to preserve their national identity since the days when Genghis Khan swept over the treeless steppes from Central Asia. When they haven't had a nation of their own to fight for (and this has been the rule rather than the exception down through history), they've been perfectly willing to fight for other people, as long as the cause seemed just. Kosciusko, for instance, served as a "mercenary" in another separatist movement—that of the thirteen American colonies. Luigi had been a part of this great martial tradition. He'd fought with the Polish Legion against the Italians and Germans in the Western Desert and at Monte Cassino. When he was wounded in Italy, nobody thought to call him a "mercenary." Then he was a patriot, as were those American "mercenaries" who served in the RAF before America entered the war against Fascism. After the war, Luigi, deprived of a homeland, wandered around from continent to continent performing, like most men, a series of not very interesting jobs that furnished him with food for his belly but gave him little satisfaction. His most recent job had been as chef to a high British official in a nearby African territory. Then Luigi's wife ran off with a man he described as "a glamorous person." Luigi, always restless, decided he would become "a glamorous person." At the time Katanga was under attack from anti-Western Congolese elements and troops from a bunch of nations which, Luigi noted, had done nothing to help Poland when it was assaulted simultaneously by Russia and Nazi Germany. The pay was good (when it came—the mercenaries were often unpaid for as long as three months at a time), and Luigi settled for a captain's commission. However, to describe him as a mercenary is to ignore Luigi's religious faith, his political convictions, his character, Poland's national history, and his people's "soldier-of-fortune" tradition. Luigi was a mercenary only in the sense that he was paid for his services, as was every U.N. soldier in Katanga. But was Luigi, after all, more a mercenary than the Swedish soldier who had no real interest in Katanga, religious or otherwise, yet who received double pay for fighting the local inhabitants of the region? And what of the Gurkhas of the Indian Army in Katanga? Nepal had no U.N. contingent in Katanga, yet these were Nepalese. The Gurkhas, mercenaries in the purest sense, had served first imperial Britain and now republican India with equal impartiality, ferocity, and skill. Finally, since the most vicious assaults on the motives and characters of the whites serving Katanga comes from the Left, let us ask this question: Whatever one may think of their politics, were those Americans who served in the International Brigade during the Spanish Civil War "mercenaries?" Of course they were not, and to suggest that they were is to dishonor the dead. The same holds true for the majority of the whites who fought for Katanga. Some were nothing more or less than paid killers. Many others were emotional cripples of one sort or another. But the majority of them fought for a variety of reasons, only one of which was money.

Luigi was always a jaunty figure around the *Leo Deux* or *Michel's* in his camouflaged battledress festooned Ridgeway-style with hand grenades, Bren gun slung over his shoulder, a red silk scarf at his throat, and a helmet on his head. He was very Polish in appearance, short and barrel-chested with sandy hair, high cheekbones, and grey eyes that glittered with splinters of light when he laughed. He laughed a lot. Sometimes it would be an old joke from the last war, or something about the railway underpass (which he commanded)—how his mixed force of whites and Katangans had thrown back an Irish attack or how he'd taken a pratfall when surprised by an exploding mortar shell. He was only solemn when the talk drifted around to Poland, the native land he knew he'd never see again.

The U.N. badly wanted Luigi's tunnel because it provided direct and covered entry into the center of the city for their Ferret armored cars. So they gave it considerable attention. In the daytime, Saabs or Canberras would come hedgehopping in at rooftop level to blast Luigi's boys with cannons and machine guns, and the Irish would lob mortar shells at the tunnel. At night, there would be more mortar barrages and probing attacks. We used to squat on the balconies of the *Leo Deux* with all lights extinguished, listening to the dull roar of explosions and the chattering of machine guns from the tunnel while tracer bullets burned across the night sky. Somebody would say "Luigi's catching hell tonight" or "Luigi'll have a thirst tomorrow." We never talked about the tunnel except in terms of Luigi. It was his personal real estate, his own small slice of Poland. Luigi had neither wife, nor home, nor nation of his own but the tunnel was his. In the tunnel with the ricochets whining like angry bees and the ground shaking from exploding mortar shells, Luigi was somebody. He was Kosciusko. He was the Polish barons standing up against the Huns and the Mongols. The tunnel made Luigi real and gave him meaning and he loved it as only a Pole could love his mistress. He was definitely "a glamorous person." Without the tunnel, Luigi was just a squat little man who used to cook other people's meals, a fellow who couldn't keep his wife in line. I often wished the errant lady could have seen him in all his glory.

We almost lost Luigi on the 13th. When he came into

the bar the next day, there was a bloody bandage wrapped around his head where a shell fragment had taken a hunk out of his skull. He was dirty, unshaven, and tired, and the going had obviously been pretty rough. But Luigi could still laugh, a great rumbling thunder of a laugh that began somewhere down by his belt buckle and gathered strength as it bounced up through his chest.

On Friday evening, Luigi did not come in for his usual *pernod* at the *Leo Deux* and we knew that things must be bad at the tunnel. There was heavy firing from that direction and from the north. Away off to the west we could hear muffled explosions and the angry stutter of automatic weapons from the Lido area, through which the Ethiopian conquerors of the golf course slowly were pressing. There were few mercenaries or gendarmes in the bar and most of those who were there were wounded. In the early days of the fighting, the bar had been packed with journalists, soldiers, and local white volunteers who spent their days in their normal civilian occupations and then went "moonlighting" with Tshombe's troops. These, again, could hardly be termed mercenaries. They were bitter men whose friends or relatives had been killed or wounded by U.N. fire, whose homes had been smashed into rubble, whose businesses had been ruined. They had an odd assortment of weapons and even odder attempts at uniforms. Nobody paid them. They fought because Katanga was their country and they hated the U.N.

Now there were few of them around the hotel. There were plenty of civilians but none with arms. The Katangan police came through checking the identity cards of the Africans in the hotel, a bad sign because it meant things were falling apart and the authorities were looking for deserters and traitors.

The night of the 15th was bad. U.N. mortar shells rained down on the center of the city all night long, bracketing the hotel and sending fragments humming into the rooms and rattling off the walls. At first I'd had to content myself with two chair cushions on the floor as a bed. But as the U.N. edged closer and the shelling became more intense, one of my more fortunate colleagues had vacated his bed and gone back to Rhodesia. So I had a place to sleep. The other bed was occupied by a former British mercenary. Things were not so good for him. If (or rather when) the U.N. captured the city, he stood a good chance of being turned over to the Leopoldville Government. If he tried to get out of Katanga, the gendarmes might well shoot him as a deserter. As the night wore on, we became quite skillful at rolling off our beds onto the floor in the split second given one between the time one heard the whistle of an incoming mortar shell and the explosion. Finally, we gave up and dragged our mattresses onto the floor and slept there. All night long the mortars came down and fragments rattled off the roof like acorns falling in the autumn.

In the morning there was no food, water, or electricity in the hotel. The lobby was jammed with taut-faced Belgians talking quietly in little knots. Mortars peppered the streets outside and the acrid smoke poured into the hotel. Dogs ran about barking crazily. Wounded gendarmes, sullen and tired, streamed south toward the one remaining gap in the U.N.'s pincers. One hard-looking mercenary in battledress with his Bren gun slung over his shoulder and a suitcase incongruously in one hand came into the hotel and disappeared upstairs. Minutes later he reappeared unarmed and in civilian clothes. There were still a few gendarme mortar crews in the area and one went into action in front of the hotel, which indicated that the U.N. was no more than a few hundred yards away. There were no more white mercenaries in evidence except for a single French officer who careened around the streets in a jeep on which a heavy machine gun was mounted. The tunnel was ominously quiet and it was rumored that it had fallen. When fire began to come into the city from the tunnel, we knew that this was the case. Luigi was gone, probably dead or captured, although there was always a chance that he'd pulled out and headed for Kipushi. I was sorry that I had not had a chance to say good-by but glad that he had had his red scarf, his few months of recapturing the brittle gaiety of World War II, of being "a glamorous person."

We knew the end was near. The Katangan Information Office, which had had its headquarters in the *Leo Deux* and had supplied us with much propaganda and, occasionally, a bit of news, had pulled out before dawn for Kipushi, where Tshombe was with his Government. These officials most ungallantly had neglected either to inform or to provide transportation for a South African woman colleague of theirs. She awoke on the morning of December 16, to find her employers gone and U.N. Indian troops within four blocks of the hotel.

Incredibly enough, Elisabethville did not fall on the 16th. This was less the result of the tenacity of the Katangan gendarmes than the extreme cautiousness of Raja. In the center, or northern front, his Gurkhas, Dogras (Indians), and Ethiopians had taken the Victory Stadium and pushed forward to the *Avenue de Ruwe*. There they were held up by scattered pockets of resistance. In a military sense, this was no front at all. Five or six gendarmes with a machine gun would barricade themselves into a house. There would be snipers scattered on the rooftops and in the gardens. Here and there an occasional civilian armed with a shotgun or a sporting rifle would fire a round or two. The U.N. soldiers would edge up slowly, clearing a street house by house. When their pressure became too great, a flying squad of gendarmes or mercenaries equipped with bazookas or recoilless rifles would roar up, establish a base of fire, and force the U.N. troops to halt. Then the flying squad would pull out and rush to some other threatened point. The Katangan mortar batteries operated in the same fashion. Both to avoid counter-battery fire and to create the impression of having far more guns than they did, they shifted their positions constantly. During all this, there would be a steady flow of refugees streaming out of the embattled area. All this fighting was in the white section of town. The native quarters to the south of the city were hit by U.N. mortars and air strikes but there was no ground fighting there until the very end. Most of the whites had fled but there were always a few who had stayed because they had no place else to go. With them were a few African servants. As the U.N. moved up, these scurried down the street in the pouring rain carrying a few belongings with them. Always there was the crazy barking of the dogs.

It was the flanks upon which Raja, attempting to complete his encircling movement, was placing the most pressure. In the west, his Ethiopians fought their way across the golf course against heavy resistance from gendarmes and mercenaries. They cleared the *Les Roches* district (machine gunning to death Guillaume Derricks, an advisory director of *Union Miniere*, his eighty-six-year-old mother, and their African servant), recaptured the Lido Hotel, and skirmished through the wooded dells surrounding the zoo. The Ethiopian right flank reached Karavia Creek, interdicting by fire one of the two routes to Kipushi. From their positions they began to fire on the *Union Miniere* compound. On the western front, the Irish and Swedes had cleared the industrial area and seized Luigi's tunnel, occupied the main railway station, and were fighting their way into Camp Massart (called Camp Tshombe by the Katangans), which was only lightly held by a rearguard of gendarmes. The Katuba and Kenya native quarters to the south were a scene of chaos. War drums were throbbing, people were rushing about aimlessly, long straggling columns of gendarmes were pulling out to the south. White civilians trying to escape by this route were arrested or turned back by the gendarmes. About the only ones able to get out were journalists, all of whom had permits from the Katangan Government. But even these often failed to satisfy the excited soldiery, although bribery usually worked.

The U.N. mortar attack on the center of the city continued on the 18th, again in a pouring rain that was a blessing because it furnished the battered city with drinking water. In the center, the Gurkhas continued their slow, methodical advance. To the west, the Ethiopians were unable to move forward because of stiff resistance in front of them. The U.N. then launched a heavy air attack against the *Union Miniere* works, claiming (after first denying the attack) that heavy firing had been directed on their troops at the Lido from the mining company's compound. A U.N. spokesman also claimed that Indian soldiers had discovered a map showing that *Union Miniere*'s telecommunications center was the headquarters for the entire Katangan resistance. *Union Miniere* denied the allegation as "false and ludicrous," stating that only mining company employees were sheltered in its offices and mill. Both sides were wrong and both right in this case. *Union Miniere*'s telecommunications had been used by the Katangan Government, but not, to my knowledge, for military purposes. Katangan gendarmes and mercenaries certainly were firing from the mining company's property but again, to my knowledge, not from its buildings.

On the west, the Swedes had captured Camp Massart, as we discovered when they fired on a car carrying three civilians out of Elisabethville. The driver of the car, Jean-Claude Cornaz, a Swiss employee of the Katangan Ministry of Economics, was killed. His two passengers, Rhodesian Federal Broadcasting Corporation newsman James Biddulph and New York *Herald Tribune* correspondent Sanche de Gramont (a Harvard-educated Frenchman), were seriously wounded. A Swedish lieutenant said his men fired on the car with a machine gun when it failed to halt at a roadblock. There was no roadblock, however. The

Swedes were simply dug in on one side of the road, the Katangans on the other, a fact of which the travelers were unaware. And the battered state of the vehicle indicated that it had been hit with either a bazooka or a 20-millimeter cannon, not a machine gun. The facts of the incident that matter are that U.N. troops fired with a highly lethal weapon on an ordinary passenger car with Rhodesian license plates in which three unarmed civilians were heading away from the combat zone. In a similar incident, the U.N. machine gunned Katangan Health Minister Jean Mwema's car, killing his wife. These incidents were typical of the type of total war waged by the United Nations, an organization dedicated to peace, in a city jammed with civilians.

While armored cars and mortars dueled in the smoke-filled streets, word came from the north that the U.N. was facilitating the advance of 1,800 Congolese troops on Kongolo, who were being resisted by the Katangan garrison. It was these Congolese troops who two weeks later were to slaughter the Kongolo missionaries. U.N. losses were unofficially put at twenty dead in Elisabethville and about fifty wounded. Katangan sources said that twenty gendarmes had been killed and 117 wounded in the last week of fighting. The city's hospitals, one of which now found itself between the opposing lines and the other exposed to Swedish fire, reported eight white civilians dead and thirty-five wounded, fifteen African civilians dead, and 121 wounded. The U.N., which declined to call its action a general offensive, reported that twelve Baluba refugees had been killed and 119 wounded in their camps by Katangan mortar fire.

Meanwhile, on the 17th, U Thant, meeting with his Congo Advisory Committee in New York, stated that he was willing to consider "reasonable" proposals for a cease-fire. This was, in effect, a denial of the five-nation plea for an unconditional cease-fire. U Thant told the Committee: "For us to stop short of our objectives at the present stage would be a serious setback for the U.N." The Committee agreed. There was no cease-fire.

But other negotiations were under way. Kennedy (with U Thant's approval) had agreed that U.S. Ambassador to Leopoldville Edmund Gullion should act as conciliator and arrange for talks between Adoula and Tshombe, provided the latter agreed not to rule out the reintegration of Katanga into the Congo. On the 17th, Tshombe cabled Kennedy:

"I await your Ambassador in Elisabethville. I am ready to hold discussions with Mr. Cyrille Adoula. Please arrange an immediate end to hostilities. Thanks to your intervention, we believe calm will be restored in the former Belgian Congo before Christmas."

It is not known whether Kennedy's overtures to Tshombe contained the promise that, if he did come to terms with Adoula, Gizenga would be dealt with by the Central Government. This may well have been the case. That other secessionist and fair-weather friend of Tshombe's, "King" Albert Kalonji of the "Mining State," was also arrested in late December. At any rate, in Leopoldville, Ralph Bunche, Linner, and Ghana's able Robert Gardiner (who was to succeed Linner as chief of the U.N.'s Congo operation) parleyed with Adoula to get him to agree to negotiate with Tshombe.

Finally, late on the 18th, Tshombe and Kibwe drove to the Northern Rhodesian town of Kitwe, where they were met by Gullion. The next day, a "suspension of fire" took effect in Elisabethville as Gullion and the Katangan delegation flew off in the American Presidential Constellation *Columbine* to the U.N.-held military base of Kitona at the mouth of the Congo River to negotiate with Adoula. Katanga's red, white, and green flag still flew over Elisabethville. The December war was over.

X

KITONA AND ITS AFTERMATH

"The President of the Province of Katanga
recognizes the indivisible unity of the Republic
of the Congo."

— Article II of the Kitona Agreement
signed by Tshombe on
December 21, 1961.

"The word 'Congolese' is a Belgian invention.
First, I am always Katangais."

— ALBERT NYEMBO, Katangan
Minister of Information, addressing
the Congolese National Assembly
on December 30, 1961.

O N HIS departure from Leopoldville to meet Tshombe
at Kitona, Adoula stated that "reconciliation is possible only if Mr. Tshombe accepts his responsibilities under
the *loi fondamentale*" and ends his "rebellion" against the
Central Congolese Government. In short, Adoula was going
to Kitona not to negotiate but to accept the unconditional
surrender of Katangan sovereignty. The only concession
Adoula made to Tshombe then or later was to agree to
meet him at Kitona rather than at Leopoldville. Tshombe
had, of course, frequently stated his willingness to negotiate with Adoula on neutral ground, since his arrest at

Coquilhatville had made it impossible for him to put much faith in a Congolese guarantee of safe-conduct. Adoula, for his part, had been unwilling to meet Tshombe on neutral territory because he regarded him as only a provincial leader. Adoula was able to accept Kitona because it was in Central Government territory. Tshombe agreed to go there only because the base was under control of U.N. forces and because he had U.S. and U.N. safe-conduct guarantees.

This statement by Adoula greatly reduced the chances of any permanent settlement emerging from Kitona. Adoula had a fair legal case in demanding that Tshombe adhere to the *loi fondamentale* since this instrument had been created at the Brussels Conference which Tshombe had attended and the Katangan leader had then accepted it. The fact remained, however, that the *loi fondamentale* was only a provisional constitution which had never been ratified. But far more important than the legal question was the actual political and military situation. Katanga had been independent in fact if not in law for nearly a year and a half. Although the Katangan gendarmerie had been mauled in the December fighting, it was still an effective fighting machine. While the U.N. at the time of the "suspension of fire" had almost encircled Elisabethville and certainly could have captured the city within a few days, the great majority of the gendarmerie and the remaining mercenaries had extricated themselves from the city and were resting and regrouping at Kipushi. The important centers of Kolwezi and Jadotville were still firmly in Katangan hands. Even had these been lost, the gendarmerie had the strength to carry on the war from the bush for months.

To expect Tshombe to surrender abjectly under these conditions was unrealistic. Even if the Katangan President had been willing to accept such terms, Tshombe knew (and Adoula, Kennedy, and U Thant must have known, unless they were woefully misinformed by their agents on the spot) that the hard core of CONAKAT, led by Munongo, would never agree to such an unconditional capitulation. Nevertheless, Adoula made his statement and flew to Kitona accompanied by Ralph Bunche, Mahmoud Khiari, and Robert Gardiner of the U.N., and by three of his ministers, Foreign Minister Justin Bomboko (an old enemy of Tshombe's), the Gizengist Interior Minister Christophe Gbenye (whom Adoula appointed Deputy Prime Minister on February 14, replacing him as Interior Minister with Cleophas Kamitatu, President of Leopoldville Province), and Justice Minister Remy Mwamba.

Tshombe, looking tired and drawn, had arrived at Kitona an hour and a half before Adoula's plane landed. With him were Gullion, Finance Minister Jean Baptiste Kibwe, and Odilon Mwanda, Katangan delegate to Brussels.

It was the first meeting between Tshombe and Adoula since the latter's rise to power in August. The talks between the two leaders on December 19, held in a hospital waiting room, were informal and friendly. The big stick was very much in evidence, however, for on the same day Ethiopian U.N. troops in Elisabethville occupied the entire *Union Miniere* compound. Both sides remained edgy, their troops still dug in facing each other.

The Congolese and Katangan delegations closeted themselves in the hospital waiting room for formal talks on the 20th, while the U.N. officials and Gullion hovered anxiously outside in the corridors. Whisky and sandwiches flowed into the room and angry voices flowed out of it. On several occasions, both Adoula and Tshombe appeared ready to break off the talks. Each time, Bunche, Gullion, Khiari, or Gardiner soothed their ruffled feathers and shepherded them back into the conference room.

Finally, in the early morning hours of December 21, after seventeen hours of almost continuous discussions, Tshombe signed an eight-point agreement officially ending Katanga's secession, although he stipulated that his action would have

to be ratified by his cabinet and by the Katangan legislature.
The Kitona Agreement reads as follows:

The President of the Province of Katanga

I. Accepts the application of the *loi fondamentale* of
May 19, 1960.

II. Recognizes the indivisible unity of the Republic
of the Congo.

III. Recognizes President Kasavubu as chief of state.

IV. Recognizes the authority of the Central Government over all parts of the Republic.

V. Agrees to the participation of representatives of the
Province of Katanga in a government commission to prepare a new constitution.

VI. Agrees to take all measures to permit senators and
deputies of Katanga Province to exercise the national functions (that is, to sit in the national legislature).

VII. Agrees that the gendarmerie of Katanga shall be
placed under the authority of the President of the Republic.

VIII. Agrees to see that the resolutions of the U.N.
Security Council and General Assembly are respected
and to facilitate their execution.

After signing the agreement, Tshombe flew back to
Elisabethville and Adoula to Leopoldville. The Kitona document, which Gullion termed a "statesmanlike agreement"
and not "punitive in any way," was not the fruit of negotiation but an unconditional surrender. On his arrival home,
Tshombe shrugged when asked if he was satisfied with it.
Kibwe murmured "not so good, not so good." Why did
Tshombe sign such an agreement? There are two possibilities. The first is that Adoula gave him a secret oral assurance to the effect that the commission agreed to under
Article V of the agreement would rewrite the Congolese
constitution to provide for a federal form of government
with considerable local autonomy. Adoula may also have
promised Tshombe substantial CONAKAT representation

in his cabinet. Nothing has taken place in the months since the meeting, however, to indicate that this was the case.

The second possibility is more likely—that Tshombe signed under duress and never intended to implement the Kitona Agreement. This duress could have taken two forms: fear for his personal safety at Kitona or the threat that the U.N., if he did not sign, would immediately end the "suspension of fire," launch a new offensive, and carry through its operations until Katanga's secession was ended and Tshombe handed over to Leopoldville for punishment.

It is unlikely that the U.S. or the U.N. would have allowed its safe-conduct guarantee to be violated to the extent of handing Tshombe over to the Congolese at Kitona. It is quite likely, however, that the U.N. and U.S. representatives did warn Tshombe he would be overthrown by force if he did not accept Adoula's terms. The U.N. was on record by the Security Council resolution of November 24, as "rejecting the claim that Katanga is a 'sovereign independent nation.' " Illegal as this resolution may have been under the terms of the U.N.'s own charter, it gave the international organization the power and the authority to overthrow Tshombe's government "by force, if necessary." There can be little doubt that this was exactly what it planned to do.

Had Tshombe been less wise and more honorable, he would have refused to sign the Kitona Agreement and flown back to Elisabethville to face a renewed United Nations offensive. He is, however, just as shrewd, tough, and unprincipled as the men with whom he has to deal. Tshombe was well aware that world public opinion was by no means solidly behind the U.S. and the U.N. He was well aware of the fact that the U.N. was deeply in the red over its Congo operation and that many member states wanted the operation ended as quickly as possible. He was aware that his gendarmerie, although still capable of

putting up a fight, badly needed a rest. Under the circumstances, it was to his advantage to play for time, as he had
frequently done before. Hence, he signed the Kitona
Agreement, in my opinion, with no intention whatsoever
of implementing it in any real sense.

Tshombe can be charged with duplicity on this count
and the charge rings true. But was it wise of Adoula and
his U.N. and U.S. advisers to insist upon an unconditional
surrender which they must have known Tshombe would not
and could not accept? It can be argued that Adoula's government was so weak that anything less than insistence on
Katanga's complete surrender would have caused its fall.
But in the long run Adoula's position could only be weakened by bringing home an agreement that could never be
implemented. If the purpose of the Kitona Agreement was
to give Adoula's government a short-term boost or to provide the U.N. with a future propaganda weapon to hold
over Tshombe's head, then the meeting at the mouth of the
Congo was a success. If its purpose was to provide a reasonable and workable means of reconciliation which both
Leopoldville and Elisabethville could accept with honor,
then it was a miserable failure. The Kitona Agreement was
not worth the paper it was written on because it failed
to take into account the fundamental structure of power
in Katanga and the Congo.

It was fairly clear that the U.N. understood this. No
sooner had Tshombe left Kitona than the international
organization began to apply heavy pressure on him to implement the agreement at once. The U.N. immediately
rejected Tshombe's contention that the agreement would
have to be ratified by the Katangan cabinet and legislature,
asserting that "as far as we are concerned, it is signed, sealed,
and delivered; there is no question of ratification."

On the 21st, U.N. vehicles patrolled into the heart of
Elisabethville to establish their right of free movement.
They failed, however, to properly police the areas already

under their control. Behind the U.N. lines, white residents were placed in the position of having to defend their property as best they could against rampaging Balubas who had broken out of their U.N. refugee camps and were after revenge, food, and loot. The U.N. had failed to keep the Balubas, whom they had invited into the camps, supplied with food, or to maintain any discipline. An estimated fifteen to twenty people were being killed each day within the camps in faction fights, and some of these were being eaten. It was calculated that about 4,000 Balubas had moved into homes abandoned by whites in the Bel Aire section alone. Most of the city continued without electricity or water.

When Tshombe reiterated that he was "only the spokesman of my people and it is up to them to decide" as to the validity of the Kitona Agreement, Adoula warned that the Central Government would use force against Tshombe again to end Katanga's secession if the Kitona Agreement was not implemented. On December 22, the Katangan cabinet decided that it was not competent to rule on the Kitona Agreement and passed the matter on to the legislature for a ruling. The atmosphere continued tense in Elisabethville as Gurkha troops arrested fifty-three gendarmes and the U.N. admitted that the Baluba refugees were "widening their arc of pillage and loot" around their camps. The U.N. finally agreed to investigate two cases of rape against Ethiopian troops and several of pillaging by the same soldiers.

On the day after Christmas, U.N. spokesman Norman Ho made a statement in Leopoldville that sent a thrill of horror up the spines of all Katangans, black and white: Ninety Congolese soldiers, the first of a force of 900, would join the U.N. forces in Kamina. The Congolese troops would wear the blue helmet of the U.N., serve with Indian, Swedish, and Norwegian troops at Kamina on an equal footing, and come under U.N. command. Such a move was certainly legal under the Kitona Agreement. But was it wise? Had Linner already forgotten the thirteen Italians murdered at Kindu? If he had, he was soon to be reminded of them by an even more horrible massacre. In fact, the movement of the Congolese to Kamina never took place (the Congolese troops showed that they disliked the U.N. as much as the Katangans did when they refused to wear the blue helmets). But the fact that the U.N. command even considered using Congolese troops showed how little it understood the situation in Katanga, how little it cared for the welfare of the territory's white population, and what little respect it had for Tshombe's pride.

The following day, the first group of Katangan representatives flew from Elisabethville to Leopoldville in U.N. planes to take part in the meeting of the Congolese legislature in accordance with the Kitona Agreement. Diplomatic relations between Belgium and the Congo were re-established on the same day, after a break that had lasted seventeen months. The first group of three senators and an equal number of deputies was led by the Katangan Information Minister, Albert Nyembo. On December 28, a second group of nine Katangan representatives arrived in Leopoldville. Tshombe made it quite clear, however, that his representatives had gone to Leopoldville to bargain for a change in the *loi fondamentale*, not to participate in the National Assembly. In Paris, Kimba, the Katangan Foreign Minister, said that Katanga was prepared to make concessions, but on the condition that "such concessions were not unilateral." Actually, the Katangan delegates did take their seats, but only after Nyembo had emphasized that they would expect concessions in return when a new constitution was framed.

The situation in Elisabethville had not improved much. On December 28, Tshombe charged that U.N. troops were preparing a new offensive against Katanga. Tshombe said it was his understanding that the U.N. would jump off if

the Katanga legislature did not meet on January 3 to ratify
the Kitona Agreement. Tshombe added that U.N. troops
had ringed the town and were preventing gendarmes from
entering the African townships. Urquhart, now senior U.N.
civilian official in Katanga (the Frenchman Georges Dumontet, perhaps the ablest of the long succession of U.N.
officials to serve in Elisabethville, now became Urquhart's
assistant), said the townships had been sealed off to prevent
looted goods from white areas reaching them and to stop
looting within the townships themselves. In an incident in
one of the townships, two Katangan gendarmes were killed
by a Swedish patrol. Katangan Justice Minister Valentin
Ilunga was arrested by U.N. troops but later released.

On the following day, Tshombe charged that Central
Government troops with the support of U.N. forces had
unleashed a new attack against northern Katanga. A U.N.
spokesman in New York denied that U.N. forces were supporting such an attack (they were correct in this) and
admitted that they had received reports of "minor skirmishing" in the area in recent days. Tshombe asserted that the
main attack, launched by nearly three battalions of Congolese, was aimed at Kongolo, 40 miles south of the Ka-
tanga-Kivu border. Tshombe added that other Congolese
troops were attacking Kapona, southwest of Baudouinville.
On New Year's Day, Tshombe repeated his charge that
Congolese troops were killing and burning in the Kongolo
district and added that he had been forced to order his
gendarmes to evacuate the town. The tin-mining town of
Manono had also fallen to Baluba irregulars. At Kapona,
he said, gendarmes had repulsed the Congolese attacks.

Now it was too much to expect that the U.N. would
make any attempt to send troops to Kongolo to separate
the Congolese and Katangan troops in accordance with
their mandate to prevent "civil war." The U.N. had already
made it quite clear that a Congolese attack on Katangans
was to be considered as a "police action" and hence not

a matter for the U.N. to concern itself with. One might
have thought, however, that the U.N. could have sent a
small body of troops to maintain the safety of local civilians, dispatched a few observers, or at least made an
aerial reconnaissance. It took none of these steps, despite
the fact that it was well aware (or should have been) that
these 1,800 troops were Colonel Pakassa's rabble that had
murdered the Italians at Kindu. One comes to the conclusion that the U.N., if it did not welcome any diminu-
tion of Tshombe's authority in northern Katanga, at least
did not care what happened in the area. Twice it had been
quick enough to kill white and black civilians alike in an
effort to impose a political solution on Katanga; seldom had
it been willing to go out of its way to maintain law and
order in remote and dangerous areas.

The first reports of the Kongolo massacre were not
released until January 16, more than two weeks after
Tshombe's charge that the district was being devastated
and his troops were withdrawing. An African seminarian
staggered into Bukavu in Kivu Province after a journey
of hundreds of miles through the bush to report that nineteen Roman Catholic missionaries (most of them Belgians)
at Kongolo had been beaten with bicycle chains, shot, and
dismembered by the invading Congolese. Parts of the bodies
were eaten. Many civilians, the seminarian said, had also
died in the massacre. The blood bath had taken place, he
said, on New Year's Eve at the Mission of the Holy Spirit.
What was the response of the U.N. to this terrible tale?
Urquhart said he had "no information." The U.N. in
Leopoldville admitted that it had no troops within 150
miles of the area and bleated about the "almost insuperable
difficulties" in investigating the massacre (yet it had always
been able to find the troops to attack Tshombe). The best
the U.N. was able to do was to offer "every possible assistance" to the Central Congolese Government in finding
the riotous troops and in preventing further incidents. In

effect, all the U.N. did was to send jets swooping over the area at a safe height. These confirmed a Red Cross report from Elisabethville (the Red Cross's intelligence apparently was better than Urquhart's) that the murderers of Kongolo were preparing to attack a mission run by White Fathers and Franciscan Sisters at Sola, just north of Kongolo. Pilots of the U.N. jets reported Congolese soldiers at Sola, huts in the village afire, and little sign of life around the mission. The idea of bringing U.N. troops into Kongolo by helicopter was rejected as "extremely hazardous."

It was not until January 23, more than three weeks after Tshombe's warning and a week after the announcement of the massacre, that a thirty-seven-year-old British major named Richard Lawson, a man of great courage, demonstrated that the difficulties of getting into Kongolo were not as "insuperable" as the U.N. had led the world to believe. Lawson, armed only with a swagger stick, jumped with a Congolese major from a light U.N. aircraft as it touched down at Kongolo, rolled across the field and took off again without stopping. The Congolese major promptly ran away into the bush and has not been seen since. Lawson, a blond and boyish former tank officer serving with a Nigerian battalion, was left alone to face the skin- and feather-clad savages of the BALUBAKAT *Jeunesse*. Although one of these patriots stabbed him in the back with an arrow (and drew a punch in the nose for his pains), Lawson was able to make an assessment of the situation in Kongolo and to rescue the one survivor of the massacre, a Belgian, Father Jules Darmont, who flew out with him when his aircraft returned. Lawson established that twenty-two missionaries had been murdered at Kongolo by five doped-up and drunken Congolese soldiers, that half the town had been burned and the rest looted so thoroughly that "there was nothing left to pillage." Most of the population had fled into the bush to avoid *Jeunesse* cannibals but three Congolese priests and thirty Congolese nuns had remained at the Holy Spirit mission.

Lawson made a second trip into Kongolo, accompanied by a Nigerian officer, Major Conrad Nwawo. From there they drove 30 miles to Mbulula where they found three nuns and eight priests. The missionaries were part of a group of seven nuns and nine priests who had fled through the bush from Sola to find refuge with a small unit of the Katangan gendarmerie. Four nuns and one priest had already been flown out to Baudouinville by the Katangan Air Force. Lawson and Nwawo were beaten by the villagers of Mbulula whom, since the pair were U.N. officers, they associated with the murderers of Kindu and Kongolo. Lawson and Nwawo, rescued by the Katangan gendarmes, offered to arrange for the evacuation of the remaining nuns and priests. But these, fearing that they would be killed if they associated themselves with the U.N., refused to go. They were later evacuated to Baudouinville on Tshombe's orders. U Thant said that the U.N. was unable to give protection to the thirty-three Congolese priests and nuns remaining in Kongolo. So ended this tragic and disgraceful episode.

In Washington, the State Department asserted that it was "deeply distressed" by these atrocities. Well might it have been, since they were the direct result of a U.N. policy to which the U.S. gave its full support. By waging war against Tshombe in the south, the U.N. had made it impossible for northern Katanga to be properly policed. The U.N. had compounded the error by air-lifting savage Congolese troops to the area. It then refused to undertake any sort of police operation in these zones which it had left open to barbarism. When the inevitable atrocities occurred, it refused to move troops in by helicopter because that would be "extremely hazardous." Lawson and Nwawo had shown that even a small group of U.N. soldiers possessed of moral and physical courage could have done a great deal to safeguard the local civilians. There were either too few such men among the U.N. forces or their political leaders were too timorous to permit them to do what most of them must have recognized as their duty: to protect lives and preserve law and order.

Meanwhile, the diplomatic pressure on Tshombe intensified. On December 30, Kasavubu called on the Katangan legislature to meet at Kamina on January 3, a move which Tshombe rejected as a "grave violation" of constitutional law. The legislature, Tshombe asserted, would meet in Elisabethville on the 3rd. Kasavubu's proposal apparently was designed to encourage the anti-Tshombe Balubas to attend (many were afraid to come to Elisabethville) so that Tshombe's lack of support in northern Katanga could be exposed.

U.N. spokesmen had repeatedly accused the Federation of Rhodesia and Nyasaland of supplying Tshombe with mercenaries and war materials, an allegation Federal Prime Minister Sir Roy Welensky had frequently and heatedly denied. Both sides were right and both wrong in this instance. One is inclined to accept Welensky's assertion that his government had at no time given Tshombe military assistance of any sort. On the other hand, white volunteers for Tshombe's forces repeatedly had passed through Rhodesia on their way from Europe to Katanga. As transit passengers, only a few of specified nationalities required visas. A few Rhodesians had volunteered as private citizens to serve Tshombe. In addition, paramilitary commodities such as gasoline, lubricants, and vehicles had legally been exported to Katanga by Rhodesia. Unquestionably, some arms and ammunition had been smuggled across Rhodesia's 1,200-mile-long border with Katanga, which was guarded by only five customs posts.

U Thant now sought to stop this by requesting that U.N. observers be posted at Rhodesian airports and roads leading into Katanga. A similar request was made to Portugal in respect to areas of Angola bordering on Katanga. Neither Portugal nor Rhodesia have any reason to love the U.N. The request to Portugal was particularly ironic since that same month the Security Council had refused to take any action in a clear case of Indian aggression (recognized even by the U.S. Government) against Portuguese Goa. Portugal and Rhodesia rejected the requests, although Rhodesia agreed to strengthen its border posts and invited U Thant to come to Salisbury for discussions on the question, an invitation he declined.

On January 3, the Katangan legislature met for exactly seven minutes before adjourning because there was no electricity and Tshombe had not arrived. On the following day, the Assembly met again with thirty-five of its sixty members (a bare quorum) present. Absent were all the BALU-BAKAT deputies and several tribal representatives who had been unable to reach Elisabethville because of disturbed conditions in the north. Tshombe told his deputies: "I leave to you the task of determining how far our concessions can go and which articles of the (Kitona) Agreement should be modified." He went on to accuse the Central Government of having several times violated the *loi fondamentale* that it requested Katanga to accept. Tshombe concluded: "Katanga must be unified with its brothers in the Congo but remain sufficiently free so that its fate will not be finally sealed on the day the shadow of Communism spreads over this country." Obviously, Tshombe was intent on keeping considerable local autonomy for Katanga and had small faith in the future of the Congo.

While Nyembo was dickering with Adoula in Leopold-ville and the Katangan Assembly was debating in Elisabeth-ville, two top State Department officials launched a new attack against Katanga. Assistant Secretary of State G. Mennen Williams, speaking in Detroit, accused the Katangan Government of fabricating "horrendous tales of indiscriminate mayhem by United Nations troops" during the December war. Unquestionably, the Katangan Information Service had played up U.N. atrocities, real and imagined, for all they were worth. Williams might have been in a better position to judge, however, had he spent some time in Elisabethville's *Leo Deux* while the U.N. mortar shells rained down during those last days before Christmas. Every newsman there had seen civilians shelled with his own eyes. Each of us had seen Red Cross vehicles destroyed by U.N. fire. Or were all of us lying? Georges Olivet, the Swiss Red Cross representative, lay in his shallow grave in testimony that we were not. Sanche de Gramont of the New York *Herald Tribune* might well have sent Williams a few pieces of the shrapnel picked from his body after Swedish troops shot up the civilian car in which he was leaving Elisabethville.

On the same night that Williams made his speech, Carl T. Rowan, Deputy Assistant Secretary of State for Public Affairs, made an even more vitriolic attack on Katanga in a Philadelphia speech. Rowan charged that Katanga was waging a "clever big-money campaign" to dispense "a string of myths" designed to gain American support. Rowan directed his attack primarily against Michel Struelens, a New York-based Belgian publicist who Rowan said had spent $140,000 in fifteen months in an attempt to put Katanga's point of view across. Rowan also strongly implied that *Union Miniere* was behind the whole problem in its attempt to create "a safe little kingdom" for its financial interests. Rowan acted as if it was a crime for *Union Miniere* to make a profit and tried to smear American supporters of Tshombe by asserting that they numbered among them "arch conservatives, people who oppose the income tax, avowed defenders of racial segregation, opponents of fluoridation of water, those who want to destroy the Supreme Court."

The *Washington Star*, in an editorial on December 29, dismissed Williams' speech as "a rehash of the familiar State

Department–U.N. line, with all of the distortions and omissions, plus a few characteristic Williams-ish embellishments." Rowan's address it saw as "filled with fascinating contradictions and McCarthy-like innuendoes." Finally, the *Star* concluded, if Struelens could get so much mileage out of $140,000, the State Department should hire him, since it achieved so much less at a cost so much greater. In the end, there were few who would agree that because one thought Tshombe had some merit to his case, one must, by definition, oppose the fluoridation of water. These two speeches could only be taken as an attempt by the Administration to muzzle opposition to its Katanga policy by smearing those who supported Tshombe through guilt by association. It failed, perhaps because Americans had experienced quite enough of these tactics under Senator McCarthy.

Back in the Congo, Adoula moved against other secessionists. On December 29, the National Assembly voted to revoke "King" Albert Kalonji's parliamentary immunity. He was arrested and placed under detention in Leopoldville. On January 8, the Assembly ordered Gizenga to return from Stanleyville to face charges of secessionist activity. Gizenga, who had been holed up in Stanleyville since October, refused to return. He was arrested after a battle between his bodyguard and Lundula's troops in which fourteen were killed, and later transferred to Leopoldville. Gizenga was censured by the National Assembly, dismissed from his post of Vice Premier, transferred to a new place of detention near the mouth of the Congo River, and legal proceedings were instituted against him.

On January 10, Linner charged in a report published by the U.N. in New York that a hard core of mercenaries was still at large in Katanga and responsible for the "continued uncertainty" of the military situation there. In addition, Linner charged that thirty-five French-speaking mercenaries two days before had reached Brazzaville en route to Elisabethville. Of these, twenty-six Frenchmen and a Span-

iard were sent back to Europe by the Rhodesian immigration authorities because their visas were not in order. Five
Belgians, an Italian, a Frenchman, a Spaniard, and a Briton,
who had valid visas, were allowed to proceed to Katanga.
Nearly three tons of camouflaged uniforms carried by their
aircraft were returned to Europe.

The importance of the incident was that it clearly demonstrated that Tshombe had no intention of implementing
the Kitona Agreement. He might send deputies to sit in the
Congolese National Assembly, he might negotiate about a
constitution, he might recognize Kasavubu until he was
blue in the face; but Katanga was in fact if not in law independent and he intended to keep it that way. While the
Katangan legislature approved seven points of the Kitona
Agreement but haggled over the one calling for it to "respect and facilitate the execution" of the Security Council's
resolutions, Tshombe fortified Kipushi and built up his
army. Said U Thant: "It is our hope that he (Tshombe)
will keep his promise; I must add, however, that our plans
and preparations for further operations to achieve total
elimination of mercenaries are going forward without
delay."

Finally, on January 12, the U.N. agreed to an International Red Cross request for an investigation into Olivet's
murder. The Katangan Government had been conducting
an investigation but had not been allowed to extend this to
territory under U.N. control, which included the spot
where Olivet's ambulance was shot up. The U.N. lamely
stated that it had not instituted its own investigation because
it did not possess "adequate legal or technical resources."
Or was the international organization in fact afraid that
such an investigation, despite "Soapy" Williams, might well
reveal that its troops had been guilty of atrocities?

On January 24, Tshombe met with Urquhart, Jose Rolz-
Bennett, a Guatemalan who has since replaced Urquhart as
chief U.N. representative in Katanga, and Dumontet to

discuss the question of mercenaries. Tshombe gave Urquhart a list of French officers who, he said, "have just been paid off with thanks." Tshombe asserted that no foreign officer held any post of command in the Katangan gendarmerie. This may well be the case. However, there is little doubt that white officers still serve as instructors and tactical advisers. On the same day, Lundula sent 160 Congolese troops to Kongolo in an attempt to apprehend the murderers of the missionaries.

After another meeting with the U.N. representatives, Tshombe announced on January 27 that he was "resolutely determined to put an end to the problem of mercenaries." With this in mind, he added, he had demanded a month to seek out "those individuals who could be suspected of being mercenaries." At the end of this month, he suggested the establishment of a joint U.N.-Katangan commission to supervise the removal of mercenaries. Tshombe also stated that the gendarmerie was commanded by Katangans and must remain so, adding that "in no case would Katangan soldiers accept being under the command of European officers of any nation." It was obvious that Tshombe had no intention of handing over his gendarmerie to either Congolese or U.N. officers for "retraining."

Several days before this, Tshombe had written to American Consul Lewis Hoffacker, asking for a visa to enable him to visit the U.S. in March, where he had been invited by his American supporters to address several public meetings. Hoffacker referred the request to Washington. Washington's reply was to ask Tshombe to file a formal application for a visa, to give details about his passport, and to state the length and purpose of his visit. Eventually, Tshombe was denied a visa on grounds that he did not have a valid (i.e., Congolese) passport. Said State Department spokesman Joseph Reap on February 15: "We believe that a visit to the United States by Mr. Tshombe at this time would interrupt and jeopardize progress towards common objectives; this

is also the view of the Central Government of the Congo."
The State Department's position, while technically correct,
obviously was yet another infringement of the right of the
American people to hear Tshombe's side of the situation.
While the U.S. could not admit the legality of a Katangan
passport since Washington recognized the Leopoldville
Government and not that of Elisabethville, there are many
ways around such a situation. For instance, political refugees fleeing from South Africa have traveled on *laissez-
passers* issued by the Indian Government. If the U.S. had
wanted to avoid the embarrassment caused by allowing
Tshombe to enter America on a Katangan passport and yet
wanted to be fair in allowing him to state his case, it had
only to suggest that the Katangan President apply for a
laissez-passer from one of his allies, such as ex-French
Congo or Malagasy. It did not, however. It simply turned
down his visa application.

Meanwhile, a *Union Miniere* team from Elisabethville
was negotiating with the Central Government in Leopoldville on how its operations could be reintegrated into the
Congo's fiscal plans. Adoula had warned the mining company that he would appropriate it unless it stopped making
payments to the Katangan Government. On February 14,
the Congolese Prime Minister stated that legally *Union
Miniere* owed the Central Government back taxes to August, 1960. He added: "We are going to recover the money
by all means at our disposal; it is up to us to decide whether
to demand retroactivity." It was not until February 20 that
the Ethiopian troops which had occupied the mining company's Elisabethville plant shortly before Christmas evacuated the works and allowed production to resume after a
stoppage of nearly two months.

On January 30, the U.N. announced that eight Congolese soldiers responsible for the Kongolo massacre had been
arrested by Lundula's troops and flown to Stanleyville, presumably for court-martial proceedings. On the same day,

Linner (since replaced as chief U.N. representative in the Congo by Ghana's Robert Gardiner) announced that he had rejected the one-month delay suggested by Tshombe to enable him to expel the remaining mercenaries from Katanga. The Swede said he had ordered Tshombe to expel his remaining mercenaries immediately and added that if the Katangan authorities did not "take urgent steps to eliminate the mercenaries, the U.N. will not hesitate to take all necessary measures to do so." It all sounded familiarly like the propaganda barrage necessary before the U.N. could launch another offensive to topple Tshombe by force.

On February 2, Adoula flew to New York where he called on the U.N. General Assembly to provide greater military assistance to end Katanga's secession. "From the beginning," Adoula said, "my government announced its absolute will to do away with the Katanga secession." He added: "We are not carrying out a war against Katanga. It is our responsibility to defend our unity and our integrity against separatist maneuverers who take their orders from abroad. Our victory over the mercenaries will be a victory of all of civilization over barbarism." Again, it appeared likely that a new U.N. attack was in the wind.

On February 5, Adoula lunched with Kennedy in Washington and was promised that the U.S. would continue to provide his government with all necessary assistance.

On February 15, the Katangan Assembly finally approved with a considerable number of conditions and reservations the eight-point Kitona Agreement. While the Assembly toned down the original statement submitted by its Foreign Affairs and Political Committee—which demanded the repeal of the *loi fondamentale*, a radical decentralization of power in the Congo, and the guarantee of ministerial posts for Katanga in the Central Government—it stipulated that it accepted the Kitona Agreement only "as being able to serve as a base" for discussion between the Congo and Katanga. In its motion, the Assembly called on the Katangan Government to solve disputes between it and Leopoldville through negotiations. Tshombe, addressing the Assembly, made "a new appeal" to Adoula. "The two of us, without any foreign interference—which was not the case, alas, at Kitona—will apply an African program, reserved to Africans and decided by Africans. The result will be peace for our people and peace for Africa," he said. Five days later, seventy-five tribal chiefs from all parts of Katanga published a communiqué in which they "disapproved of the conduct of the United Nations toward the Katangan people" and alleged that the U.N. was in the Congo to help the United States appropriate for itself Katanga's copper and south Kasai's diamonds. In late February, the gendarmerie retook Kongolo and Kabalo and fanned out against Baluba terrorist gangs in the north.

By March, 1962, although the last nine mercenaries had officially left Katanga three weeks before, it was clear that the Kitona Agreement was a dead letter. Adoula had made no concessions to Tshombe and the Katangan leader was still too strong to accept an unconditional surrender. While the arrests of Gizenga and Kalonji unquestionably strengthened the Central Government, these moves gave Tshombe pause: What was to prevent Adoula, once Katanga had been reintegrated into the Congo, from arresting him?

Despite his fears, Tshombe, accompanied by Kibwe and Public Works Minister Gabriel Kitenge, flew to Leopoldville on March 15, after first obtaining iron-clad safe-conduct guarantees from the U.N. Tshombe told reporters that the purpose of his visit was "not to capitulate but to try by means of frank and sincere discussion to save a country that has suffered for almost twenty months." Reconciliation between the Congo and Katanga, he said, was necessary "both for ourselves and for the whole of Africa."

Adoula, in a deliberate snub to Tshombe, flew to Coquilhatville for discussions with the Congo's other five provincial leaders, before talks between the two began on March

18. After a week of secret discussions, during which the tightest security precautions were observed, the talks were suspended when Tshombe asserted, as he had at Kitona, that no new agreement could be binding until approved by the Katanga Assembly.

Said Adoula: "The Katanga crisis has never been more serious." The Congolese Prime Minister asserted that while Tshombe was "stalling for time," his colleagues in Elisabethville were buying arms and hiring mercenaries. Calling the talks "a comedy," Adoula said his government would use "all the means in our power" to end Katanga's secession. He added that he was "linking his government's life to the question."

On March 27, U Thant took the occasion of the appointment of Lieutenant General Kebede Gebre, Ethiopian Chief-of-Staff, to replace McKeown as U.N. military commander in the Congo to assert that the U.N. had plans "for the next stages" if the talks broke down. He denied, however, that the use of force was contemplated.

The talks between Tshombe and Adoula were reopened in Leopoldville, where they dragged on into April without making noticeable progress.

The U.S. and the U.N. were by now more firmly than ever committed to intervention in the Congo and the crushing of the secessionist movement in Katanga. The only factors delaying such a move appeared to be financial considerations and some political pressure from Britain, France, and Belgium, all of which had grave doubts about the U.N.-U.S. policy in the Congo. *Union Miniere*, anticipating a third and perhaps final U.N. attack on Katanga, was dickering for terms with Adoula.

Tshombe, meanwhile, was reorganizing and building up his forces for a third test of strength with the U.N. The financial problems of the international organization appeared to be playing a major role in delaying U.N. action against Tshombe. Should the American Government agree, as Kennedy proposed it should, to buy half of the $200 million U.N. bond issue, and should at least a portion of the rest be subscribed to by other nations, it appears likely that the U.N. will again attack Tshombe.

Since Kitona, Tshombe has acted on the assumption that the U.N. will run out of funds and withdraw from the Congo before it has ended Katanga's secession. With this in mind, he has done everything in his power to play for time, to prevent a clash between his forces and the U.N., to persuade Adoula that he intends to reintegrate Katanga with the Congo.

It remains to be seen who will win this waiting game.

Epilogue: MYTH AND REALITY

"To save succeeding generations from the
scourge of war . . . to reaffirm faith in
fundamental human rights, in the dignity and
worth of the human person, in the equal rights
. . . of nations large and small.

> —From the Charter of the
> United Nations.

"The United Nations died in Katanga."

> —MOISE TSHOMBE, December 16, 1961.

ONLY A fool would deny the desirability of union between the Congo and Katanga. The arguments for
this are both political and economic. Union is desirable politically because the African states want it and because both
the U.S. and the U.N. have staked their prestige on the
establishment of such links. If Katanga is not reunited with
the Congo, both the U.N. and the U.S. will suffer crushing
psychological defeats. This, of course, is the fault of the
U.N. and the U.S., not of Katanga. The international organization and the Kennedy Administration have placed
themselves in this position because they have followed a
policy of expediency that is both shortsighted and unethical.
More of this later.

There is more substance to the economic argument. We
have seen that Katanga is the richest of the six provinces
that once constituted the Belgian Congo. We have seen that
its fabulously wealthy mines once supported the colonial
budget to the extent of more than 30 per cent of its total.

Apologists for U.S. and U.N. policy maintain that the Congo without Katanga will never become solvent. They may be right. But even a superficial examination of the country's economy reveals that the Congo will be in deep financial trouble even if Katanga's secession is crushed.

During the first six months of last year, the revenues and expenditures of the Congolese Central Government and of the six provincial governments including Katanga were as follows:

	Revenue	Expenditure	Deficit
		(in millions of dollars)	
Central Government	27	40.8	13.8
Leopoldville Province	8.4	28.8	20.4
Orientale Province	.18	24	23.82
Equateur Province	.42	7.8	7.38
Kivu Province	——	2.4	2.4
Kasai Province	——	4.2	4.2
Katanga Province	42	42	——

These statistics, provided by Belgium's Center for Socio-Political Research and Information, indicate that the integration of Katanga with the Congo would not solve the latter's financial problems. They also go a long way toward showing why in an economic sense Katanga has no desire to be affiliated with the Congo. For the first six months of 1961, the Central Government and the five provinces ostensibly under its control had a combined income of $36 million and combined expenditures of $108 million, a total deficit of $72 million.

Nor, of course, could the Congo extract all of Katanga's revenues from her even if she were reintegrated with the Congo, since Leopoldville would then become responsible for the administration of Katanga. Under the colonial regime, half of Katanga's contribution to the Central Government was returned to her. Even if this proportion were halved again—and Katanga could not possibly be administered for anything less than this—Elisabethville's subsidy to the Central Government and the other five provinces over the six-month period in question would amount to only $31.5 million. This would still leave a combined deficit of $40.5 million. In short, Katanga would be impoverished and the rest of the Congo not significantly enriched.

Even this rather unpromising situation would not come about unless Katanga's industrial complex was captured intact. It is unlikely that this would be the case. The U.N.'s military action in December caused considerable damage to Katanga's economy. Any further attempt to forcibly reintegrate Katanga into the Congo could only result in the implementation of the scorched earth policy that the Katanga Government has threatened. In addition, further fighting in Katanga, particularly any attempt to introduce Central Government troops, would result in the almost total exodus of Katanga's whites. The U.N. and the U.S. may be able to wash the Kindu and Kongolo massacres out of their memories. But Katanga's whites, reduced in number from 35,000 to about 8,000 by the U.N.'s policies, have not forgotten. They are the ones who would have to live under the unstable conditions created by the U.N. The vast majority of them would leave if Central Government troops were brought in. Their departure would delay the reactivation of Katanga's economy if not irreparably damage it.

Thus it is clear that the Congo's economic health depends less upon the reintegration of Katanga than upon the re-establishment of order and productivity in the other five provinces and the adoption of a policy of fiscal responsibility by the Central Government. Under the Security Council's resolution of August 9, 1960, the U.N. certainly had the authority to assist the Central Government in doing this. Although it did its best in this regard, it failed miserably.

The excuse used by the U.N., the U.S., and the Central Government to cover this failure has always been that it was impossible to accomplish these ends before terminating

Katanga's secession. This simply does not hold water, as events have proved. The U.S. has always underlined the point that Leopoldville could not smash Kalonji and Gizenga until it had dealt with Tshombe. The falseness of this claim was demonstrated by the ease with which each of these leaders was taken into custody at a time when Katanga's secession was just as real in fact if not in name as it was a year before. Gizenga was always a paper tiger with whom the State Department was fond of conjuring. Lumumba's heir never had a real base of power in Stanleyville because it was not his tribal homeland. As the Central Government discovered when it finally moved against him, his support was limited to a personal guard of less than 200 troops backed by a few hundred members of the Lumumbist Youth Movement. His arrest and imprisonment cost exactly fourteen deaths. Linked to this question was the U.N.'s and the State Department's fear that if action was taken against Gizenga, Russia would intervene unilaterally in the Congo and Central Africa would become another Korea. A small knowledge of logistics and a cursory glance at the history of direct Communist military intervention elsewhere in the world would have taught these nervous gentlemen that this was nonsense. Where has direct Communist military intervention taken place? In Korea, East Germany, Indochina, Hungary, and Tibet. Each of these countries is contiguous to a Communist-controlled land mass. Khrushchev would no more have launched massive military intervention in the Congo than he did in Egypt during Suez or in Lebanon during the American landing there. The logistics of the Congo's geographical position are such that he would have taken a severe beating had he done so. He, if not the U.S., obviously realized this. Khrushchev let Gizenga go without a murmur. So much for the paper tiger Gizenga and the threat of Russian intervention. Kalonji in fact was a far more formidable opponent because his regime in South Kasai is based on his own Baluba tribe.

This problem was solved by arresting him while he was in Leopoldville, far out of the reach of his supporters.

The fact remains, however, that it would be desirable for Katanga to be a part of the Congo. There are many things that are desirable but are not possible. To confuse the two is to prepare the ground for serious psychological defeats. We have already explored the factors in the Katangan situation—historical, linguistic, tribal, geographic, economic, and political—that militate against such unity. A return of Katanga to the Congo immediately after its secession could only have been possible (and then not probable) had some sort of order and stability been re-established in the Congo. Paradoxically, the U.N., which was unable to accomplish this task itself, prevented the one group who might have done so from returning to the Congo: the Belgians.

The Congo was Belgium's creature. It had neither ethnic nor geographical meaning. It was one territory only because the Belgians carved it out of Africa's heart seventy-seven years ago. The Belgians provided the essential link that gave all the parts of the territory at least the semblance if not the reality of unity. Most of them fled from the Congo during the unhappy events of the mutiny. As the situation quieted, many of them wanted to return. The U.N. in general and Dayal in particular opposed this. The Belgian Government itself, under the terms of the treaty of friendship, assistance, and cooperation attached to the *loi fondamentale*, had both the right and the obligation to supply the Congo with the technicians and advisers necessary to keep the new nation orderly and productive. Many of the Congolese themselves favored the return of these Belgian civil servants who had forgotten more about the Congo than the most brilliant U.N. civil servant will ever know. The U.N. was unable to provide the Congo with doctors, teachers, technicians, or administrators in anything like the number or the quality necessary. Yet the international organization adopted a hostile attitude toward a member nation that had been instrumental in the creation of the United Nations and erected every obstacle against the return of Belgians as either private citizens or as government employees. By so doing, the U.N. made a difficult job almost impossible and delayed perhaps by years the recovery of the Congo. Both New York and Washington must bear a heavy responsibility for this.

The U.N., having destroyed the Belgians as a possible factor in the reintegration of Katanga into the Congo, then proceeded to place obstacles in the path of reconciliation between the various Congolese leaders. Tshombe's secession was never absolute. The Katangan constitution stipulates that "The State of Katanga adheres to the principle of association with the other countries of the ex-Belgian Congo on condition that they are themselves politically organized in an atmosphere of law and order." Secession took place only because Tshombe and other federalists were unable to obtain a realistic constitution. From start to finish, he has asserted his willingness to negotiate on the subject. He played a leading role at the Tananarive Conference that laid the first foundations for a reconstituted Congo. He showed his good faith by attending the Coquilhatville Conference, where he was arrested after U.N. representatives had made it clear to the Central Government that they could get a better deal by working through the international organization. The Congo envisaged at Tananarive had many weaknesses. The U.N. and the U.S. didn't like it because it didn't happen to fit doctrinaire theories of political science. But it had two great advantages: It was a Congolese solution to a Congolese problem and it recognized the fact that political power in the Congo now and for the foreseeable future rests not in Leopoldville but in the provinces. In any case, Tananarive was only a beginning. Had it been properly nurtured, a more unified and stable Congo might have grown from it. But the U.N. was never able to face the fact that if a solution to the Katanga problem was difficult with Tshombe, it was impossible without him.

The U.N.'s plan, despite frequent disclaimers, has been and is to forcibly compel the reintegration of Katanga into the Congo. This was shown by O'Brien's statement in September, when he said Katanga's secession was "ended." It was shown when the U.N. flew Bochely-Davidson, the Central Government's gauleiter, into Elisabethville a few hours later. It was demonstrated again in the Security Council resolution of November 24, 1961, which rejected Katanga's secession. This plan was and is unworkable, for the simple reason that the U.N. lacks the military forces necessary to implement it. The present U.N. force in Katanga of 9,000 men is barely large enough to secure Elisabethville. But Jadotville and Kolwezi, the country's two most important cities, are still firmly in Katangan hands. Even if the U.N. were to receive sufficient reinforcements to enable it to capture the principal cities and towns, the war would be far from over. What the U.N. and the U.S. have never been able to understand is that when you make war on Tshombe, you make war not on a government or on a political party but on the Lunda, one of the largest tribes in Central Africa. In addition, each of Tshombe's cabinet ministers has the support of his own tribe. Even if the U.N. troops had the skill and the stomach to pursue the gendarmerie into the bush and destroy it, they would still have the problem of dealing with the rebellious tribes. In any event, a political solution created by force would not survive the departure of the bayonets that imposed it. The U.N., already deeply in the red on its Congo operation, cannot keep troops in Katanga forever. Some time this year, they will have to be withdrawn. Once they are gone, Katanga will rebel again. The Central Government probably could not keep Katanga within the Congo by force. If it did succeed in doing so, the bloodshed and misery caused in the process would be immense.

As well as being unworkable, a solution imposed by force is unethical. Tshombe's Government is far from an ideal one. But it does rule. It has maintained reasonable order, created a workable multiracial society, and kept the wheels of economic and social progress turning. In the two years of its existence, it has acquired most of the characteristics of a nation as understood by international law. The mere fact that Katanga seceded from the Congo gave the U.N. no right to crush it. The unity of the Congo was never more than a myth created and maintained by the Belgians. The *loi fondamentale*, setting forth the unity of the Congo, was only a provisional constitution that has yet to be ratified by the Congolese National Assembly. Most of its other clauses have been violated by the Congolese themselves, so it seems strange that the U.N. should insist that the clause referring to the unity of the Congo is sacrosanct.

In addition, the secession of any one of a nation's parts from the whole is recognized by international law as the internal affair of the nation involved. Had the U.N. existed two centuries ago, would it have been right for it to prevent the secession of the thirteen American colonies from Britain or that of the South American nations from Spain and Portugal? More recently, would it have been right to prevent Norway's secession from Sweden and the excision of Northern Ireland from Eire? What about the division of Imperial India into Pakistan and the Indian Union? Was Syria wrong to secede from Egypt? Were France and the Indochinese wrong to split Indochina into four nations? In Africa itself, were France and the Africans wrong in 1958 to divide two great territories, French West Africa and French Equatorial Africa, into twelve separate and independent nations? Was Senegal wrong to secede from the Mali Federation in 1960? Should U.N. troops have been used in each of these instances to impose an unwanted and impossible unity? The answers to these questions must be in the negative. Were the U.N.'s actions in Katanga just and logical? Were they calculated to promote the establishment of law and order locally or to preserve world peace? Equally certainly, the answer to these questions must be in the negative.

International law, which we claim is the foundation of our society and the only hope for a peaceful world, is quite clear on the question. It establishes that once rebels or secessionists have established themselves firmly in a definite portion of territory and have acquired a reasonably stable government of their own, a duty of nonintervention arises in their favor. These rights are not dependent on diplomatic recognition. Once the proscribed situation exists, the rights exist.

There is one important exception to this canon of international law. This is that the central government of a nation may request and receive assistance from other nations against its rebels if it can prove that the rebellion itself has been inspired or is being supported by external powers. This was the reason invoked by the U.N. when it went to the assistance of South Korea when it was invaded by North Korea in 1950. Eight years later, the U.S. again invoked this clause to move into Lebanon.

Although the U.N. has never formally stated that its intervention in Katanga is based on the supposition that Tshombe's rebellion is inspired from abroad, it has strongly implied this by the issue it has made of the presence of foreign mercenaries. Tshombe unquestionably made an important political mistake in recruiting mercenaries from South Africa and the colonial powers. This act damned him in the eyes of most African nationalists and gave substance to the allegation that he was no more than a white man's puppet. More recently, he has been equally unfortunate in the support given him by far-out reactionaries and neo-fascists in Africa, America, and England. The U.S. Government, in particular, has used this fact to tar all those opposed to the U.N.'s actions in Katanga with the same brush. But Tshombe had no alternative to the former and he has no control over the latter. In August, 1960, having dismissed the mutinous *Force Publique*, Katanga needed to create a new army. Had the U.N. not exerted immediate pressure on him to end Katanga's secession, the regular Belgian army officers on duty in Katanga would have been sufficient to train his gendarmerie. As it was, Tshombe was faced with the task of defending himself almost immediately. As a rebel, he was fighting not only for his own life but for his nation's existence. For this, he needed a trained force of men. So he hired mercenaries. Under the circumstances, he had to take them where he could get them. As a result, he ended up with an army composed at least partially of white supremacists and neo-fascists. The fact that Tshombe's need for an effective military force coincided with the hatred of these men for the U.N. should not conceal the fact that Tshombe's support in Katanga, particularly the southern half of the country, is immense. He is, after all, the lawfully and popularly elected leader of Katanga. Had his regime been propped up only by the mining interests and a group of mercenaries which never even in the wildest dreams of the U.N. exceeded 500 and seldom in actuality amounted to more than a fifth of that figure, surely it would have toppled of its own weight under assault by U.N. troops in September and December of 1961. How is it that a couple of hundred ill-trained and loud-mouthed soldiers of fortune of a dozen nationalities have been able to achieve so much more than thousands of American "mercenaries" have been able to accomplish in Laos?

In any case, the presence of mercenaries, military advisers, or whatever you choose to call them, does not, in international law, constitute inspiration or support of rebellion by external powers. International law is quite clear on one point: When foreign assistance (in this case, United Nations troops) is obtained for the purpose of imposing a political solution by force that could not be reached by normal democratic means (elections or a plebiscite), such intervention is illegal. There can be little doubt in any competent observer's mind that a plebiscite in the portion of Katanga under Tshombe's control would overwhelmingly confirm secession. This does not mean that a feeling of Katangan nationality is widespread. Most Katangans, like most Congolese, still think of themselves primarily as members of a tribe. But there has been a growth of Katangan nationalism in recent months. Paradoxically, it is the U.N.—in seeking to destroy this—which has largely created it. The fighting in September and December of 1961 did more to create a Katangan nation in the minds of those simple tribesmen than a hundred Tshombes. Katangans—black and white—have fought and died in defense of their homes against the white and brown soldiers of the United Nations. Out of this suffering and blood and passion has been born a Katangan nation. It is ironic to think that if Tshombe is the father of Katanga, Conor O'Brien, Ivan Smith, and U Thant have been its midwives.

The U.N. recognized Katanga's position under international law in the Security Council's resolution of August 9, 1960. This asserted that the United Nations "reaffirms that the United Nations forces in the Congo will not be a party to or in any way intervene in or be used to influence the outcome of any internal conflict, constitutional or otherwise." The resolution of February 21, 1961, authorizing the "use of force, if necessary, in the last resort" to prevent civil war does not and cannot affect this fundamental principle. Thus an action taken to secure the expulsion of white mercenaries cannot legally be used to impose a political solution on Katanga.

This was undeniably Hammarskjold's interpretation of the situation. In a 4,000-word summary of the situation leading up to the entry of U.N. troops into Katanga in August, 1960, Hammarskjold had this to say about Katanga's secession: "This is an internal political problem to which the United Nations as an organization obviously cannot be a party. Nor would the entry of the United Nations force in Katanga mean any taking of sides in the conflict to which I have just referred. Nor should it be permitted to shift the weight between personalities or groups or schools of thought in a way which would prejudice the solution of the internal political problem. I believe all this can be avoided if the United Nations maintains firmly its aim and acts with clarity and tact."

Unfortunately, the U.N. did not maintain its aim. It acted with neither clarity, nor tact, nor honesty.

On August 12, 1960, Hammarskjold made an even more explicit statement when he said that the United Nations could "not be used on behalf of the Central Government to force the provincial government of Mr. Moise Tshombe to a specific line of action."

Yet last year a U.N. spokesman said the U.N. force had acted to end Katanga's secession on the request of the Central Government. On several occasions, the U.N.'s legal position was reaffirmed and explained to Tshombe by various U.N. representatives, including Ralph Bunche, who told Tshombe in July, 1960, that the U.N. force "has received strict instructions not to intervene in the internal politics of the country." Had Tshombe not trusted the sacrosanct nature of the Security Council's resolution and the statements of the international organization's representatives, he unquestionably never would have allowed the U.N. to enter Katanga.

The U.N. was right, both morally and legally, to come into the Congo. It had a great task to perform there, the successful completion of which would have reflected great credit on the organization. This was, first, to restore order, second, to secure the withdrawal of the Belgian forces from their Congolese bases (since their presence there, although legal, was no longer politically possible), third, to encourage the return of Belgian technicians and to replace those who would not return, and, fourth, to see that the economy and the social services continued to function. The U.N. was totally successful in the second instance and partially so in the first. It accomplished little in either the third or the fourth instances.

Should Hammarskjold have insisted on the entry of U.N. forces into Katanga? Legally it appears that he should not have done so. The U.N. was invited into the Congo by the Leopoldville Government. Tshombe repeatedly stated that he did not want the U.N. in Katanga, which by then had seceded from the Congo. To bring U.N. troops into Katanga on the basis of an invitation from the Congo was a clear violation of international law since it constituted intervention in recognizing that Katanga was part of the Congo. If it was necessary for reasons of world politics to break international law, then the U.N. should have established only a nominal presence in Katanga in the form of a small military force and a few advisers. In fact, the U.N. poured its military forces into Katanga, the only peaceful portion of the Congo, with the obvious intention of either overthrowing the lawfully elected regime or of imposing a political solution by force. The Security Council resolution of November 24, 1961, which rejected the independence of Katanga, was both a violation of the U.N.'s own charter and illegal under international law. In addition, U.N. representatives in Leopoldville and Elisabethville stretched even these mandates to the breaking point in their attacks on Katanga.

The September attack, badly managed and made in bad faith, was particularly indefensible. If the object was to arrest mercenaries, what purpose could be served by attacking and killing Katangan troops defending public buildings? Why were U.N. troops sent to arrest Katangan cabinet ministers, who could hardly be described as white mercenaries? As has been mentioned earlier, Linner apparently had no knowledge of the U.N.'s plan of attack, and it appears likely to O'Brien that Hammarskjold did not. Why then did Khiari order the offensive? Since the U.S. pays about a third of the U.N.'s running costs (in 1961, $22.3 million of $64 million), finances half of the Congo operation ($77.5 million paid or pledged so far; in contrast, only 88 of 104 members of the U.N. have paid their assessed share of the cost of the Congo operation), and is considering the purchase of $100 million worth of U.N. bonds, the American people have a right to know the answer to this question. The U.N., assuming that it had exhausted all avenues of negotiation, had more justification for attacking in December than in September since the freedom of movement of its forces was severely threatened by Katangan roadblocks. But once these roadblocks were cleared and freedom of movement between its various strong points re-established, why did it feel compelled to launch air and mortar attacks on the center of a city crammed with civilians and to attack industrial targets? Obviously, the only intention was to punish Tshombe and to force Katanga's political reintegration into the Congo, a goal achieved on paper at Kitona.

The role and responsibility of the U.S. in the situation is clear and heavy. The U.S. gave the U.N. its full diplomatic and financial support and it intervened in a military sense by providing air transport to bring U.N. soldiers from Leopoldville to Elisabethville during the fighting. It is customary for U.S. Government spokesmen to disavow responsibility for the U.N.'s acts in Katanga, to say that it does not make U.N. policy but loyally tries to carry it out. Yet during the December fighting, the U.S. made it quite clear under what terms a cease-fire could take place in Katanga. When Tshombe complied with those terms, he was flown to Kitona in an American plane and accompanied by an American diplomat. Obviously, the U.S. was calling a good percentage of the shots.

Why was the U.S. so eager to involve herself in the military suppression of Katanga, an act it must have known was illegal under international law? We have already mentioned the spurious fear of Gizenga and Russian intervention. It is worthwhile to ask why, if Katanga's independence so strengthened the Red puppet Gizenga and threatened a pro-Western Leopoldville government, Russia not only did not veto Security Council resolutions aimed at Katanga but vociferously supported them? The answer to this would seem to be that Russia realized from the start that a Red Congo was neither possible nor desirable. Marxist theory and Congolese realities do not coincide. As the London *Times* once put it, "the Russian debut in Leopoldville was unhappy, and the exile in Stanleyville little better." What was both possible and desirable was chaos in the Congo, preferably prolonged for as long as possible. By refusing to pay for the U.N.'s Congo operation while encouraging the attack on Katanga, Russia was placed in the pleasant position of seeing the most stable and pro-Western portion of the Congo blasted by the U.N. at a cost of $51 million a year to the U.S. and at none to herself! From the Russian point of view, this policy was infinitely successful in a larger sense in that it drove a wedge between the U.S. and the other fourteen NATO powers, which, with the exception of Canada and Norway, either entertained serious reservations about America's Congo policy or were frankly antagonistic to it. This is not to imply, of course, that America's foreign policy should be dictated by its European allies. However, particularly in questions relating to Africa, an area where they have had so much more experience than we, virtually unanimous NATO disapproval of U.S. policy should have given Washington pause for serious thought.

The U.S. clearly adopted its strong and illegal position regarding Katanga's secession in the hope of pleasing the Afro–Asian nations. In December, when flying to Katanga, I found myself in the company of a high, Washington-based State Department official with considerable responsibility for making American policy (he was not going to Katanga, but continuing on to Salisbury). Our conversation went something like this:

Q. Why are we as a nation supporting the suppression of Katanga?

A. The President has questioned almost every African leader who has visited Washington as to his views on Tshombe; all of them regard him as a stooge.

Q. Have any of them ever visited Katanga or met Tshombe? Do any of them have any real knowledge of the situation?

A. Most of them don't know much about the situation, but they feel strongly about it.

Q. What you're saying is that it's better for America to be popular than to act either morally or intelligently?

A. I wouldn't put it that way. We just feel that America should be in the mainstream on questions such as this.

Q. But surely Washington must realize that there is no alternative to Tshombe in Katanga, that if you remove him and allow Leopoldville to set up a Baluba regime under Sendwe or to install a gauleiter, thousands will die?

A. Maybe. But that would be Africans killing Africans.

Q. And that's desirable, is it?

A. It's better than white mercenaries killing Africans.

This unfruitful conversation ended quickly. If it was representative of official American thinking—as it appeared to be—there was little profit in further talk. Nor can there be much of a future for America when its government would rather be popular than just. It is obvious that the U.S. hopes its position on the Katanga question will generate enough support among the Afro-Asian nations to forestall Russian moves to establish a troika system in place of the office of the U.N. Secretary-General and to delay Red China's admission to the international organization. Yet the Afro-Asian nations following the Communist line have given no indication that they intend to alter their position on these questions. Nor is there anything to indicate that the conservative African nations (such as the ex-French republics) had any intention of shifting to the Left in this regard. In point of fact, the U.S. has alienated two of these, ex-French Congo and the Malagasy Republic, who are supporters of Katanga.

U.S. and U.N. intervention in Katanga might have been justified—if one assumes, as the Communists do, that the end justifies the means—had it produced reunion with the Congo on a workable basis. This it has not done. By allowing Adoula to impose unacceptable terms amounting to unconditional surrender, the U.N. and the U.S. have only made it certain that Katanga will revolt again. The U.N., deeply in the red on its Congo operation, cannot stay in Katanga forever. Tshombe's policy now appears to be to attempt to comply with the form but not the substance of the Kitona Agreement, to send delegates to Leopoldville, to expel most of his white mercenaries, and to pay lip service to Kasavubu, the *loi fondamentale*, and the unity of the Congo. But as surely as night follows day, when the U.N. withdraws from Katanga, Tshombe will recall his deputies, new mercenaries will fly in, and the standard of revolt will be raised again. Had the U.N. and the U.S. convinced Adoula of the necessity of granting Tshombe liberal terms, it might have been possible to reunite Katanga and the Congo. This opportunity was missed. Consequently, the U.N.-U.S. Katanga policy is doomed to failure. It is unethical and it won't work. The Congo's chaos will be prolonged and differences between America and her allies exacerbated. Nobody wins by this except the Communists.

As far as the situation in Katanga itself is concerned, neither the U.N. nor the U.S. are capable of playing a constructive role as long as they follow their present policies. The blue helmet and armband of the U.N. have become symbols not of hope but of oppression. The sight of an American plane produces not cheers but fists shaken in rage. It takes a big man, nation, or organization to admit it has been wrong. But to continue to follow a wrong policy rather than admitting to error is only to compound a wrong.

It is easy enough, especially in a case where ethics have been so flagrantly violated and the practical aspects of the problem so completely ignored, to show where the U.N. and the U.S. have gone wrong. What can be done to make the situation right, to deal justly with Katanga and at the same time re-establish the reputations of the U.N. and the U.S.? The U.N. must first recognize that it acted illegally (through the Security Council resolution of November 24, 1961) by "completely rejecting" Katanga's declaration of independence. The right of Katanga to self-determination —after nearly two years of autonomy—must be recognized. It is, after all, larger, more populous, wealthier, and just as stable as a good proportion of the members of the United Nations. Having done this, the U.N. should make every effort possible to demonstrate to both Adoula and Tshombe the advantages to both of a Congo federation or confederation. The Kitona Agreement cannot be the starting point of such an agreement. Adoula must be made to realize that concessions are necessary to bring Katanga into the Congo. After every possible avenue of negotiation has been exhausted and a reasonable period of time has elapsed (say, six months or a year), if Tshombe does not then agree to bring Katanga back into the Congo, a plebiscite should be held on the matter in Katanga. Such a plebiscite should be supervised by the United Nations, preferably by a commission made up of French Africans. During the balloting, both the U.N. force and the Katangan gendarmerie should be confined to their barracks. Such a plebiscite should be conducted on the basis of Katanga's eight provinces, the only condition being that no province should be allowed to secede unless it is contiguous to the other secessionist provinces. Such an arrangement would give the Balubas of Grands Lacs, Luvua, and Tanganyika provinces the opportunity to rejoin the Congo if they so desired. In addition, Katanga should be compelled under the terms of the secession agreement to remit $40 million per year (roughly its contribution under the Belgians) to the treasury of the Central Government for a term of ten years. Other powers which do a considerable trade with Katanga, such as Britain, Belgium, and the U.S., should be signatory to such an agreement to make sure that these funds are paid over and to guarantee the borders of both Katanga and the Congo. A customs union should be established between the two countries and a nonaggression treaty signed. For a stipulated period of perhaps five years, provision should be made for regular discussions between the Congo and Katanga in an effort to recreate unity. To allay fears that Katanga might become an outpost of white supremacy allied with the Federation of Rhodesia and Nyasaland, Katanga should waive her right to amalgamate with any nation other than the Congo, and immigration of whites into Katanga should be strictly controlled. A small U.N. observer force on the Katanga-Congo border might be desirable to reduce the probability of a clash between the two countries. Such a solution would be far from ideal. No compromise is ever perfect. But it would at least recognize the reality that the Congo is unable to prevent Katanga's secession by force. At least it would be better than the state of hatred, illegality, and near-chaos that exists today.

The implications of what the U.N. has done go far beyond Katanga. By breaking its own charter, the U.N. has not only compromised its usefulness but placed in question its very future existence in an explosive world that needs its potential power for peace. The first fruits of this evil seed flowered in December, while firing was still going on in Elisabethville, when India invaded Goa and the Security Council turned down a Western bid for a cease-fire.

Chief U.S. Delegate to the U.N. Adlai Stevenson expressed his shock at the Security Council's decision when he said that "we have witnessed tonight an effort to re-write the [United Nations] charter to sanction the use of force in international relations when it suits one's own pur-poses. This approach can only lead to chaos and to the dis-integration of the United Nations." In an emotion-charged speech, Stevenson pointed out that "the League of Nations died, I remind you, when its members no longer resisted the use of aggressive force." Yet it was the Security Coun-cil's reliance on the use of force in Katanga which made possible if not certain the decision on Goa. By its actions in Katanga, the U.N. invalidated international law and substituted for it the theorem that it is better to be popular than to be just. If that is the sort of world which we—meaning the U.S. and the U.N., for the latter still has a role to play—are building, then we are going back to the jungle. Dutch New Guinea may provide the final test. If the U.S. fails to stand up for the rights of the Papuans, a small and unimportant people, then there is no hope either for us or for the world, and we might as well start digging.

Loyal Americans and supporters of the United Nations are doing neither their government nor the international organization any favor if they support them when they are wrong. It was right for the U.S. and the U.N. to con-demn British and French aggression at Suez. It was equally wrong, both morally and legally, for the U.N. and the U.S. to intervene aggressively in Katanga.

The story of Katanga is a doleful tale bristling with false morality and injustice. It is still an unfinished story. Let us hope that it is a story that will not be repeated in other times and other places.